D0219664

ARMIES OF THE POOR

Armies of the Poor

*Determinants of Working-Class
Participation in the
Parisian Insurrection of
June 1848*

MARK TRAUGOTT

Princeton University Press
Princeton, New Jersey

For Fritz and Lucia
and Patti
and to the memory of
Jean-Baptiste Faivre

CONTENTS

CONTENTS

LIST OF ILLUSTRATIONS

LIST OF TABLES AND MAP

PREFACE

INSOFAR as I can specify its precise point of origin, this study grew out of a routine rereading of "The Class Struggles in France, 1848-1850" by Karl Marx. Like its companion essay, "The Eighteenth Brumaire of Louis Napoleon," it is a classic in its style, but a classic flawed—or so it seemed on reconsideration—by its reliance on the concept of the *lumpenproletariat*. Embedded within a rigorous analysis of the class forces that shaped the events of 1848 are references to a "nonclass" defined in terms of the *absence* of bonds of solidarity grounded in the constraints of material life-conditions.

Although I reserve for Chapter Two a discussion of the likely reasons for Marx and Engels's use of this explanatory tactic, its theoretical implications should be spelled out immediately, for they provided the principal motivation for this research. Its significance in Marx's analysis of 1848 can perhaps best be conveyed by analogy to "The Eighteenth Brumaire." There Marx presented the Second Empire as a regime deriving in important ways from the opportunism of lumpenproletarians operating at different levels of French society. But such a characterization leaves an essential question unanswered: how, from the perspective of class analysis, can one satisfactorily explain the efficacy and longevity of a regime perceived to have so insubstantial a social base? Despite efforts by Marx and later analysts to qualify and amplify his basic analysis, the question has remained sufficiently problematic to generate an entire line of revisionist argument emphasizing the potential autonomy of the state and of the political sphere from the determining influence of the economic infrastructure. This, at least, is one way to reconcile Marx's disparagement of what he saw as the initiating force behind the Second Empire with the general theory's tendency to assume the class determination of history.

In the case of "The Class Struggles in France," the description of the forces of repression in the June Days as essentially lumpenproletarian in composition poses a similar problem. This is not to assert the inherent implausibility of a thesis that holds that the members of such a nonclass may be politically volatile. But Marx alerts us to the possibility of an anomaly in his reasoning by referring to a set of material interests to explain the political stance of insurgents in the June Days and, in an abrupt turnabout, invoking not a difference in but the *lack* of clear-cut material interests to account for the opposing political stance of their repressors.

My interest in this apparent anomaly was heightened by the at least superficial parallel presented by a line of argument that, in the literature on collective behavior and social movements, is often referred to as the "riffraff" thesis. Conservative analysts of urban unrest have frequently asserted that insurgent forces, far from representing the solid elements of the working class, were drawn in disproportionate numbers from the most marginal segment of the lower classes—those least integrated into stable networks of social relationships and possessing neither a well-defined position in the economic system nor the sense of political efficacy that is seen as its natural concomitant. Given the regularity with which riffraff explanations have been shown to be in error when subjected to empirical test, it seemed fruitful to ask whether the mirror-image view presented by Marx's lumpenproletariat thesis might not be equally misleading.

It seemed all the more important to sort out these possible contradictions because the work of Marx and Engels—both the general theory and their specific analyses of concrete historical situations—has been so influential in the branch of sociology devoted to the explanation of revolutionary social movements. Fortunately, in the case of the French Revolution of 1848, an obvious point of reference for such an investigation existed in the research of Tilly and Lees (1975) on the

June insurgents. From the outset, I had the benefit not only of this published work but also of Charles Tilly's advice on sources, the availability of archival materials, and the most promising avenues of inquiry. It is fair to say that without his help, this study would not just have been different; in all probability, it would not have been done at all. Of course, there is no historical sociologist working in the area of social movements who has not been influenced in some degree by Tilly's broad-ranging and path-breaking contributions. But in my case the debt is far more direct. Tilly generously provided me with his own patiently accumulated data sets, with a detailed coding scheme for nineteenth-century occupations indispensable to the comparison of the relevant groups, and, at various critical junctures in the research process, with invaluable information, criticism, and encouragement. It is a genuine pleasure to have this opportunity to thank him for a disinterested generosity and intellectual openness that are all the more appreciated since the position I have advanced is in a number of respects critical of his own.

As the focus of my research came to center on the Mobile Guard, the group most clearly implicated in the June repression and the one that Marx had explicitly labeled lumpenproletarian, my principal resource was an article by Pierre Caspard (1974). His work represented the only serious analytical treatment of this militia and was the source of the "cohort hypothesis" that is so much at issue in the argument developed below. Caspard's article was instrumental in a number of other respects, not the least of which was that it established the existence of documents from which a description of the social composition of the Mobile Guard could be derived. The twenty-four uncatalogued registers of Mobile Guard enlistments were rediscovered by Caspard while he was serving as an archivist in the Archives historiques du Ministère de la Guerre at Vincennes. Without them it is hard to imagine how a direct test of Marx's propositions would be possible, particularly in view of the loss of most Parisian municipal records with the burning of the Hôtel de Ville in 1871.

But even knowing of the existence of these documents, I had yet to find them. I approached the problem with the naïveté of the sociologist. To my untutored eye, the state of French archives bordered on the chaotic. I learned that where catalogues of a given period existed at all, they were typically incomplete. Instead of a single, comprehensive system arranged by substantive categories, I discovered a great many separate listings, more often organized according to the date of the documents' acquisition or the agency of their bureaucratic origin. It goes without saying that the catalogues were themselves unindexed.

Under such circumstances, the researcher is utterly dependent on the expertise and good will of the archivists. Although my search for documents took me to the Archives nationales, the archives of the Paris Prefect of Police, the Bibliothèque nationale, and several more obscure locations, by far the greater part of my primary research was conducted at the military archives at Vincennes. There the entire personnel, and especially Madame Combes, spared no effort to assist me. From the beginning, they were inordinately patient with my claim that the Mobile Guard documents existed, even though the latter did not then appear on their general list of holdings. At a later point in the research, perhaps resigned to my stubborn insistence that more extensive sources must be present, they granted me the rare privilege of making my own exploration and inventory of relevant documents in the stacks. It was only thanks to their efforts that I was able to assemble a satisfactory description of the Mobile Guard for comparison with the June insurgents.

As yet, however, my research merely negated some of the bolder claims of Marx and Engels concerning the June Days, ground already broken by the work of Price (1972), Caspard, and Tilly and Lees. What was needed was to affirm an argument that could provide a comprehensive alternative explanation consistent with the historical sequence as I had come to understand it. It was Theda Skocpol who, as a reviewer of an early article manuscript on these basic findings, pointed me in a new and more constructive direction with her trenchant criticisms and her mention of Katherine Chorley's *Armies and the Art of Revolution* (1943). Her frank and unerring assessment of the limitations of my essentially descriptive line of argument are what turned me toward the "organizational hypothesis," a return to the archives, and my ultimate focus on a paired comparison between the Mobile Guard and the National Workshops. More than anyone else she is responsible for the intellectual inspiration of what is most original in this work.

Again in the concluding phase of this research, the mutually reinforcing criticisms of Theda Skocpol and Richard Hamilton steered me toward a much clearer and stronger statement of the implications to be drawn from my empirical findings. Although neither of them is likely to be entirely satisfied with the result, the changes that I made on the basis of their suggestions have greatly improved the coherence of my argument.

In the period of the initial data collection, I was fortunate to find two excellent research assistants, Carla Hesse and Susan Fisher-McCloud. Each of these undergraduates brought to her work an enthusiasm and intelligence that would have been remarkable in an advanced graduate student.

I have also had the benefit of advice from a number of historians and sociologists at various points in the preparation of the manuscript. These include Peter Amann, Ron Aminzade, Jonathan Beecher, Robert Bezucha, Rick Gordon, Gareth Stedman Jones, Robert Liebman, and Ted Margadant. They offered criticisms and suggestions bearing on everything from possible new sources of information to the reconceptualization of basic issues. One of the most difficult problems I had to face was how to phrase my argument in such a way that it would speak to the concerns of both historians and sociologists. This has necessitated a series of uneasy compromises that, I fear, will satisfy neither group completely. Many historians will be dismayed by my use of social-scientific jargon, though I have struggled to keep this to a minimum. They may also be disappointed to find that I have *not* attempted a reinterpretation of 1848 in the historian's sense but have instead used this case to test propositions about revolutionary mobilization. As a result, I have simultaneously narrowed the focus to a brief four-month phase of the French Second Republic and attempted to generalize beyond the confines of the period under consideration. I can only hope that these readers will feel that in applying sociological theory and methods, I have treated the history of the period with the care and respect it deserves.

The fact remains that throughout this work, I have primarily addressed an audience of sociologists. This is the justification for the lengthy summaries of events and descriptions of social conditions that will surely seem elementary or tedious to those already versed in the literature. It seemed crucial, however, not to abstract the causal process under scrutiny at too preliminary a stage or to let the analysis stray too far from the day-by-day unfolding of the events in which it is rooted. Sociologists, in turn, may be disappointed to learn that no "theory of revolution" in the general sense is advanced but only a grounded interpretation of a finite set of historical events whose implications I try carefully to circumscribe in the conclusion.

The general structure of the book is readily summarized. Chapter One presents a brief overview of the period in order to familiarize the reader with the events and persons discussed subsequently. The next two chapters concern the Mobile Guard. Chapter Two relates its history and provides a sociological description of its membership in comparison with the general Parisian population and with the June insurgents. Chapter Three considers those organizational factors that, I argue, determined its political orientation in the June Days. The two chapters that follow concern the National Workshops, which furnished a large share of the personnel that manned the June barricades. In parallel fashion, Chapter Four reviews the workshops' history and social composition, and Chapter Five provides the elements of an organizational analysis of their June orientation. A concluding chapter recapitulates and sharpens the general argument and attempts to draw the appropriate inferences concerning revolutionary mobilization.

Whatever the shortcomings of this book, it is certain that they would have been infinitely more serious without the precious assistance tendered by the scholars already mentioned. I would also like to acknowledge the help of the members of the Comparative History Seminar at the University of California, Santa Cruz, who provided valuable feedback on my first efforts to conceptualize the problem and who, along with the Faculty Research Committee of that university, supported this research in its exploratory phases. This work was also funded by a small grant from the American Philosophical Society and a fellowship from the National Endowment for the Humanities that made possible the expansion of the project at a crucial stage.

Mark Traugott
Santa Cruz, 1984

ARMIES OF THE POOR

ONE

The June Days of 1848 in Historical Perspective

THE French Revolution of 1848 is generally regarded as the key event in the broadest sustained outburst of revolutionary activity that the modern world has witnessed. It was quickly followed by violent upheavals in Belgium, Austria, Hungary, and several German and Italian states. During this "year of revolution," few regions of the Continent were left untouched by efforts to effect at least constitutional reform.[1] But although the revolution in France appeared to serve as both precipitant and model for its successors, no other European movement produced as sweeping a program of social change as that originally envisioned by the founders of the Second Republic.

In 1848, as so often in the insurrectionary history of France, the nation appeared to bend to the initiative and will of its capital. The revolutionary process begun with the February Days achieved its culmination and definitive reversal in the Parisian insurrection of June 1848. Just as the February Days, in toppling the monarchy of Louis Philippe, triggered a burst of radical activity that quickly spread across Europe, so the June Days set in motion a wave of reaction that would ultimately erase most of the political and social gains so recently achieved. The election of Louis Napoleon Bonaparte as President of the Republic in December 1848 merely confirmed the recision of the reform program undertaken by the democrats and presaged the return to autocratic rule. For all practical purposes, the fate of the French Second Republic had been settled in the streets of Paris through a test of strength between forces that on both sides can be characterized as "armies of the poor."

3

This label applies more obviously to the Parisian Mobile Guard, a full-time armed force whose members were overwhelmingly of working-class origins. Created in the wake of the February Days, the Mobile Guard was intended as a compromise between a citizens' militia and a unit of the regular army.[2] Yet, despite its origins and contrary to the expectations of most contemporary observers, in June it outdid the National Guard and the troops of the line in its enthusiastic defense of the moderate republic.

It is perhaps less obvious why the Parisian National Workshops should be termed an "army of the poor." There can be no question that the members of this all-volunteer, civilian corps, constituting the better part of the city's unemployed, were poverty-stricken. But, in a more than metaphoric sense, they also constituted an irregular army, for in order to instill discipline, the workshops were organized along the strict, hierarchical lines of a military unit. Long before the outbreak of the June Days, contemporary opinion noted their martial cast with varying degrees of pride or apprehension. The moderate majority of the Provisional Government had called for the formation of this institution in the hope that it might serve as "a praetorian army."[3] *Le Constitutionnel*, a moderate republican daily, reflected the anxieties of the middle class when it termed the National Workshops "the army of anarchy."[4] The Commission of Inquiry, appointed in the aftermath of the June Days to investigate the causes of the insurrection, branded the workshops' organization a form of "armed socialism."[5]

It would, of course, be as inappropriate to adopt uncritically the views of these contemporary sources as to accept at face value the exaggerated claims of Marx and Engels that the insurgents represented a class-conscious movement on the part of proletarianized Parisian workers. The purpose of this study is to retrace the origins and document the actual composition of the groups that participated in the June insurrection as a preliminary to elucidating the connection between social organization and political orientation. Since any such understanding must take account of the larger social context, it will prove helpful first to outline the economic conditions that prevailed in 1848.

THE PARISIAN ECONOMY IN THE MID-NINETEENTH CENTURY

In the 1840s, the majority of the French population lived in rural areas and would in fact continue to do so through the remainder of the nineteenth century.[6] Urban areas, which most statistical sources of the period generously define as agglomerations of 2,000 or more people, had, however, grown at an accelerating pace. Yet even in the cities, the expansion of what was ambiguously called the "industrial economy" was gradual and uneven. In contemporary French usage, the term *industriel* described the application of human industry in the production of goods (as opposed to the provision of services or the cultivation of the soil). It embraced but was by no means limited to the large-scale, often capital-intensive manufacture of commodities by wage-earning, proletarianized workers. This factory mode of production, which the twentieth century has come to associate with the concept of industrialization, was in fact the exception rather than the rule in mid-nineteenth-century France where most industrial workers were members of skilled trades, employed in small workshops.

The failure to address this ambiguity in the meaning of "industrial" has seriously hampered efforts to explain the relationship between economic factors and the social movement activity of the nineteenth century. In the work of Marx and Engels, for example, both meanings were used and often confused. In a general way, the modern, more specific meaning of industrial was emphasized in their more theoretical writings, linking the conditions of factory production to the development of class consciousness among workers. In accounts of historical cases and notably in their analyses of the period of the French Second Republic, however, the label "industrial" (and, for that matter, the still more restrictive term, "prole-

5

tarian") was applied to a Parisian working class that in no way fulfilled this more specific usage of the word.[7]

In interpreting the established pattern of French economic development in the nineteenth century, authors differ sharply as to whether change or continuity constituted the dominant trend. Both the persistence of handicraft production and the gradual advance of market penetration, proletarianization, and industrial concentration were realities of the times. Which aspect of this complex picture is ultimately emphasized depends in part on one's point of reference. According to whether the French economy is being implicitly compared cross-sectionally with the already advanced development of English industrialism or longitudinally with its own state at the time of the Revolution of 1789, it will be judged backward or dynamic, stable or in flux.

O'Brien and Keyder (1978) have offered as an alternative to this essentially quantitative mode of comparison an assessment in more qualitative terms. In their view, the French economy's course of development in the nineteenth century creatively exploited its own distinctive strengths. Where England moved in the direction of large-scale production of intermediate quality goods aimed in part at an export market that it virtually controlled, France capitalized on its traditional advantage in the fabrication of commodities of exceptional quality, largely for domestic consumption. In this sense, the two countries were committed to different paths toward economic expansion. If, for example, the use of coal and the introduction of power-driven machinery was less extensive in France in the 1840s than it had been in England even a generation before,[8] this cannot simply be interpreted as a lag in industrialization. It may instead be seen as an enlightened strategy of differentiated development in the face of competition from a more precocious and powerful rival.

Even considered in its own terms, French economic development in this period was uneven in its geographical and sectoral distribution. By 1848, large factories existed in France, but these were concentrated for the most part in the textile

6

centers of the north and northeast regions: Lille, Rouen, and, on a smaller scale, Mulhouse, Le Creusot, Reims, Troyes, St.-Etienne, and Roubaix (Audiganne 1849: 984-85). Outside these pockets of factory organization, the urban labor force was primarily engaged in small-scale handicraft production, a situation that remained unchanged at least through the end of the Second Empire.

Nowhere was this predominance of artisans more striking than in Paris. Although it was the industrial center of France (in the nineteenth-century sense) with a total population of roughly one million and by far the largest working class, factory work was almost unknown there (Duveau 1948: 73; Audiganne 1849: 992-93; Audiganne 1854: 169). The capital attracted a diverse and highly skilled labor force, plying the full range of urban trades. Here the elite of the working class produced the luxury goods and specialized services on which the far-flung reputation of Paris was based. These workers had been recruited from all corners of France as well as neighboring countries. A steady stream of in-migration had nearly doubled the population of Paris in the first half of the nineteenth century.[9]

The worker newly arrived in the capital of the 1840s faced a number of immediate difficulties in gaining a sense of orientation. Although the tendency was for the western part of the city to be more middle-class, and for the greatest concentration of workers to be found in the east, this division was never sharp or complete.[10] Due to the steady growth of population, housing was continually in short supply. The recent migrant was likely to settle for a time in one of the *maisons garnies* offering furnished rooms on a monthly, weekly, or even nightly basis.[11]

It was the chance of employment, particularly at the privileged wage levels that obtained in Paris, that was the capital's principal attraction. Though a number of trades were already under pressure from mechanization or changes in work organization, in Paris most retained a traditional craft organization that neither the universalistic legal reforms of the French

Revolution nor the labor repression of the Restoration and July Monarchy had been able to eradicate (Sewell 1980). Young males of thirteen or fourteen years might enter a trade as apprentices. The apprenticeship relation remained rather intimate, both because the number of openings was limited by convention and because the apprentice was often fed and housed by his master. Over a period of four to six years, the neophyte acquired the requisite skills and standards of the craft until, once judged a competent practitioner in his own right, he was elevated to journeyman status. By mid-century the traditional *tour de France*—the year-long journey through the provinces spent polishing one's skills and learning regional variations in technique—had largely disappeared. More commonly, the newly credentialed craftsman would remain in his master's shop or seek employment elsewhere in the city.

Shops were small. In half of all those enumerated in the Paris Chamber of Commerce's 1848 survey, the owner worked alone or was assisted by a single worker. Only one in ten shops employed more than ten workers (Chambre de Commerce de Paris 1851: Table 3). Except in the very largest enterprises, masters would typically be found working side by side with their employees.

The journeyman provided his own tools, which, in these labor-intensive trades, might cost the equivalent of two to four weeks' wages. He worked to the standards current in the profession, was personally responsible for the quality of his product, and was familiar with virtually the entire range of processes and techniques available. He switched from one task to another according to the requirements of the job, for, with few exceptions, the division of labor remained rudimentary. Along with any fellow workers, he retained discretion over the pace of his work and was able to intersperse bench work with "breaks," discussions, singing, and interactions with customers (Aminzade 1981: 67).

In 1848, systems of remuneration by the task, by the hour, and by the day coexisted. Earnings were appreciably higher in Paris than in the rest of France, but so was the cost of living. In times of prosperity, the average worker's family enjoyed a slim margin of safety in the struggle for survival, but this could be instantly erased by rising prices or a wave of unemployment.

The journeyman who practiced a skilled craft continued to dream of owning his own shop. The relatively egalitarian organization of the workplace and the small scale and capital requirements of the typical enterprise lent an air of plausibility to this aspiration. Though the social distinctions between master and journeyman were real and growing, in France the worker still tended to identify first with other practitioners of the same trade and only secondarily with his status equals in different trades. He might work shoulder to shoulder with one or several members of his craft association by day and mingle with them in larger numbers at the corner bistro or neighborhood cafe that same evening.

Of course, this picture of artisanal autonomy is highly idealized. Changes in work process, labor force composition, and the organization of the enterprise had begun to erode the egalitarian quality of work relations and workers' sense of collective control. But in Paris, in 1848, these changes were matters of degree and for the most part concentrated in certain trades. In a sector like "Thread and textiles," where by 1848 a clear majority of workers were women, wages were appreciably lower, shop sizes much larger, and prospects for mobility practically nil. In the cyclically active construction sector, large numbers of unskilled *hommes de peine* or common laborers were employed by subcontractors in a system of *marchandage* (Bezucha 1983). In the clothing trades, the growth of the market for ready-made garments encouraged a narrow division of labor in tailors' workshops and resulted in an increase in sweated labor (Johnson 1975).

Such changes in the organization of production were but one factor adversely affecting the prospects for upward movement. Since the French Revolution, the legal attack on workers' corporations had removed the traditional barriers to entry into the craft sector and diluted members' monopolistic privileges. Workers would discover that the new mobility this made possible was a double-edged sword, allowing downward as well as upward movement (Sewell 1980: 140-41). In the absence of systematic intergenerational data for the first half of the nineteenth century, the standard judgment that the fortunes of the working class were on balance in decline should perhaps be treated as intelligent surmise rather than established fact. There can, however, be little doubt about the net effect of the short-term economic contraction of the 1840s. At a time when the rate of bankruptcies among small businesses was sharply rising, the opportunity for journeymen to break into the ranks of entrepreneurs was sharply curtailed.

Still, in Paris, in 1848, the impact of long-term changes was gradual and affected only certain groups of workers, whereas the short-term dislocations were typically treated as temporary setbacks without lasting impact on career expectations. On the whole, the Parisian labor force continued to be dominated by skilled artisans whose relative autonomy and collegial organization set them apart from the many workers in French provinces and foreign countries who had already experienced the consequences of proletarianization.

ECONOMIC CRISIS AND THE FEBRUARY REVOLUTION

These conditions helped determine the response of Parisian workers to the economic crisis that overwhelmed the French economy in 1847-1848. At one and the same time, it resembled and was distinct from the pattern of old-regime crises. Its origins can be traced back to dislocations in the agricultural sector that began with the arrival of the potato blight in 1845 and were greatly exacerbated by the disastrous wheat harvest of 1846.[12] By late spring of 1847, the price of grain had doubled from its precrisis level of nineteen francs per hectoliter (Labrousse 1956: v-vi; Clough 1964: 158). Food and tax riots, attacks on shipments of grain, an increase in begging, and an acceleration of urban in-migration were among the consequences of this rapid rise (Stearns 1974: 34; Quentin-Bauchart 1920: 129).

The aggressive importation of foreign grain and a bumper crop of wheat in the fall of 1847 produced a sharp decline in the price of bread by the start of 1848, but not before the reverberations of the agricultural crisis had spread to the commercial sphere. Shortages and price fluctuations encouraged hoarding and speculation. The purchase of grain on foreign markets depleted gold reserves, eroded the value of the franc, and precipitated a drastic tightening of credit. Interest rates rose from 3 percent to the unheard-of level of 5.5 percent, deflation began to affect the price of nonfoodstuffs, and soon France was experiencing a liquidity crunch of major proportions.

These developments in the realm of finance inevitably had an adverse effect on French industrial production. Business circles were demoralized, and the population at large quickly revised its economic expectations downwards. The agricultural crisis had already reduced rural purchasing power. In urban areas, the average working-class family was forced to allocate an increasing share of its budget to subsistence needs. This further reduced demand for the very industrial goods that provided its source of livelihood, setting in motion a reverse multiplier effect that gradually diffused throughout the economy. French capitalists, faced with a depressed domestic market and highly restricted access to credit, curtailed industrial production, swelling the ranks of the unemployed and placing irresistible pressure on the level of wages. The petty-bourgeoisie and working class were the hardest hit, and the crisis was more severe in Paris than in France as a whole. The annual total of bankruptcies in the capital rose from 691 in 1845 to 931 in 1846 and 1,139 in 1847. A disproportionate share of these failures occurred in small businesses (Tudesq 1956: 27). Petty theft increased by more than 60 percent, and arrests for begging nearly trebled (Cherest 1873: 171). Meanwhile, the weakened state of markets in securities and bonds constrained the government's borrowing power, and the state itself was threatened by a fiscal crisis (McKay 1933: xxiii; Quentin-Bauchart 1920: 129; Ponteil 1955: 55).

What had begun as an old-style crisis in the agricultural sector had thus enveloped all realms of the French economy. Yet by the end of 1847, the prospects for economic recovery seemed to be improving. The plentiful wheat harvest of the previous fall promised a reduction in food prices while the maneuvers of the Bank of France succeeded in arresting the rise in the discount rate and the contraction of credit. Whether, like England, France might have escaped further economic calamity will never be known, for it was just at this juncture that the February Revolution broke out in the capital. Uncertainty about the future, until then largely economic, now became political as well. The prominence of working-class activists and socialist doctrines in the February Days further sapped the confidence of business circles, restricted the circulation of capital, and provoked an unparalleled collapse of the French economy. The value of government bonds resumed its only briefly interrupted downward course. Between March and June, the level of unemployment among Parisian workers attained 54 percent overall, surpassed 70 percent for entire sectors such as furniture-making, and reached as high as 90 percent in specific trades.[13]

In following this three-step progression from agricultural to commercial to industrial dislocation, the mid-nineteenth-century crisis in France conformed neither to the old-regime prototype described by Labrousse nor to the cyclical pattern of boom and bust that Marx associated with more developed forms of capitalism.[14] Its idiosyncratic character can be partly ascribed to the intervention of noneconomic forces after February. In effect, the crisis of 1845-1847 prepared the ground for a revolutionary outburst that greatly amplified, in its turn, the economic crisis. It is instructive to note that in England, where the initial economic downturn occurred simultaneously but no comparable revolutionary movement ensued, the crisis never attained the dimensions observed in France, and recovery was already underway in 1848. This suggests that in order to understand the distinctive quality of the French case, it will prove helpful to consider the course of political developments in this same period.

Chronology of the Early Second Republic

The following descriptive account of the political events leading up to the June Days in Paris purports to be neither original nor complete. It is, instead, an intentionally selective summary, emphasizing popular agitation in the first several months of the French Second Republic. Its purpose is to introduce those names and dates, events and issues, that are the elements out of which the analysis of later chapters is fashioned.[15]

Like the economic preconditions discussed in the previous section, the political origins of the French Revolution of 1848 reach back months or years before the outbreak of overt conflict. The major precipitant was the movement for liberal reforms instigated in 1847 by the French bourgeoisie. A wide array of parties and factions collaborated in a campaign whose primary demand was for a lowering of the property qualification that would have extended the vote to 200,000 additional members of the middle class.[16] This coalition included members of the dynastic opposition like Odilon Barrot who were formally loyal to Louis Philippe, the Orleanist king, though not to his Prime Minister, François Guizot. It enjoyed the support of republicans of no fixed political attachments like the celebrated romantic poet Alphonse de Lamartine. It embraced moderate republicans like Adolphe Crémieux, Louis Antoine Garnier-Pagès, Armand Marrast, and the rest of the group aligned with the liberal newspaper *le National* as well as more radical republicans like Alexandre Ledru-Rollin, Ferdinand Flocon, and the circle associated with the ultraliberal newspaper *la Réforme*. Its left wing consisted of populist socialists like Louis Blanc. The campaign was opposed by the parliamentary majority, composed of Bourbon legitimists and Orleanist loyalists. The basis of political support for these last

13

groups was neither as geographically concentrated nor as vocal as that of the party of reform, and their position was
weakened by their association with a government unpopular
for the vacillation of its policies, the harshness of its treatment
of domestic opposition, and its growing reputation for cor-
ruption.

In order to circumvent the July Monarchy's prohibition on
large-scale political assemblies, the organizers of the reform
campaign adopted the fraternal banquet as a vehicle for mobilization efforts. The first such affair, held in Paris in July
1847, was soon imitated in cities and towns all over France.[17]
If, at these formally apolitical functions, speakers rose to propose lengthy "toasts" that sometimes touched on matters of
widespread current interest, this bending of the spirit of the
laws was never sufficiently blatant to invite repression. Plans
for a great culminating banquet, to take place in Paris on 22
February 1848, had drawn the capital's working class into
what had originally been a predominantly middle-class movement. Anxious to preserve their waning influence and perhaps
intimidated by government pressure, the moderate organizers
of the banquet hastened to secure a new and smaller site
outside the popular twelfth ward, to reschedule the event in
the middle of the work week, and to raise the price of admission in the hope of discouraging workers from attending.
When the government, alarmed by what had grown into a
symbolic confrontation, published its resolve to prevent this
assembly by force if necessary, the organizers backed down
completely. With the agreement of both republican newspapers, the banquet was canceled in favor of the presentation
of a formal protest to the parliament.

But the bourgeoisie's decision to relent came too late to
quell the working-class ferment touched off by the reform
campaign. When 22 February arrived, most workers took the
day off to parade in the streets. For the most part, troops were
held in reserve out of public view, but in one incident before
the Palais Bourbon a company of dragoons, ordered to clear
the square, sheathed its weapons and was cheered by the

crowd. Incidents of rock-throwing and ritual barricade-building punctuated a day that both sides spent in an apparent attempt to gauge the seriousness of the opposition.

On Wednesday, 23 February, the situation deteriorated. Troops were deployed at key locations, and a command was issued for the beating of the *rappel*, the drum call used to summon the National Guard. The response was mixed at best. Most units refused to support the government. A few actually assembled in the Tuileries to petition the king to accept the proposed reforms, thus dealing a sharp blow to the morale of the regular troops. Barricades were erected in far greater numbers than the day before, and it appeared for a time that Louis Philippe would be forced to effect a compromise with the liberal coalition. In the event, all possibility for compromise was eliminated by one of those incidents that suddenly transforms reformist protest into hardened resistance. A crowd had drawn up before the Ministry of Foreign Affairs facing a detachment of the fourteenth regiment of the line. A rifle was accidentally discharged from an unknown quarter, and the apprehensive soldiers opened fire. In minutes, some fifty unarmed protesters lay dead, and the revolution had begun in earnest.

Word of the "massacre of the Boulevard des Capucines" quickly spread, and through the night the populace prepared for full-scale battle. The king had assigned command of the Paris garrison to Marshal Bugeaud, passionately hated for his role in the suppression of the Paris riots of April 1834. His early-morning attack on 24 February failed to take the insurgents by surprise and, with some 1,500 barricades now in place, military operations soon were stalemated. In these unsettled circumstances, many units of the army and National Guard fraternized with the rebels and were surrounded and disarmed. One such episode at the Château d'eau resulted in a brief but fierce battle.

Having concluded, perhaps prematurely, that a military solution was impossible, Louis Philippe belatedly aimed at conciliation by dismissing Guizot and selecting Louis Adolphe

Thiers to form a new government. Thiers insisted that Barrot, a leading figure in the banquet campaign, join his ministry and that the troops be cleared immediately from the capital. When even these measures failed to calm the crowds, and with enthusiasm for the declaration of a republic beginning to mount, Louis Philippe, who had given the democratic movement just the combination of weak resistance and grudging acquiescence that allowed it to mobilize a victorious coalition, now resolved to abdicate in favor of his grandson.

On the eve of the 24th, less than forty-eight hours after the outbreak of hostilities, the king and his immediate family left Paris to seek refuge in England. Regular troops and the Municipal Guard fought on briefly, but the Prefecture of Police and the Tuileries were soon overrun, and the last symbols of monarchical power defiled.

Meanwhile, at an emergency session of the Chamber of Deputies, the first steps were being taken toward a redefinition of the form of the French state. The Duchess of Orléans was in attendance in the vain hope of winning recognition for her nine-year-old son, the Count of Paris, as king and of herself as regent. This option was quickly discarded after speeches by Pierre Marie (a member of the dynastic left), Ledru-Rollin, and Lamartine counseled the formation of a provisional government to decide the political fate of the nation. Its mandate would be to reestablish order and to set up procedures for consulting the people on the definitive form of government. The chamber had been invaded by large numbers of armed citizens, and speakers were often unable to make themselves heard over the tumult. In this confusion, the names of nominees to take part in the Provisional Government were shouted out to the mixed reaction of those present. The nominating process was soon adjourned to the Hôtel de Ville, traditional site for the consecration of new governments. The final list of eleven names, read to the acclamation of the assembled crowd, included the seven already put forward at the Assembly and a few additions worked out in a compromise between the rival republican newspapers, *le National* and *la Réforme*. Its moderate majority consisted of seven men. In addition to Lamartine, Crémieux, Garnier-Pagès, and Marie, already mentioned, this group included the eighty-year-old Jacques Dupont de l'Eure, whose republicanism dated back to the Great Revolution; Dominique François Arago, a distinguished astronomer and longstanding republican; and Ferdinand Flocon, editor of *le National*. To the left of the moderates stood Ledru-Rollin, Blanc, Armand Marrast (editor of *la Réforme*), and the worker Albert.[18] Though they were a minority and not at all a coherent one, their views initially carried considerable weight because they coincided more closely with the demands of the armed workers who now controlled the streets of the capital.

This eleven-member government, which assumed authority on the evening of 24 February, began its deliberations immediately. Its first order of business was the declaration of France's Second Republic. The hesitation of the majority, which would have preferred to leave the question to the formally expressed voice of the people, was overcome by the urgent protestations of the revolutionary crowd. A long list of ministerial posts was quickly filled, mostly with men who possessed republican credentials.

The initial decrees of the Provisional Government were intended to ensure the democratic character of the revolution. The Chamber of Peers was abolished. Freedom of the press and the rights of free assembly and association were proclaimed. Universal suffrage was decreed. The ranks of the National Guard were opened to all adult males. The Mobile Guard was established as a people's militia that would maintain order in the capital. The radical Marc Caussidière assumed control over the Prefecture of Police and set about organizing a republican police force whose members, drawn exclusively from the barricades and secret societies, were called *montagnards* in evocation of the first French Revolution.

At the same time, the Provisional Government addressed a number of pressing social concerns. The death penalty for political offenses and the practice of imprisonment for debt were abolished. The Luxembourg Commission was created to deal with the problems of labor. Perhaps most important, the Provisional Government responded to the insistent demands of the workers who had made the revolution by guaranteeing the right to work and moving to establish "national workshops" in which the unemployed could find an assured source of livelihood. In those first days, the revolutionary momentum was irresistible. It assumed concrete form in the crowds of armed citizens who continually occupied the Place de Grève and in the endless delegations of workers who streamed into the Hôtel de Ville to pledge their support, present petitions, and exert their influence on the decisions of the Provisional Government. Much against its will, the moderate majority was compelled to adopt a series of reforms far more sweeping than any of the instigators of the banquet campaign had originally envisioned. Almost immediately a division arose between proponents of a "democratic revolution," limited to a restructuring of governmental institutions and the extension of political rights, and those who proposed a "democratic and *social* revolution" that would fundamentally transform relations among members of French society.

During the first two weeks of the Second Republic, while popular enthusiasm continued to soar, the Provisional Government was forced to come to grips with the problems of implementing the reforms to which it was now committed. With elections initially set for early April, aspirants to public office who until the overthrow of Louis Philippe had perhaps been staunch adherents of one or another variety of monarchy were discovering in themselves avid republican sentiments. The terms "republican of the eve" (of the February Days) and "republican of the morning after" entered the vernacular to distinguish between those rare political figures whose advocacy of democratic government was longstanding and the far greater number whose republican leanings developed only with the revolution itself.

The period of the early Second Republic was punctuated by the three great *journées* or popular interventions that occurred at approximately one-month intervals on 17 March, 16 April, and 15 May. With each step in this progression, of which the June insurrection represented the culmination, the political influence of radicals diminished, and peaceful protest gave way to increased reliance on armed force. The first and most successful of them was actually a counterdemonstration. On 16 March, members of elite companies of the National Guard assembled before the Hôtel de Ville. Their purpose was to protest the dilution of their all-bourgeois units under the Provisional Government's decree opening the ranks of the National Guard to all adult males. The government, anticipating the popular reaction to this challenge to the egalitarian ethic of the revolution, was unreceptive. Its representatives informed the leaders of the protest that the democratization would proceed as planned. Rebuffed in their demands, the petitioners were obliged to walk a gauntlet of jeering working-class radicals who had been forewarned of the objective of the demonstration. The radical response did not end there. The Parisian democratic clubs organized a massive counter-demonstration for the very next day.

By contemporary estimates, upwards of 100,000 workers marched through the streets of Paris and to the seat of government in a show of strength calculated to forestall further attempts to reverse the revolutionary momentum. Some of the instigators—notably that master of intrigue, recently released from prison, Auguste Blanqui—clearly hoped to intimidate and possibly unseat the moderate majority of the Provisional Government. The protest had practical objectives as well: to demand the removal of all troops from the city; to force postponement of the date set for electing officers of the National Guard; and, most important, to postpone the election of representatives to the Constituent Assembly.

At issue on 17 March was the degree of republican fervor with which the revolution would be prosecuted. Despite internal divisions, the Provisional Government presented a united front before the crowd, refusing to give its assent on the spot. Soon thereafter, however, it was announced that troop with-

The Demonstration of 17 March (*l'Illustration* 1848: 84)

drawals would begin shortly and that both sets of elections
would be rescheduled. Formally a standoff, this confrontation
actually represented a radical victory.[19] The left's ability to
mobilize the masses and extract concessions from a government in which moderates predominated gave telling evidence
of the power it then wielded. Its ascendancy was, however,
short-lived. Coming less than three weeks after the conclusion
of the February Days, the *journée* of 17 March, which Ménard
(1904: 72) bitingly termed the "last glorious day of the democratic party," marked the height of radical influence.

One segment of the working-class population was already
being weaned from its radical sympathies through the skillful
use made of the National Workshops. Under their youthful
director, Emile Thomas, these havens for the unemployed had
been organized along military lines. Positions of responsibility

20

were reserved for cadres loyal to the moderate republic, though low-level officers were elected by the rank and file beginning on 26 March. Late in March, Marie, who as Minister of Public Works was Thomas's superior, reviewed the assembled members of the National Workshops and attended a reception for its officers. His speech on this occasion was a plea to the workers to maintain order and pledge their support to the Provisional Government. From the audience came the suggestion that a Club of Delegates of the National Workshops be formed, an idea that Thomas and his assistants would skillfully exploit as a means of coopting members.

By early April the lines of political cleavage were beginning to be drawn more clearly. The Provisional Government tried to anticipate the possibility of popular intervention. Despite the assurances Lamartine had given the workers on 17 March, troops were repositioned in the Paris region throughout April. In the first week of that month, two battalions of Mobile Guardsmen were moved into the Hôtel de Ville where they might offer some protection to the government. Philosophical differences among the liberal and moderate members of the government were increasingly subordinated to the common preoccupation with the threat of the crowd.

The radical workers, meanwhile, mobilized for the electoral campaign. Not only did they draw up slates of candidates to represent Paris in the Constituent Assembly; they also raised money through the democratic clubs to dispatch delegates to proselytize in rural areas. The great event of this period was the demonstration of 16 April. In the minds of most participants, its purpose was to galvanize support for liberal republicans in the elections to be held one week later. Radical leaders like Blanqui, however, hoped that it might be used to stage a *coup de main* against the moderates in the government. These plans were thwarted by the defection of several key leftists. Armand Barbès, a veteran revolutionary and arch-rival of Blanqui, chose to appear in his capacity as commander of the twelfth legion of the National Guard rather than as a leader of the demonstrators. Ledru-Rollin, who as Minister of the

Interior was the obvious figure around whom the radicals might have formed an alternative government, threw in his lot with his more conservative colleagues by calling out the National and Mobile Guards to serve as a hostile escort for the column of demonstrators. When the marchers reached the Place de Grève situated before the Hôtel de Ville, their reception by representatives of the Provisional Government was notably cool. Even Blanc, one of the initiators of the affair, had moderated his stance at the last moment, apparently in fear that direct popular action might leave him outflanked by the ultraleft.

The progressive polarization of French politics proceeded apace throughout the period. At each stage, the lines of cleavage reached deeper into the class structure and left opposing sides further apart. The February Revolution had enjoyed at least the passive support of virtually the entire Parisian population. By mid-March, the interests of the middle and lower classes had visibly diverged. In the month that followed, various factions within the working class would part company. One group, including most members of the large-scale organizations newly created by the Provisional Government (Mobile Guard, National Workshops, and democratized National Guard), was content to consolidate the political gains and limited economic reforms ushered in with the democratic republic. An increasingly strident current of opposition, centered in the Luxembourg Commission, now constituted the left wing of the workers' movement, seeking potentially far-reaching changes under the banner of the "social republic." Between these ever more clearly opposed alternatives, the bulk of the Parisian population remained as yet uncommitted.

In this still fluid state of affairs, the elections held on Easter Sunday, 23 April, favored the moderates. The institution of universal manhood suffrage gave France by far the most broadly defined electorate in its history. This, along with a turnout of over 80 percent of eligible voters, amplified the voice of rural France. The Constituent Assembly of 1848 contained more landlords, clergymen, and aristocrats than any elected under the Orleanist monarchy. Of some 900 representatives, only thirty-four (by the most generous estimates) were members of the working class. The largest block—350 to 500, according to various sources—consisted of nominal republicans. This categorization is probably meaningless, however, since candidates of the most diverse political persuasions had assumed the protective coloration of republicanism after the February Days. Radical republicans, with less than 10 percent of all seats, were far outnumbered by both Orleanists and Legitimists. Indeed, the proportion of monarchists of various stripes exceeded one third of the entire body.

Yet the conclusion drawn by so many analysts, Marx among them, that these elections represented the triumph of politically backward rural areas over the progressive cities is simplistic. It fails to take account, for example, of the electoral results in Paris, where only one of twenty radical candidates put forward by the Luxembourg Commission won a seat in the Assembly. Parisians preferred all ten of his colleagues in the Provisional Government to Louis Blanc and gave twice as many votes to those perceived as most conservative, like Garnier-Pagès and Marie, even though they were less well known (Stern 1862: II, 580-81; Garnier-Pagès n.d.: 320-22).

It was in part the lack of time and resources to organize their electoral campaign that accounted for the radicals' defeat in the capital as in the countryside. Still more important, Parisian workers continued to be oriented to their individual trades rather than to a superordinate sense of class identity and therefore ran so many independent occupational slates that the working-class vote was fractioned and rendered ineffective.[20] But at the same time, the Parisian working class remained deeply divided in its political loyalties. One segment witnessed the 4 May ceremonies surrounding the installation of the Constituent Assembly with pride and satisfaction, pleased with the changes that the moderate republic had accomplished so swiftly. For another, these same events confirmed its fear that the Revolution of 1848, like that of 1830, had been stolen from the workers and turned against them.

The period between 23 April and 15 May produced a steady increase in levels of popular agitation. The Constituent Assembly had formally declared France a republic, but it had also redelegated the power relinquished to it by the Provisional Government to a more conservative five-member Executive Commission. Socialists like Blanc and Albert had been purged and, despite his role in the *journée* of 23 April, Ledru-Rollin was voted in by a slim majority and only because Lamartine refused to serve unless his colleague were retained. They were joined by Arago, Garnier-Pagès, and Marie, the three more conservative holdovers from the Provisional Government who had garnered the highest vote totals in the recent elections. Ministerial duties were also reshuffled. Marie, perhaps hoping to avoid political controversy, surrendered the public works portfolio. It was entrusted to a former leader of the banquet campaign, Ulysse Trélat, along with, as subsequent events permit us to infer, an unofficial mandate to bring a quick end to the nagging problem of the National Workshops.

The trend to the right was immediately apparent to radical workers. It was matched by a change in the tone of their public demonstrations. The leftists' attempts to promote the organization of work and the establishment of workers' cooperatives through the Luxembourg Commission had produced no concrete results. Efforts to exert their political influence through the petition process and the ballot box had been stalemated. Parisian workers now confronted a government that, though set in place by universal suffrage, seemed intent on dismantling even those more modest reforms introduced since February.

A demonstration planned for 15 May offered the occasion for a renewal of conflict. Its nominal purpose was to present the Assembly with petitions advocating French intervention on behalf of Polish democrats. On this relatively innocuous pretext, the organizers were able to attract some 30,000 Parisians to the staging area on the Champ de Mars. Certain leaders, however, clearly hoped to provoke a confrontation with the new regime. As their intentions became obvious in the course of the march, the less committed participants, reluctant to join in an overt challenge, slipped away. By the time the columns reached the Pont de la Concorde, their number had dwindled to a mere 2,000. With the acquiescence of the National Guard commander, they were able to force entry into the Assembly chambers and disrupt proceedings with impromptu speeches that quickly broadened from the Polish situation to the failings of past and present governments and finally to a demand that troops be withdrawn from the Paris region. Confusion reigned and was merely intensified when above the tumult could be heard the beating of the *rappel*, summoning loyal units of the National Guard to the aid of the captive representatives. The invaders hastily declared the Assembly dissolved, proclaimed a new Provisional Government, and headed for the Hôtel de Ville to see to its installation. Nearby units of the National and Mobile Guard soon were able to regain control over the chamber. A detachment

The Invasion of the Assembly, 15 May (*l'Illustration* 1848: 145)

under the command of Lamartine set out in pursuit of the radicals, most of whom were arrested at the Hôtel de Ville.

The 15 May invasion of the Assembly brought the latent social conflict into the open and virtually precluded all possibility of its resolution by peaceful means. The radicals had set the stage for insurrection but, by moving prematurely, not only failed in their immediate objectives but also alienated a large part of their potential mass following and deprived themselves of many visible and able leaders who at the time of the June Days would still be held in jail. Among members of the Constituent Assembly, the policy of compromise adopted by the Executive Commission was completely discredited, and political initiative passed into the hands of an increasingly intransigent coalition of conservatives. At the latter's insistence, the Luxembourg Commission was disbanded, though its members would continue to function informally as a center of mobilization for those disillusioned with the recent turn of events. Even more significant, the Assembly pressured the government into a plan to phase out the National Workshops completely. Apprehension at the thought of an organized body of 100,000 destitute workers blinded the institution's critics to its success in isolating members from the radical cause. As late as 21 May, during the parade that marked the Festival of Concord, cries in favor of the "social republic" by columns representing the *corporations* of Paris met with a stony silence from the National Workshops' delegation. By the first week of June, however, a rapprochement had taken place, leaving most of the rank and file in open sympathy with the radical camp.

This sudden shift in political orientation can be directly attributed to the government's initial efforts to disestablish the National Workshops. Director Emile Thomas, who had earlier balked at a plan to restrict the institution's size, was forced to submit his resignation to the Minister of Public Works and spirited from the capital by night. To supervise the dissolution process, Léon Lalanne was brought in as his replacement. The new director enjoyed the confidence neither of Thomas's handpicked cadres nor of the rank and file. For the workers, these changes symbolized the government's lack of commitment to a program of social and economic reforms. With the disbanding of the two most politically sensitive working-class organizations, the Luxembourg Commission and the National Workshops, their previously antagonistic memberships closed ranks. Their collaborative efforts included a popular banquet, electoral agitation, and the almost daily demonstrations that would continue up to the June Days.

Thanks in part to this new spirit of cooperation, the working-class alliance succeeded in winning four of eleven seats in the Parisian by-elections held on 6 June, a far better showing than in April. Elsewhere in France, however, the radicals actually lost ground. In a political climate tending rapidly toward reaction, many of the gains made since February were wiped out. The democratic clubs were closed and new restrictions placed on the right of assembly and the freedom of the press. The new administration of the National Workshops began a census of members, preliminary to reducing their number. Delegates from the rank and file met frequently with representatives of the now defunct Luxembourg Commission, and on 18 June they issued a joint statement affirming their continued support for the ideal of a democratic and social republic and protesting against the erosion of social welfare provisions.

The final rupture was precipitated by the 20 June meeting of the Assembly, which took up proposals for the reform of the National Workshops. The debate was marked by inflammatory speeches on both sides. It resulted in the Assembly's directive that its Special Committee on the National Workshops develop a plan for their immediate dissolution. The report of these proceedings, published in the official newspaper, *le Moniteur*, on the following day, aroused the apprehension and anger of the workers. The government chose 21 June to publish a decree adopted a week earlier obliging all workshops' members between the ages of eighteen and twenty-five years to enlist in the army or be struck from the rolls. It was also the day set for the imposition of a plan that would send contingents of older workshops' members to outlying provinces to participate in rural work projects. This swift implementation of policy changes removed any lingering doubt as to the government's resolve to do away with the National Workshops and, with it, all inclination on the part of the radicals to compromise.

At 8 A.M. on 22 June, a crowd of some 1,500 workers assembled behind their workshops' banners on the Place de la Bastille. Under the leadership of Louis Pujol, a lieutenant in the National Workshops, a column of marchers made its way to the seat of the Executive Commission. There Pujol and four workers were able to secure an audience with Marie. A heated exchange ensued. When asked what would happen if the workers refused to comply with the new directives, Marie flatly replied: "If the workers don't want to leave for the provinces, we will make them leave by force. . . . By force, do you hear?"

Throughout that day, workers paraded through the city, carrying placards and shouting such slogans as "We Won't Go!" and "Bread or Lead!" On their rounds, they attempted to call out the National Guard and to fraternize with the Mobile Guard and army units. That evening, several thousand workers convened on the Place du Panthéon. Contingents sent to all popular districts succeeded in mobilizing a mass following. By 9 P.M., the square before the Hôtel de Ville was filled with a crowd of 100,000. In the absence of any sign of accommodation on the part of the government, the decision was made to resist by force of arms, and rendezvous was given for six o'clock the next morning.

For those who gathered early on 23 June, the day's slogan had changed to "Liberty or Death!" The crowd proceeded toward the column of the Bastille, as if to consecrate an insurrection that all now recognized as imminent. Construction of the first barricades began by 10:30 A.M. By mid-afternoon, the streets of the working-class districts in the east were studded with massive barriers, many of them topped with the

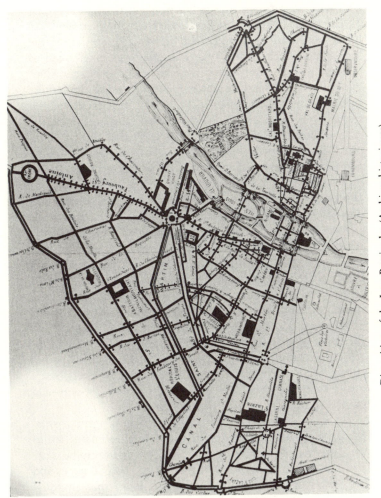

Disposition of the June Barricades (Archives historiques)

banners of National Workshops' companies or National Guard legions. More than 1,000 were eventually erected, due in part to the military authorities' decision to hold back army units in order to give the insurrection a chance to take definite form. This was the self-conscious policy of Minister of War Eugène de Cavaignac, whom an obviously ineffective government had hastily entrusted with dictatorial powers. Remembering the lesson of the February Days, Cavaignac was determined to commit his forces only in massed formations in order to eliminate all chance of having whole units disarmed by the people.

As a result, the insurgents initially controlled about half the surface area of the city, including many strategic points in the central districts. This early advantage enabled them to hold out through four days of fighting against the better trained and numerically superior forces of the government. The latter represented a mix of different units. Although information concerning the activities of the National Guard remains impressionistic, it appears that those legions drawn from well-to-do sections of the city sided with the forces of order, whereas the others either joined the insurrection or declined to take any part in the fighting. Some thirty-six battalions of army troops were present from the beginning, although, perhaps recalling their February disgrace, they proved hesitant in the initial combat. Most prominent in the fighting were the approximately 15,000 Mobile Guardsmen whose allegiance in the event of a popular insurrection had been a matter of intense speculation on all sides. As news of the conflict spread, a huge influx of irregular volunteers from the provinces poured into the capital. These, however, were for the most part held in reserve or assigned noncombat duties.

For its part, the insurrection mobilized only a minority of the Parisian working class. The most liberal estimates set insurgent strength at only 40,000 to 50,000, figures to be compared with a total labor force of well over 200,000 males and 300,000 workers of both sexes.[21] It is likley that an equal number participated in the repression as members of the National and Mobile Guards while the majority of the working class remained uninvolved. It is worth noting that even among

Column of Arrested Insurgents (*l'Illustration* 1848: 208)

members of the threatened National Workshops, most abstained from the fighting, neutralized in part by the government's decision to continue their pay through the four-day
conflict.

No match for their opponents in numbers or material strength,
the insurgents gradually gave ground. By Saturday, 24 June,
their progress had been halted. By Sunday, 25 June, the rebellion had largely been contained within the faubourg St.
Antoine, and the outcome was a foregone conclusion. On 26
June, the last resistance was overcome.

The June Insurrection in
Historical Perspective

Marx described the June Days as "The most colossal event
in the history of European civil wars" and as "the first great
battle . . . fought between the two classes that split modern

society" (Tucker 1978: 601, 589). For Tocqueville they represented "not a political struggle . . . but a class struggle, a sort of 'Servile War' " (1971: 169). Rare as it may be to find these two acute observers of nineteenth-century French politics in such clear agreement, one cannot accept these statements at face value. At least if we take literally their implication that the dividing line between insurgents and repressors in June was strictly one of class, the work of Gossez (1967), Price (1972), Caspard (1974), and especially that of Tilly and Lees (1975) shows them to be demonstrably in error. This is most apparent in the case of the insurgents. This group, which Marx referred to as "the armed proletariat," is shown by data based on arrest records and reproduced in subsequent chapters to have represented a broad array of members of the lower classes. In Langer's words, the June insurrection was "not in any sense a revolt of a class-conscious industrial proletariat, but rather an uprising of skilled as well as unskilled workers made desperate by hunger and want" (1969: 350). For their part, the leading elements in the June repression will be shown to have possessed a virtually identical social composition. My initial purpose must therefore be to describe the sociological identity of the opposing camps in considerable detail and demonstrate the limited utility of strict class analysis in explaining their alignment in June.

Yet this attempt to correct the errors of the widely accepted view of the June Days as a class war is only a preliminary task. By far the greater part of the present work is devoted to the exposition of an alternative sociological explanation of the array of forces in the June insurrection. I propose to do this by following the organized groups that were most central to the insurrection and repression, respectively, through the four-month sequence of events sketched in this chapter. This involves retracing the history of the Parisian Mobile Guard and National Workshops from the moment of their formation to their confrontation in June. In each case, an initial chapter outlines the history, the internal structure, and the sociological makeup of the respective organization; a second makes use of this material to ground an explanation of its ultimate role in the insurrectionary struggle. A concluding chapter attempts to make the comparative dimension of this work explicit and to draw out its implication for the sociological understanding of revolutionary conflict.

TWO

The Constitution and Composition of the Parisian Mobile Guard

THE insurrection of February 1848 brought the Orleanist Monarchy to a spectacular, if unexpected, end. For months previous, Louis Philippe had refused to make the sort of timely concession that might have blunted the popular appeal of the reform movement. Only in the final days of confrontation, when a display of indecision could do the greatest damage to the morale of his defenders, did the king begin to vacillate. It was his initial reluctance to commit the forces at his disposal that gave time for disaffection to spread among the legions of the National Guard and ultimately to the regiments of the line. With only 5,000 men of the Parisian Municipal Guard willing to put up a spirited defense, the advocates of reform were able to score a sudden, virtually uncontested victory in the capital. Barely forty-eight hours after the outbreak of overt hostilities, a despondent Louis Philippe composed a two-line statement of abdication and, dressed as a commoner, fled Paris to seek eventual refuge in England.[1]

The Provisional Government formed to oversee the creation of France's Second Republic inherited a chaotic situation. With its deliberations frequently interrupted by popular groups exhilarated by their recent triumph and intent on seeing their often contradictory demands promptly enacted into law, the government soon became acutely conscious of the lack of reliable social-control forces (Freycinet 1912: 20-21, 26-27). Those that had been associated with the July Monarchy were worthless. The Parisian Municipal Guard was discredited in the eyes of the people precisely because it had remained loyal to the deposed regime, and one of the first acts of the new government was to decree its abolition.[2] The army had suffered in the estimation of the people due to its initial resistance, however halfhearted, to the February revolution. Internal morale was dismally low due to the fact that a number of units had been disarmed by the insurgents.[3] The legions of the Parisian National Guard, it is true, either remained passive or joined the rebels outright, thus sealing the fate of the July Monarchy (Crémieux 1912: 120-45). But although its early support for the change of regime enhanced its revolutionary legitimacy, this part-time militia was not deemed to be suited organizationally to the enforcement of law on a regular basis.[4]

According to Caussidière, the radical who took possession of the office of Prefect of Police on his own initiative, the people of Paris spontaneously assumed responsibility for the maintenance of order in the city.[5] What troubled the members of the Provisional Government was the revolutionary crowd's willingness not only to see to the protection of property but also to intervene in their own official debates. The situation called for the creation, without delay, of an effective police force that would enjoy the confidence of the government and could claim legitimacy in the eyes of the people.

This was the object of the decree promoted by Lamartine and promulgated by the Provisional Government at 7 A.M. on 25 February providing for the establishment of the Mobile Guard.[6] Enlistments were to be opened immediately to male residents of Paris between the ages of sixteen and thirty years. Recruits were to be armed, clothed, and quartered at public expense and to receive in addition the sum of 1 franc 50 centimes per day.[7] Volunteers signed on for a period of one year and one day by presenting themselves at their local *mairie*. Two 1,058-man battalions were to be recruited from each of the twelve Parisian wards to produce a full complement of some 25,000 men.[8] Officers in this democratic militia were, according to the provisions of the founding decree, to be elected by the volunteers. Until such time as the battalions reached half-strength, organization and instruction would be provided by cadres detached from the regular army on a purely temporary basis.[9] Despite its formal title,[10] the Mobile Guard was to be an exclusively Parisian force whose deployment was strictly limited in geographical terms.[11]

In the face of the inherent difficulties of coordinating a massive recruitment drive undertaken in great haste, many of these formal provisions were honored in the breach. The sense of urgency is conveyed in Garnier-Pagès's revealing, if somewhat self-serving, assessment of the Provisional Government's motives in setting up the Mobile Guard:

> The foundering of all organized forces left only one means of safety: to draw from the masses themselves the elements of order and discipline; to contain, direct, and govern the people with the people. . . . Audacious to the point of temerity, impulsive, flirting with destruction, running to rebellion as to a recreation, deprived of work, wandering through the streets hunger-stricken, the children of Paris were a new element of turmoil. To assemble them, group them, clothe them, give them shelter and bread, all the while transforming them into an intelligent and devoted force was to accomplish an act at once political and humanitarian. (n.d.: I, 320)

By creating a citizens' militia, poised between the professionalism of the regular army and the democratic precepts of the National Guard, the Provisional Government sought simultaneously to solve three of its most pressing problems. It hoped to mitigate the economic crisis in the capital by employing as many as 25,000 jobless Parisians. Politically, this might also help neutralize the most volatile segment of the street population, caught up in the exhilaration of the February victory. And, if the Provisional Government's ultimate purpose should be fulfilled, it would have succeeded in transforming the recruits of the Mobile Guard into the reliable armed force of which it could expect at any moment to be in urgent need.

From the Barricades of February to the Barricades of June

For all these reasons, the Provisional Government made a self-conscious effort to recruit members of the Mobile Guard from among the youthful insurgents who had manned the February barricades. During the four months that followed the declaration of the republic, these men were forged into a fighting force that assumed the leading role in repressing a large-scale popular insurrection. To understand the causes of this dramatic transformation, it will first be necessary to reconstruct the Mobile Guard's role at critical junctures in the history of the early Second Republic.[12]

In the first month of its existence, the demands of recruiting, organizing, equipping, and training a military force created virtually overnight absorbed all energies and limited the public presence of the Mobile Guard. Enlistments had been opened on 26 February, but not until mid-March did the first battalions reach half-strength and petition Commanding General Duvivier to authorize the election of officers (Archives historiques Xm 34, 17 March; Xm 32, 20 March). Only after the twin demonstrations of 16 and 17 March did the Minister of the Interior begin to call upon the Mobile Guard to provide crowd control in the capital.[13] As of 1 April, Lamartine has stated, the Mobile Guard "could as yet count only a few battalions, and those without uniforms" (1849: II, 252). It assumed a more active role when in the first week of April two battalions, now described as "well armed and well equipped," were installed by Marrast in the Hôtel de Ville (Stern 1862: II, 166). From that point on, these troops would be frequently employed to disperse popular demonstrations (Chalmin 1948: 52).

With the *journée* of 16 April, the Mobile Guard made its definitive entry on the Parisian political scene. The timing was most appropriate, for the Mobile Guard's rise to prominence thus coincided with a critical shift in revolutionary momentum. General Duvivier received requests in writing from Marrast and in person from Lamartine to dispatch four battalions of his best prepared troops to the Place de Grève.[14] In this, its first engagement in a major popular disturbance, the Mobile Guard's loyalty to the constituted authorities was unshakable. This steadfast adherence to the cause of order turned out to be of pivotal significance. The demonstrators' plan was to descend in a column along the quays that stretched from the Louvre to the Hôtel de Ville. At the moment when the march departed from its staging area, the seat of the Provisional Government appeared to be only weakly defended, the square before it utterly deserted. Just as the head of the column reached the Place de Grève, units of the 10th legion of the National Guard made a last-minute appearance (Lamartine 1849: II, 328-29). As if on signal, Mobile Guardsmen descended the many narrow streets running perpendicular to the quays, thus cutting the main body of demonstrators into numerous uncoordinated segments (Regnault 1850: 298). Only then did the National Guard turn out in massive numbers to join with the Mobile Guard in shouting, "Long live the Republic!" and "Down with the Communists!" With their bayonets fixed in place, they formed a veritable gauntlet through which the disconcerted demonstrators were forced to file in silence (Stern 1862: II, 178; Regnault 1850: 299). The contrast with the *journée* of 17 March, when members of the democratic clubs had been acclaimed for promoting much the same kind of symbolic march, could not have been more pointed.

The first real test of the allegiance of the Mobile Guard had given complete satisfaction to Commanding General Duvivier, who seized the opportunity afforded by the next day's review to address his congratulations to his men.[15] Thenceforth, the government did not hesitate to muster the Mobile Guard to deal with the most compromising situations, a need that arose with increasing frequency now that politics in the capital had begun to polarize. The radicals' response to the humiliation of 16 April was to call for an armed procession two days later, a move that could not fail to be interpreted by the Provisional Government as a call to insurrection. The beating of the *rappel* at 6:30 on the appointed morning brought the National Guard out in force to join eight battalions of Mobile Guardsmen massed on the Place du Carrousel (McKay 1933: 54, n. 24). Confronted with this concentration of armed defenders, the prospective demonstration evaporated, leaving behind, in Garnier-Pagès's retrospectively confident turn of phrase, "only the certainty of the absolute devotion of the National and Mobile Guards" (n.d.: II, 236).

The threat of a radical *coup de main* preoccupied the authorities from this point on. The Fête de la Fraternité, scheduled for 20 April to allow the government to review its loyal troops, seemed to offer the dissidents a made-to-order opportunity. But any such plans were forestalled by the show of strength and solidarity by which the armed populace affirmed its support of the moderate republic on that day. Lilacs sprouted from the muzzles of shouldered rifles. As they passed before the reviewing stands, marchers plucked the flowers and showered them over the attendant dignitaries. Perhaps 200,000 paraded in a steady stream that lasted over twelve hours.[16] Among them marched the great majority of Mobile Guardsmen, still basking in the glory of their baptismal engagement and anxious to make a show of their allegiance to the Provisional Government.[17] This display of apparent good will on the part of the most diverse segments of the Parisian population was sufficiently ambiguous to allow Raspail and Caussidière on the one hand (Duveau 1967: 93) and Lamartine on the other (1849: II, 337) to congratulate themselves on the outcome.

The elections held on Easter Sunday, 23 April, removed any lingering doubts as to the direction in which political consciousness was evolving in the nation at large. The electoral influence of rural France had been greatly magnified by universal suffrage, and the Constituent Assembly returned by the most democratically organized electoral process Europe had ever witnessed was decidedly conservative. But the swing to the right was not merely the result of a split between the cities and the countryside, for even in Paris the moderates held sway.

Duvivier, whose visibility derived wholly from his role as commander-in-chief of the newly formed Mobile Guard, received the eleventh highest vote total of the thirty-four candidates elected in the Département de la Seine.[18] This indirect expression of the approval of their fellow citizens did not escape the notice of the members of the Mobile Guard. The elections, meanwhile, had other, more direct consequences for a portion of the corps. When the workers of Rouen learned of the defeat of radical candidates, they rose in anger. A two-day outbreak of street fighting was severely repressed by the regular army and National Guard. The 19th battalion of the Mobile Guard, dispatched to Rouen, arrived on 29 April, after the rebellion itself had been reduced but in time to render loyal service in restoring order.[19]

The Mobile Guard soon became the strong right arm of the Provisional Government, assigned on at least a weekly basis to quell disorders in Paris and its outskirts. On 29 April, it was sent against the workers of Belleville, who, according to the mayor's office, were threatening an uprising (Archives historiques F1 6, 29 April). Soon thereafter, it was placed on alert during the government's dispute with the workers of the Chemins de fer du Nord and asked to protect the work projects underway in the Champ de Mars.

The allegiance of the Mobile Guard was further tested in the *journée* of 15 May. For a month previous, the radicals had watched the revolutionary surge decline. The Constituent National Assembly had been convened in Paris on 4 May and had wasted no time in displaying its conservative colors. The left concluded that the survival of the social revolution hinged upon a show of mass support impressive enough to reverse the recent trend of political affairs. Failing that, the most militant leaders of the popular movement were prepared to challenge the legitimacy of the National Assembly as the sovereign governing body of France. The pretext chosen for the event—a call for solidarity with Polish freedom fighters—possessed the democratic appeal and political disinterestedness necessary to forestall the opposition of the authorities and to attract the broadest possible constituency.

When the crowd of demonstrators approached the National Assembly, they encountered a mixed force of defenders composed of National and Mobile Guardsmen.[20] A contingent of Mobile Guardsmen under recently appointed Commanding General Tempoure had been subordinated to "the people's general," Commander-in-Chief Courtais of the National Guard. It was Courtais who, after parleying with the leaders of the march, agreed to admit a small delegation of petitioners through the grillwork surrounding the Assembly courtyard. At the crucial moment, the entire crowd of demonstrators pressed forward through the gates and forced entry into the enclosure. Tempoure, incensed at this violation of the Assembly's security, initially refused to relay Courtais's command that Mobile Guardsmen sheathe the bayonets with which they were confronting the crowd. He acceded only when Courtais reiterated his direct order and agreed to put it in writing.[21] Meanwhile, the crowd had penetrated the Assembly chamber proper, and the sovereign deliberative body of the French nation was occupied without serious resistance.

After an uproarious series of exchanges on the crowded floor, the impromptu declaration of the Assembly's dissolution, and the departure of the most militant radicals for the Hôtel de Ville, the moderates managed to reassert control over the Palais Bourbon. According to Tempoure, having managed to elude his captors, he slipped out of the chamber, addressed brief exhortations to the several Mobile Guard units he found milling in the environs of the Assembly, and led them against clusters of demonstrators grouped around the Palais. His version is confirmed by Tocqueville's testimony that Mobile Guardsmen were the first agents of order to appear in the assembly hall and that with the aid of a recently arrived column of National Guardsmen they succeeded in clearing the floor of interlopers (1971: 153; see also Ménard 1904: 121; Girard 1964: 307). The demonstrators' initial reaction, according to Stern (1862: II, 265) was to cry out "The Mobile Guard! We've been betrayed."

According to the Lamartine (1849: II, 438), it was he himself who rallied the Mobile Guardsmen and led them into the chamber with bayonets fixed. More certain is the fact that, once the Assembly had been rescued, it was he and Ledru-Rollin who headed the force dispatched to the Hôtel de Ville, another mixed contingent that included units of the Mobile Guard (Lamartine 1849: II, 441-45; Archives historiques F1 15, especially the report of Clary, commander of the 2d battalion; Ligne 1923: 296). With the ouster of the new revolutionary government hurriedly installed by the rebels and the arrest of the principal leaders, the leftist movement of Paris was effectively decapitated and the undisputed sovereignty of the National Assembly reestablished.

On 15 May, the party of order contracted an enormous debt to the soldiers of the Mobile Guard, who had not merely remained loyal but had seized the initiative in parrying the threat to the moderate republic. Thereafter, the rapid polarization of Parisian politics would require the Executive Commission to draw upon the services of this corps with increasing regularity. On the 21st, the Mobile Guard participated in the Fête de la Concorde, a review of armed forces loyal to the government that, in light of the narrow escape of less than a week previous, possessed something of the character of a celebration. Tocqueville (1971: 162) found the attitude of its members equivocal on that day, but he might have been more assured had he paid less attention to shouts and slogans and more to their actual conduct when called upon to serve. On 23 May, the Guard was sent against the protesting butchers of the *abattoire de Grenelle*, and on the following day it was asked to police the *banquet de la constituante* at the Hippodrome. Two days later the Director of the National Workshops was removed from office under highly unusual circumstances, setting off a long series of disturbances among the Parisian unemployed. From 26 May on, the correspondence collected in the Mobile Guard archives is replete with orders for the dispatch of forces in strengths as great as ten battalions. The Prefect of Police complained that "a mute agitation reigns in the National Workshops," and the Executive Commission, fearing that the safety of the Minister of Public Works was endangered, ordered the workshops' headquarters at the Parc Monceaux surrounded (Archives historiques Xm 32, letter of Trouvé-Chauvel, 25 May; Xm 32, order of 27 May). When the Minister emerged unscathed, the force was reduced to two battalions and assigned to keep watch over the installation of the new director of the workshops, but an anxious Executive Commission simultaneously requested that two battalions be sent to its own seat at the Petit Luxembourg (Archives historiques Xm 32, order of 27 May, 6:50 P.M.). These dispositions were reaffirmed the following evening in anticipation of workers' assemblies at the gates of the city (Archives historiques Xm 32, letter from Pagnerre, 28 May). The anxiety of the Minister of Public Works clearly showed in his letter of 29 May, inquiring after the contingent of Mobile Guardsmen he had been promised for the defense of the ministry (Archives historiques Xm 32, letter of Trélat, 29 May). It was in this period that the Mobile Guard's existing responsibilities for picket duty at such strong points of the capital as the Prefecture of Police, the Ministry of War, and the Jardin des Plantes was extended (Archives historiques Xm 32, 30 May, 5 June). When the government responded to the rising incidence of unrest with a new law against tumultuous gatherings, it merely served to redouble the number of disturbances that the Mobile Guard in turn was asked to disperse.

The daily record of correspondence maintained by the commanding officers of the Mobile Guard reveals an unbroken stream of troop displacements intended to bring order to an increasingly turbulent city (Archives historiques Xm 46, Nos. 915-1155). The Minister of Public Works continued to call upon the Mobile Guard to police collisions between members of the National Workshops and nonmember workers in Courbevoie (Archives historiques F1 9, letter from Trélat of 20 June). The Prefect of Police also assigned the Mobile Guard responsibility for crowd control in connection with protests against the recently instituted workshops' policy of payment "by the task" rather than by the day (Archives historiques F1 9, letter from Trouvé-Chauvel of 21 June). On the eve of the June insurrection, the Mobile Guard was also sent against the hatters of the quartier Ste. Avoye and the Mont de Piété.

What this incomplete catalogue of social control incidents demonstrates is that well *before* the arrival of the June Days a wedge had been driven between those erstwhile comrades-in-arms of the February barricades, the Mobile Guardsmen and the unemployed workers of Paris. By 22 June when the members of the National Workshops resolved to resist the government's plans to dismantle their organization, the Mobile Guard had compiled an unambiguous record in the field. In every one of its innumerable confrontations with workers, it had remained unswervingly loyal to the regime in power.

During the June Days themselves, the 15,000 men of the Mobile Guard were generally acknowledged to have led the repression.[22] The regular army appears to have displayed little enthusiasm in the early fighting.[23] Tocqueville contrasted its hesitancy with the positive zeal of the Mobile Guard:

> I noticed that the soldiers of the line were the least eager of our troops. Memories of February appeared to weaken and paralyze them, and they seemed a little afraid that the next day someone might tell them that they had done the wrong thing. Without any doubt the keenest were those very Mobile Guardsmen whose fidelity we had questioned so seriously. (1971: 198-99)

Despite the dissenting opinions expressed by a few observers, the great majority of sources placed the Mobile Guard in the foremost rank of the repression.[24] Stern describes the youthful impulsiveness with which its members joined the fray:

> The courage of the children of the Mobile Guard in this first and terrible test cannot even be imagined by those who were not there to witness it. The sound of the gunshots, the whistling of the bullets seemed to them a new

44

game which brought them joy. The smoke, the smell of powder excited them. They charged at a run, climbed over crumbling paving stones, clung to every scrap of cover with a marvelous agility. Once launched, no order could hold them back. It required only this transport of youth and this mad thirst for glory, sustained by the brilliance and calm of their army officers, to sweep along the regiments of the line and the mass of the National Guard. If the Mobile Guard had passed over to the insurrection, as was feared, it is virtually certain that victory would have passed over with it. (1862: II, 391)

Casualty figures confirm the prominence of the Mobile Guard in the June combat. The best available data indicate a total of over 700 wounded, including 195 dead.[25] In four short months, the Mobile Guard had developed from a rag-tag collection of February insurgents to a formidable fighting corps that delivered victory in June to the forces of order.

EXPECTATIONS OF MOBILE GUARD POLITICAL ORIENTATION

In the aftermath of the June Days, the volunteers of the Mobile Guard were feted by the Parisian population and showered with honors by a grateful nation. The popular weekly, *l'Illustration*, published engravings of several who had distinguished themselves in the repression and reported that the most celebrated actresses and singers of the capital were vying for the favors of these youths of sixteen or eighteen (1848: 210-12). No less than 108 Mobile Guardsmen were awarded ranks in the Légion d'honneur for heroic conduct in the June Days. The public thus acknowledged extraordinary services rendered to the moderate republic at the same time that it found an outlet for its collective sense of relief, greatly heightened in the case of the Mobile Guard by the fact that up to the last minute its loyalty had remained so much in question.[26]

True, the new troops seemed unruly. The battalion registers are filled with notations of Mobile Guardsmen brought before

Imp.ᵉ par la Machine Perrot

He: "Amanda, at last I know the motive (*mobile*) for your conduct."
She: "Yes, it's true, I love a Mobile, and I forbid you to be a
    barricade between us."
(*le Journal pour rire*)

disciplinary councils for offenses ranging from absence without leave to theft and insubordination. The correspondence
preserved in the Mobile Guard archives documents almost
daily infractions of public and military law by individual members of the corps. Yet, as suggested by the evidence previously
cited, in all preliminary tests as in the June Days themselves,
there occurred not a single instance of a collective Mobile
Guard defection in the face of duty. The record is unambig-

uous. When ordered to confront popular forces in defense of the moderate republic, the Mobile Guard discharged its responsibilities without hesitation. Why then, throughout this period, was it the persistent belief of observers from all points on the political and social spectrum that in the event of insurrection the Mobile Guard would side with the rebels?

Stern, for example, described the indeterminacy of Mobile Guard loyalties as perceived on the eve of the *journée* of 16 April:

> In the ranks of the Mobile Guard, there was never any question but that they would fight. But against whom? They were not too sure themselves, and if the truth be known, they were not too concerned.[27]

Balleydier (1848: 48) has indicated that one month later, "the anarchists were already counting on this youthful guard." Stern also reported that on 15 May, as the small band of insurgents marched on the Hôtel de Ville to declare a revolutionary government, it attempted to win over the troops stationed there by telling them that the National Assembly had been dissolved, that 80,000 workers were about to arrive, and that the Mobile Guard had joined in the coup. The last two claims were pure fabrications, yet plausible enough in the view of the 4,000 to 5,000 armed guards assembled in the Place de Grève to cause them to disperse.[28]

Once the attack on the National Assembly had been repulsed, the tide of revolutionary forces sharply receded. Yet, despite the Mobile Guard's key role in that affair, doubts about its loyalty continued to be expressed. The Fête de la Concorde on 21 May provided Parisians with the occasion for publicly declaring their adherence to the moderate republic. Tocqueville, who witnessed the events from the reviewing stand reserved for members of the Assembly, observed that

> The various exclamations which we could hear from the battalions of the Mobile Guard left us full of doubts and anxiety about the intentions of these young men, or rather

children, who, more than anyone else at that time, held our destinies in their hands.[29]

This view seems not to have been a mere excess of caution in one who identified with the authorities, for it was rather optimistically shared by the militant organizers of the "twenty-five-cent banquet," the popular feast planned as a focus of the radicals' mobilization efforts in early June. An orator of the Club de la rue Albany was reported by the Prefect of Police to have affirmed that the Mobile Guard would attend in force, even if it had to overcome the resistance of its officers (Archives historiques Xm 32, 9 June). On 9 June, the daily summary prepared by the Prefect of Police for the Executive Commission noted that "numerous reports concerning the unfavorable disposition of the Mobile Guard have come before us."[30] Thus, the belief that the Mobile Guard would defect persisted among both moderates and radicals right up to the June Days. The incontrovertible evidence of Mobile Guard loyalty in April and May was either ignored or rationalized. Falloux, the conservative who was to play so important a role in bringing on the June insurrection through his attacks on the National Workshops, noted that

> A few of the [Mobile Guard] battalions had obeyed the voice of duty on 15 May, but this youthful militia, composed for the most part of Parisians, had on that day been subjected to [only] a brief test and its state of mind remained extremely doubtful.[31]

Lefrançais, who fought with the insurgents in June, confirmed the fact that those defending the barricades were counting on the support of the Mobile Guard both for the material aid it would provide in the fighting and for the neutralizing effect its example might have on the National Guard (1902: 52). Like certain other leftist commentators (cf. Renard 1907: 78), he claimed that the Mobile Guard wavered in the early hours of the June insurrection.

Representatives of the government also found cause for concern in the information that filtered in immediately before the fighting began. A police report of 22 June, for example, detailed how a crowd of 250 to 300, marching through the streets to mobilize the people, raised a cry of "Long live the Mobile Guard!" when it passed before one of the barracks housing the corps. Fifteen minutes later, another column, this time 500 strong, was similarly active in the eastern part of the city. When questioned as to their intentions, members of the latter group told police spies that they would "take up arms against the National Assembly and be seconded by the Mobile Guard" (Archives nationales C 930, Nos. 689, 698; C 933, No. 2452). Although in retrospect there is little to suggest that efforts to win over its members achieved any concrete result, one cannot assume that the insurgents' perception of Mobile Guard sympathies was totally unfounded. Many indicators of the attitude of individual members of that corps were ambiguous at best. For example, the same police report of 22 June quoted a corporal in the Mobile Guard, responding to the inquiries of a crowd assembled behind the Hôtel de Ville, to the effect that if a serious engagement with the people arose, his comrades would take their arms and equipment and flee. Rumors and scattered bits of information contributed to the muddle of hopes and fears as the June confrontation neared:

> The Mobile Guard, comprising 15,000 to 16,000 men, inspires no confidence. These are children of the working-class sections. Can they be made to march against the people? Will they fire on their parents, their brothers? It is known, moreover, that the workers are counting on them, that they are riven by factions. They have elected several declared supporters of Louis-Napoleon Bonaparte as their commanders. There is talk of a plot being hatched in their ranks in favor of the prince. It is said that the battalion commanders met on the 18th and 20th [of June] to decide collectively if they would fight and on which side of the barricades.[32]

It seemed all the more likely that the rumored confabulation had actually taken place in the light of a 5 April meeting of a group calling itself the Club de la Garde nationale mobile. Anticipating the results of the legislative elections, its members debated the question, "What would be the duty of citizens if the National Assembly should stray into a static pattern and fail to extirpate in a radical manner all abuses—in a word, if it should not be republican in the broadest meaning of the term?" The unanimous response of those present was "Insurrection, insurrection in this case being the most sacred and holy of duties" (Archives nationales C 930, No. 570).

Parisian leftists, much like the secret police, seem to have formed their impressions of Mobile Guard loyalties from fragmentary evidence supplied by haphazard sources. Marx would later chide the Parisian lower class for the illusions it permitted itself on this score:

> The workers *cheered* the Mobile Guard as it marched through Paris! . . . They regarded it as the *proletarian* guard in contrast to the bourgeois National Guard. Their error was pardonable. (Marx 1973: II, 53, author's emphasis)

But this condescending judgment was made with the full benefit of hindsight. One can only assume that what Marx was willing to pardon in the workers he must also have been willing to pardon in his collaborator. Engels, the member of the pair who specialized in military and insurrectional tactics, produced a number of newspaper accounts in this period, working largely from press dispatches. In one of the earliest, written on 27 June, he republished the erroneous version of events according to which

> The eleventh battalion of the mobile guard which attempted to join the insurgents was wiped out by the troops and the national guard. (Marx and Engels 1976: VII, 135)

It is true that he was skeptical enough to append the words, "So at least goes the story." But on the following day, as more detailed information became available, he was obliged to modify his tone. He claimed, on the one hand, that "Only those detachments of the mobile guard that consisted of *real* workers changed sides" (Marx and Engels 1976: VII, 143, author's emphasis). Yet he also maintained, somewhat anomalously in view of his earlier attitude, that

> The organized lumpenproletariat [i.e., the Mobile Guard] has given battle to the unorganized working proletariat. It has, *as was to be expected*, placed itself at the disposal of the bourgeoisie [emphasis added].[33]

In fact, the expectation that the Mobile Guard would turn died hardest among the insurgents. According to Stern (1862: II, 422), it was only during the second day of actual combat that the rebels abandoned the hope of winning over the Mobile Guard. This reassessment was prompted not merely by the failure of their proselytic efforts but also by the positive ferocity with which the Mobile Guard gave battle. Its reputation for cruelty itself played an important role at several junctures in the fighting.[34]

Yet not even its ardor in the repression fully dispelled the impression that Mobile Guard loyalties had been hanging in the balance. Well after the fact, Engels insisted that the insurgents had been "within a hairsbreadth of victory," for if they had managed to form a provisional government they would thereby have succeeded in

> doubling their number not only by people from the captured parts of the city joining them but also from the ranks of the mobile guard, who at that time needed but a slight impetus to make them go over to their side. (Marx and Engels 1976: VII, 164)

Still more insistent was Tocqueville. Writing nearly three years later, he eschewed the temptation to revise retrospectively what had been his vivid impression on the eve of the June Days. Completing a passage previously cited, he wrote of the combat initiative of the Mobile Guardsmen, whose fidelity we had questioned so seriously and, I still say, even after the event, so rightly, for it would have taken very little to make them decide against instead of for us. True, once involved, they performed prodigies of valor. They were all those children of Paris who give our armies their most undisciplined and rash soldiers, for they rush toward danger. They went to war as to a festival. But it was easy to see that they loved war in itself much more than the cause for which they fought. (1971: 199)

In stressing the essential indeterminacy of Mobile Guard loyalties as perceived by the authorities, the insurgents, and the population at large, Tocqueville was merely providing a typically accurate sounding of public opinion. But this nearly universal belief in the susceptibility of the Mobile Guard to radical appeals was grounded in a flawed logic to which the sociologically informed analyst of today must remain particularly sensitive: contemporary observers of all stripes reasoned from the attitudes, attributes, and behavior of member individuals to the attitudes, attributes, and behavior of social groups as if the latter were a mere extrapolation of the former. Thus, before the June Days they *assumed* the collective stance of the Mobile Guard from the fact that the sympathies of many members appeared naturally to be engaged on behalf of fellow workers. They *deduced* the Mobile Guard's wavering loyalties from the conduct of specific individuals that was seen as consistent with the aims of leftists. Above all, they *inferred* the radical tendencies of the Mobile Guard from the observation that members' most salient social and economic characteristics were shared with the prospective insurgents. In doing so, they ignored the formative influence that bonds of solidarity and organizational constraints exerted upon individuals once incorporated into the Mobile Guard. They consistently undervalued the new, collective identity being forged among the recent recruits and the direct evidence of its efficacy provided by the record of Mobile Guard loyalty in the preliminaries to the June Days. Although the next chapter will analyze in detail the organizational techniques through which this sense of collective identity was created and maintained, it will prove helpful first to establish the sociological character of the Mobile Guard and to demonstrate that its aggregate properties cannot explain its June conduct.

Contemporary Views of Mobile Guard Composition

If social origin and prior experience were perfect predictors of behavior, then one might well have expected to find the Mobile Guard ranged alongside the June insurgents, for its members had to a considerable extent been recruited from the barricades of February. Garnier-Pagès, one of the more conservative members of the government that created the Mobile Guard, described its social and political origins in these terms:

> The constituent elements of the Mobile Guard were essentially revolutionary. Drawn from the barricades, they bore the mark of their origins: they had the intrepid quality, but also the turbulence and fickleness of the people. (n.d.: II, 110)

Caussidière, the left-wing Prefect of Police, held much the same view:

> The Mobile Guardsmen who issued from the barricades of February turned their arms against the barricades of June and stained the working-class quarters with the blood of their families.[35]

Ménard, who fought with the insurgents in both February and June, grudgingly recognized that the Mobile Guard "contained a certain number of youths who had their first taste of battle with the People in February."[36] Similar observations were made by contemporary observers not associated with the revolutionaries. General Rébillot asserted that:

The quickest and most valiant adversaries of the June insurgents were these regimented youths most of whom had, alongside them, erected the February barricades.[37]

The identification of the Mobile Guard and the February insurgents corresponded, in short, both to the intention of the Provisional Government and the perception of a broad spectrum of contemporary public opinion. The recruits themselves took pride in the role they had played in toppling the July monarchy and were not above exploiting these credentials if it seemed to their advantage. When, for example, delegates from the 15th battalion addressed a letter to their commander-in-chief pleading for the speedy delivery of the uniforms they had long since been promised, they emphasized how it was

> sad and painful to see men lacking necessities, possessing as their entire wardrobe nothing but what they are wearing, namely the clothes that sustained the ravages of the barricades of February 1848. (Archives historiques Xm 35, 31 March)

Even Marx, whose bitterness toward the Mobile Guard gives a special edge to his commentary, acknowledged its revolutionary origins:

> And so the Paris proletariat was confronted with an army, drawn from its own midst, of twenty-four thousand young, strong, foolhardy men. It gave cheers for the Mobile Guard on its marches through Paris. It acknowledged it to be its foremost fighters on the barricades. (Marx and Engels 1959: 298)

The assumption that the Mobile Guard would revert to its revolutionary origins seemed all the more plausible, since the corps was widely believed to be host to a variety of political factions.[38] The youth of Mobile Guard recruits was another trait that incited frequent comment from the right, left, and center. Garnier-Pagès, for example, conveyed the sense, now of hope, now of suspicion, with which the "respectable citizenry" regarded the new militia:

> [The Mobile Guard] presented at its origin the strangest of spectacles. It was an unforeseen mixture of young, honest, and capable workers swept away by the ardor of the age and devotion to their country; and of vagabonds, those who prowl about the gates of the city, now attracted by the pay of 1 franc 50 centimes and by a guarantee of refuge. (n.d.: II, 109)

The liberal Stern described them as "undisciplined, jeering children, most of them already corrupted by the vagrancy of the big cities" (1862: I, 443). She expanded upon this characterization in a later passage:

> Recruited, as we have seen, on the morrow of the barricades, the Mobile Guard was composed, nearly in its entirety, of the turbulent swarm that had previously been thought beyond all discussion, of those children, the vagabonds of alleys and street corners, who are called "urchins of Paris." The rest were a mix of men of all conditions. . . . At the time of which I am speaking, most of them were still in rags and tatters, many lacking shirts and shoes. (1862: II, 165)

The gist if not the tone of these remarks by supporters of the moderate republic is in general agreement with the views of Marx, for whom the Mobile Guard consisted of "former beggars, vagabonds, rogues, gutter-snipes and small-time thieves."[39] The difference is that whereas the former tended to call attention to the similarities between insurgents and Mobile Guardsmen as if to underscore the sense of surprised relief felt within the party of order following the June Days, the latter stressed the discontinuity between those groups. Given the Mobile Guard's prominent role in the repression, Marx seemed anxious to draw the clearest possible distinction between the stratum of true "proletarians" who would stand in the vanguard of socialist revolution and the members of this arm of reaction. His general theory, after all, tended to equate class position and political consciousness. Having, as we saw in the preceding chapter, already exaggerated the degree of both economic and political development among the insurgents, Marx now yielded all the more readily to the temptation to minimize economic and political development among the Mobile Guardsmen. The latter were vilified and set apart, their revolutionary role in February forgotten or discounted. After the June Days, Marx flatly asserted that the Mobile Guardsmen

> belonged for the most part to the *lumpenproletariat*, which in all big towns forms a mass sharply differentiated from the industrial proletariat, a recruiting ground for thieves and criminals of all kinds, living on the crumbs of society, people without a definite trade, vagabonds, *gens sans aveu et sans feu* [people without tie or home], varying according to the degree of civilization of the nation to which they belong, but never renouncing their *lazzaroni* [dregs] character. (Marx and Engels 1959: 298)

With the nebulous concept of the lumpenproletariat, Marx had found the means of contending that, though "drawn from [the proletariat's] own midst" the Mobile Guard was not *of* the proletariat.

THE EMPIRICAL INVESTIGATION OF MOBILE GUARD COMPOSITION

Conjecture as to the social composition and resulting political orientation of the Mobile Guard long remained without empirical foundation. No serious inquiry into the class origins of its members was undertaken at the time of the Second Republic or for a century thereafter. Chalmin (1948) appears to have been the first to examine the surviving documents and render an informed judgment. Since, however, his intention was to write a descriptive history of the Mobile Guard rather than an analytical précis, his summary of its composition remained impressionistic:

> One finds in its ranks men deriving from just about every milieu: adventurers, deserters, sailors and soldiers from the army or from disciplinary battalions who were extremely discreet about their past, unemployed workers, the turbulent idle, Parisian urchins, students abandoning their studies, young men happy to play soldier and to hold a rifle. (1948: 43)

Not until the work of Caspard (1974) was an attempt made to determine the social background of the Mobile Guard with the explicit objective of establishing its connection, if any, with the corps' participation in the June Days.

For this purpose, Caspard constructed a categorization scheme based on levels of skill and instruction as indicated by rates of pay and literacy. He found that unskilled workers and those in marginal occupations constituted only a minor segment of the Mobile Guard and were represented at lower rates overall than among June arrestees (1974: 84). In the skilled categories that Caspard points to as supplying the bulk of Paris's industrial lower class, fewer contrasts occurred apart from a relative overrepresentation among Mobile Guardsmen of highly skilled workers from commerce and the professions (1974: 85-87). Caspard was led, in short, to conclude that "it is not possible to subscribe without reservations to the thesis of Marx" that the Mobile Guard was predominantly composed of lumpenproletarians.

Caspard also reported that although most Mobile Guardsmen were recent arrivals in the capital, they were in the aggregate more likely than the general population to be Parisian by birth (1974: 94-96). The significance of this finding remained unclear, however, as it was not possible to control this comparison by age, the single factor that Caspard himself found to offer the clearest distinction between the Mobile Guard and the relevant reference groups.[40]

In effect, whereas the average age of Mobile Guardsmen

was found to be a mere 21.5 years, that of June arrestees was no less than 34 years according to Caspard's figures (1974: 88-89). The concentration of Mobile Guard enlistments among very young Parisians meant that broad swaths of certain of the city's age cohorts—one in six of all 19-year-olds, one in eight of all 17-, 18-, and 20-year-olds—were inducted, casting grave doubt on Marx's insinuation that they represented an isolated mass of marginal individuals. The striking discrepancy in the ages of Mobile Guardsmen and insurgents has, moreover, served as the point of departure for a theory of the genesis of Mobile Guard political orientation that I shall here term the "cohort hypothesis." It associates the youth of volunteers with limited occupational experience, lower pay, lower status in their profession, and thus a potential for estrangement from the older generation of artisans under whom they had worked. In this view, their alleged marginality was less a matter of class than of cohort. In the economic crisis sweeping France, these young men were the first to be let go. Gossez has also suggested that the Mobile Guard recruited youths more literate and skilled than the average worker but also more exposed to the hardships of a depressed economy (Gossez 1956b: 446). Caspard has neatly summarized the cohort hypothesis in this portrait of Mobile Guard volunteers:

> Young without being children; Parisians, but of recent date; skilled workers, but without professional experience; intensely exploited by their employers, but also by their seniors; educated and open to the currents of ideas which agitated the capital, but without having yet had time to become impregnated with the ideology of the older workers, the conduct of the Mobile Guardsmen, while not uniformly hostile to the Parisian proletariat and its aspirations, would evolve more and more toward the incomprehension and finally the antagonism which was expressed in the course of the June Days. (1974: 96)

Thus, the net effect of this earlier research was to propose that class-based explanations be replaced with alternatives built around differences in age.

My reanalysis of the data contained in the Mobile Guard battalion registers has confirmed the essential descriptive statistics reported by Caspard (Traugott 1980b). It also led, however, to an interpretation of Mobile Guard behavior at odds in certain respects with the cohort hypothesis. Replication of Caspard's previous research, applying techniques of sampling and data analysis that better satisfy the standards current in the social sciences, was merely one of the objectives of the present research.

A second was to produce data on Mobile Guard composition that would be directly comparable with the existing studies of the two principal reference groups: the general Parisian population and the June insurgents. For this dual purpose, I was fortunate to possess two invaluable resources. The first is the intensive survey conducted by the Paris Chamber of Commerce at precisely the historical moment on which our attention has been focused. It documented in great detail the characteristics of the Parisian "industrial" labor force.[41] This investigation has also made use of the important research on the June insurgents published since the appearance of Caspard's article.[42] The study by Tilly and Lees has been of special value, in part because those authors developed a comprehensive coding system that expanded on the Chamber of Commerce scheme. By adopting their categorizations, it was possible to code the occupation of a far greater proportion of Mobile Guardsmen (2,747 of 3,845) and make direct cross-comparisons of their occupational distribution with that of the insurgents.[43]

A third major objective of my analysis was to examine the correlates of differential participation in the Mobile Guard on the part of various sectors of the Parisian economy, thus complementing the work of Tilly and Lees on June arrestees and permitting a more systematic, comparative investigation of the origins of revolutionary and counterrevolutionary political orientation.

The primary source for this research has been the set of twenty-four leather-bound battalion registers held in the French military archives at Vincennes.[44] These enlistment records were typically begun in the first days of March. Two Mobile Guard recruitment stations had been set up in each Parisian *mairie* as early as 26 February (Archives historiques Xm 32, letter of 1 March), but these hastily made arrangements produced a situation so chaotic that Commanding General Duvivier complained that

> Enlistments have been carried out prematurely and by the ward mayors. Anyone was accepted, anyone enrolled: men over fifty, cripples, even women. (Archives historiques F1 3, letter of 12 March)

It is thanks to his insistence that extensive written documentation be carefully maintained that it is today possible to reconstruct the recruitment process and establish the composition of the Mobile Guard in its broad outlines. By perusing these records in our minds, as it were, it should be possible to convey to the reader not only an impression of the character of the Mobile Guard but also an appreciation for the quality and range of the documents on which this study is based.

Imagine, for instance, as many as 150 volunteers waiting their turn in line before an officer seated at a desk in the reception hall of a ward *mairie*. To each prospective recruit the officer would read a statement of the conditions of enlistment and pose a series of simple questions, recording the responses in the battalion register (Archives historiques Xm 32, letter of 1 March). This information included the individual's name, the date and place of his birth, and the date of enlistment.[45] On the basis of a cursory medical examination, a series of descriptive physical characteristics was also entered. The recruit was then asked to sign the register, a task accomplished by some in the flowery script of the nineteenth century, by others in large, shaky, childlike scrawls, and by not a few with simple "Xs" witnessed by two literate neighbors in line.

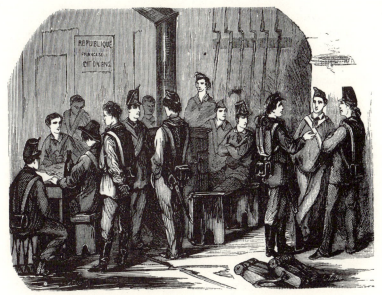

A Mobile Guard Post at the Time of the Corps' Formation
(Garnier-Pagès n.d.: II, 105)

Other information was added as time went on. A complete
record of the individual's military service—promotions and
demotions, unauthorized absences, disciplinary proceedings,
combat duty, wounds, hospitalizations, decorations, and so
forth—was carefully maintained right up to a final entry noting the date and reasons for discharge. Most important, given
the primary focus of the present research, a number of battalions began in August or September to record the previous
occupation of all their members.[46] It is those data that permit
us to establish the class origins of Mobile Guardsmen.

Glancing through these battalion registers, we are able to
glean further impressions of recruitment standards and prac-
tices. In a few cases, for example, a birth certificate, obtained
from a provincial records office, is joined with a ball of red
sealing wax to the matriculation papers of a volunteer who
did not appear to meet the minimum age requirement of sixteen years. In some cases, a date of birth that indicated that

the recruit was only fifteen at the time of enlistment was crossed out or simply ignored.[47] The reader's eye might be caught, for example, by the entry for Charles Potts, who signed on as number 199 in the 1st battalion and served as a corporal in the June Days. It was only in October 1848 that his name was struck from the records because a belated check revealed that he was not a French citizen.[48] Here and there we discover sequences of three to six men of similar age and identical occupation—perhaps neighbors or co-workers in the same shop—who may have been let go at once by their employer and decided to enlist and serve as a group as well. In some cases the records show that they remained close friends over the succeeding months, as when several were jointly arrested and brought before a disciplinary council for participation in the same barroom brawl.

We are often able to retrace in some detail the careers of individual members of the corps. There was, for instance, more than one Marx whose name can be associated with the events of June 1848. While Karl was writing diatribes against the Mobile Guard, Samuel and Jacob Marx were distinguishing themselves in that very organization. These brothers signed on together on 10 March as matriculation numbers 26 and 30 in the 13th battalion. Jacob, twenty-six years of age, had been born in Metz; Samuel, younger by seven years, was born in Hamburg, Germany. After submitting to a perfunctory medical examination, each signed his name in a legible, unadorned style and was accorded the rank of private first class. Just one week later, Samuel was elected corporal by his peers, his older brother among them. Neither attracted the further attention of the recording officer, for reasons good or bad, until the June Days themselves in which the 13th battalion played a particularly active role. On 25 June, Jacob became one of its first casualties. He is mentioned by name in the official report of battalion commander Camuset as having died heroically in the assault on a barricade in the faubourg du Temple. For his part, Samuel received the cross of the Legion of Honor for valor in the June fighting. How he responded to the loss of a brother, to his newly won status, or to the growing indiscipline of the Mobile Guard in the wake of its June victory cannot be found among battalion records. They show simply that when the corps was reorganized in February 1849, Samuel seized the opportunity to return to civilian life.

The richest documentation naturally describes the heroes of the June Days, for many were written up in contemporary newspapers and magazines, thus providing a useful supplement to and cross-check of official records. One case in point is private Henry Friedl (according to the register of the 7th battalion) or Henri Friel (according to a poster celebrating the victors of June).[49] His date of birth is listed as 18 June in one source and 16 June in the other. Both agree that the year was 1825 and the place Paris, though the recording officer of the 7th battalion incorrectly concluded that he was twenty-three at the time of his enlistment on 19 March 1848. We learn that he was the son of Georges Friedl and Juli Schmidt, French of German extraction, who had been living in the third ward at the time of Henry's birth. When he enrolled in the Mobile Guard, Henry himself lived at 10 rue Baillif in the 4th ward, the one from which the 7th battalion was recruited. He gave his former occupation as "piano maker," one in which 68 percent of all workers were unemployed in 1848. As a soldier he distinguished himself by plucking an insurgent flag from atop a barricade in the faubourg St. Denis. By opportunely performing this feat before the eyes of General Lafontaine, he earned a decoration for valor. But the record of his accomplishments in battle does not end there. On the following day he joined his lieutenant in the capture of eleven insurgents from a fortified construction site. Still later in the fighting, he was wounded in the right arm by a shot fired from the upper story of a building occupied by the insurgents. Without hesitation, he climbed three flights of stairs in pursuit and "after a bloody fight" managed to make a prisoner not only of his attacker but also of a lieutenant in the National Guard who had gone over to the rebels. He was a member of a group singled out for decoration by Citizen Sénard, president of the National Assembly. Confirmed in his rank of private first class at the time of the February 1849 reorganization of the Mobile

Mobile Guardsman Henry Friedl
(*l'Illustration* 1848: 210)

Guard, he stayed on even when the 7th battalion was absorbed by the 6th in the further reorganization of April 1849. For reasons that remain obscure, he seems to have been unhappy with this change, for two days later he requested and was granted an immediate discharge.

Quite similar is the story of Friedl's friend and comrade-in-arms, François—or as our celebratory poster would have it, Pierre—Charlemagne. Both sources agree that his date of birth was 17 March 1825, but this time the recording officer errs by underestimating his age at the time of his enlistment on 31 March as twenty-two years. The residence of his parents, Joseph and Rose Irma, and his own place of birth was Lurcy-Lévy in the Allier. Friedl and Charlemagne had shared the apartment in the rue Baillif until first one and then the other joined the Guard at a two-week interval. Charlemagne indicated that he was a "porcelain painter," a skilled occupation in which 59 percent of all workers were then unemployed. He had already earned acclaim in 1847 in the Haute-Vienne, where he received a medal for his courage in fighting a fire. In June 1848, not to be outdone by his former roommate, he captured an insurgent standard, was wounded in the face, and briefly made prisoner by the insurgents. His exploits commanded the attention of no less distinguished an observer than Commanding General and Minister of War Eugene Cavaignac. The general, in his eagerness to reward such bravery, tore the cross of the Legion of Honor from the lapel of Colonel Charras, who happened to be standing at his side, and pinned

Mobile Guardsman François Charlemagne
(*l'Illustration* 1848: 211)

it on Charlemagne's breast. Cavaignac's impulse was later confirmed by bureaucratic action, but Charlemagne remained a private (though briefly demoted to second-class status) through the reorganizations of 1849. In May of that year he was elected corporal, and it was in that rank that he asked to be discharged in December. With the issue of his certificate of good conduct, Charlemagne disappears from our view.

But enough of heroes and paragons of military virtue. What of goats, and cowards, and rogues? The archives of the Mobile Guard provide us with an ample supply, though their service records, except under the heading of disciplinary proceedings, are often rather abbreviated. An alarming number of men were expelled from the corps for offenses ranging from petty theft to desertion in the face of duty.[50] Pierre Mazin Juhelle will serve as representative of this group. Originally from Calvados, he was seventeen when he appeared on 3 April to enroll in the 5th battalion. Although most of the adjacent entries in the register include the usual interlinear notations on recruits' previous residences, parents' names, and occupations, in Juhelle's case even the spaces set aside for anthropometric descriptions have been left blank, presumably because his departure under less than honorable circumstances occurred in late June, before the battalion register was brought up to date. His entire record contains a bare minimum of information with the sole exception of a concluding note penned in an almost illegibly small hand. It indicates that Juhelle was formally expelled from the Mobile Guard in early August 1848 "for having abandoned the company during the insurrectionary days of 24, 25, and 26 June 1848." Though documentable cases of Mobile Guardsmen going over to the insurrection are virtually unknown, a sizable number deserted the corps, either before or after the June Days, without serving their one year and one day. My examination of the battalion registers shows that they amounted, in fact, to 8.4 percent of all those who signed on prior to 22 June. Whereas nearly all these men were granted amnesty by a ministerial decree of 1 July 1850, Juhelle, for having failed in his soldier's duty at the proverbial moment of truth, was among the few to whom this clemency was denied.

Illustrative cases of this type give us an initial idea of the variety of Mobile Guard experiences, allow us to assess the quality of the available documents, and help bring our subject to life. Still, no manageable number of case studies can convey a balanced sense of the make-up of the Mobile Guard as a whole. The kind of systematic statistical summary required for analytical purposes can be based only on an explicitly defined, representative sample. Although a detailed explanation of sampling procedures has been reserved for the Methodological Appendix, it is perhaps worthwhile to note here that the Mobile Guard sample used in this research consists of six battalions (comprising 3,845 individuals) selected to represent the full range of variations in the quality of the available data, the activity of Mobile Guard units in the June Days, and the socioeconomic and politicial divisions of the Parisian population.

As an initial step in assessing the collective sociological identity of the Mobile Guard, the occupational distribution of its members was compared with that of the general Parisian population. For this purpose, the occupations listed in battalion registers were coded within the thirteen categories used in the Chamber of Commerce's survey of 1848. Table 2.1 arrays the data for each of the six sampled battalions alongside the figures for the Parisian ward from which that battalion was recruited. Although all wards displayed gross similarities in the proportion of workers associated with various sectors, appreciable differences do occur as the result of residential or commercial concentrations of specific types of workers or enterprises. Note that these variations in the concentration of economic sectors by ward are also reflected in the occupational distribution within Mobile Guard battalions. Thus, although Chevalier (1950: 20) stressed that occupational heterogeneity was the rule in all Parisian wards and that localization, where it did occur, was more characteristic of individual streets or neighborhoods than of entire quarters, he also noted, for example, the preponderance of joiners and cabinetmakers that

Table 2.1

Occupational Distribution: Mobile Guard Battalions and Corresponding Parisian Wards (Percentage)

Sector	1st Battalion	1st Ward	5th Battalion	3d Ward	8th Battalion	4th Ward	16th Battalion	8th Ward	19th Battalion	10th Ward	23d Battalion	12th Ward
Food	6.0	6.2	5.6	4.4	6.6	5.0	3.2	2.4	4.1	7.0	3.5	5.7
Construction	27.4	30.8	16.2	16.7	17.4	9.3	17.0	20.2	28.4	35.1	27.1	24.0
Furniture	8.5	6.3	11.1	8.3	3.9	3.8	31.3	40.8	10.8	8.8	5.2	2.9
Clothing and shoes	9.4	13.3	19.2	20.0	22.0	41.9	4.7	3.8	11.8	12.8	13.4	9.0
Thread and textiles	8.5	1.5	7.7	9.9	7.2	8.2	5.6	4.2	4.4	0.7	9.7	11.2
Leather	0.9	0.2	0.9	2.2	0.3	1.5	0.0	0.3	0.3	0.2	3.2	19.5
Carriage-making	10.3	20.7	1.7	6.2	2.6	3.6	1.2	2.2	4.4	6.8	3.0	4.1
Chemicals, ceramics	1.7	0.8	1.3	5.1	2.0	1.5	2.3	3.2	3.0	2.3	4.5	3.3
Base Metals	17.5	11.4	12.8	6.5	11.8	4.0	16.4	16.3	8.8	6.1	10.7	9.5
Precious metals	1.7	2.4	3.8	4.1	8.9	3.4	6.1	1.4	6.8	0.8	5.2	0.5
Cooperage, basketry	2.1	1.3	4.7	1.6	3.9	3.5	4.4	1.2	3.7	2.3	3.2	3.3
Fancy goods	2.1	2.9	9.4	9.2	5.3	5.8	1.8	2.9	4.7	3.5	2.5	1.1
Printing	3.8	2.1	5.6	6.0	7.9	8.5	6.1	1.1	8.8	13.6	8.7	6.0
TOTAL	99.9	99.9	100.0	102.2	99.8	100.0	100.1	100.0	100.0	100.0	99.9	100.1
(N)	(234)	(14,106)	(234)	(15,407)	(304)	(8,207)	(342)	(32,352)	(296)	(9,961)	(402)	(10,471)

Sources: Archives historiques (Xm); Chambre de Commerce (1851: Tables 5-16).
Note: Reprinted, by permission of the publisher, from Traugott (1980a: 700). Data on ward populations include both resident and transient male workers.

typified the faubourg St. Antoine, part of the 8th ward. Table 2.1 bears out this observation, for it shows that in the 8th ward furniture trades employed 41 percent of the general labor force and 31 percent of the Mobile Guardsmen in that district, percentages well in excess of those found elsewhere in the capital.

In general, the practitioners of any given sector were distributed according to one of three basic patterns. Certain sectors—"Food" is probably the best example—employed large numbers of workers in enterprises that were, by their very nature, dispersed throughout the city. This combination of aggregate size and decentralization precluded marked local differences. Other sectors—for instance, "Leather"—involved very few workers, typically in enterprises of moderate size, a circumstance that favored strong between-ward variations.[51] Still others—especially those that operated on a large scale like "Construction"—were subject to perceptible variations due to the location of a few large enterprises in specific trades.

By employing a sample that embraces six of twelve Parisian wards, selected for the variety of their socioeconomic composition, much of the nonsystematic variation reflected in Table 2.1 has been controlled. This is apparent in Table 2.2, which represents the distribution into economic sectors of (1) the six-battalion Mobile Guard sample in its entirety; (2) the six corresponding Parisian wards, aggregated; and (3) the population of Paris as a whole. In general, the fit between columns 1 and 2 suggests that the composition of Mobile Guard battalions closely conformed to that of the Parisian quarters from which they were recruited. At the same time, the remarkable convergence between columns 1 and 3 indicates that the methods used to recruit the Mobile Guard resulted in a corps that faithfully reproduced the socioeconomic distribution of the Parisian working class at large.[52] Taken together, these findings cast grave doubt on any view of the Mobile Guard as a highly differentiated segment of the urban lower classes and intensify our interest in understanding the role it assumed in the June Days.

The central issues are posed in their starkest form by con-

Table 2.2
Occupational Distribution: Mobile Guard and the Adult Male Parisian
Population, Aggregated
(Percentage)

Sector	1 Mobile Guard: Six- Battalion Sample	2 Chamber of Commerce: Wards 1,3,4,8,10,12	3 Chamber of Commerce: All Paris
Food	4.6	4.5	3.9
Construction	22.4	22.3	19.6
Furniture	12.0	18.6	14.0
Clothing and shoes	13.2	13.1	14.8
Thread and textiles	7.2	5.5	5.4
Leather	1.0	2.9	2.1
Carriage-making	3.6	6.6	5.2
Chemicals, ceramics	2.6	2.9	3.2
Base metals	12.8	10.9	10.8
Precious metals	5.6	2.0	5.3
Cooperage, basketry	3.7	1.9	2.0
Fancy goods	4.0	4.1	8.6
Printing	7.1	4.7	5.3
TOTAL	99.8	100.0	100.2
(N)	(1,812)	(90,504)	(204,925)

Sources: Archives historiques (Xm); Chambre de Commerce (1851).
Note: Reprinted, by permission of the publisher, from Traugott (1980a: 701).

trasting the June defenders of order with the insurgents whom
they helped repress. A juxtaposition of the occupational distributions of the formations representing revolution and reaction most directly tests the proposition that class origins
account for the decisive difference in the political orientation
of these groups. Such a comparison can be effected thanks to
the detailed studies (Price 1972; Tilly and Lees 1975) that
have been based on the records of arrests made in Paris immediately following the defeat of the June insurrection. Tilly
and Lees in particular, by extending the Chamber of Commerce classification scheme to include service workers, those

employed in commerce, professionals, military veterans, and a host of miscellaneous occupations, have made it possible to increase greatly the percentage of those in the Mobile Guard sample who could be included in direct comparisons.

Table 2.3 displays the occupational distribution of these representatives of opposing camps. Column 1 refers only to those Mobile Guardsmen who fought in June and whose occupations were listed in the battalion registers. Column 2 is taken from Tilly and Lees's classification of insurgents arrested at the time of the June Days.[53] Even casual inspection reveals that these two groups bear a remarkable resemblance with respect to previous occupation. This holds true not only in the categories borrowed directly from the Chamber of Commerce inquiry but also among nonindustrial workers whether of higher or lower status. The principal exception to this general correspondence is in the relative overrepresentation of former military men in the Mobile Guard. Of course, the preference of men with a service background for an organized militia offering premium wages hardly seems surprising. A number of further discrepancies—for example, the relative overrepresentation in the Mobile Guard of thread and textile workers (4.9 percent versus 3.3 percent among the insurgents) and of precious metal workers (3.7 percent versus 2.4 percent) and the underrepresentation of transport workers (2.0 percent versus 4.1 percent) and to a lesser extent metal workers (8.0 percent versus 12.2 percent)—are of sufficient magnitude in both absolute and relative terms to merit further investigation. Yet they take little away from an overall impression that the Mobile Guard, far from constituting a highly differentiated group, was actually a rather broadly based fighting force that, both among industrial and nonindustrial sectors, was essentially indistinguishable from the insurgents themselves.

Although it forces us back to the thirteen Chamber of Commerce categories, it is helpful to convert these percentages into rates of participation based on the total number of male workers in each sector of the industrial economy.[54] Although the raw rates reported in Table 2.4 reflect the difference in ab-

Table 2.3

Occupational Distribution: Mobile Guard and June Arrestees
(Percentage)

Occupational category (Tilly and Lees)	1 Mobile Guard: Six-Battalion Sample	2 June Arrestees
Food	3.7	4.0
Construction	15.0	18.2
Furniture	8.1	6.9
Clothing and shoes	8.7	10.3
Thread and textiles	4.9	3.3
Leather	0.7	1.6
Carriage-making	2.4	1.6
Chemicals, ceramics	1.7	1.3
Base metals	8.0	12.2
Precious metals	3.7	2.4
Cooperage, basketry	2.4	1.1
Fancy goods	2.5	2.0
Printing	4.7	4.5
Transport	2.0	4.1
Services and others	14.1	13.1
Liberal professions	2.2	2.8
Commerce	6.6	7.6
Military	8.5	3.0
TOTAL	99.9	100.0
(N)	(2,696)	(8,371)

Sources: Archives historiques (Xm); and raw data from Tilly and Lees (1975: 190).

Note: The format of Table 2.3 resembles that of a table previously published in Traugott (1980a: 702). The percentages by sector reported here for June arrestees differ, however, because they are based exclusively on Parisians who reported an occupation.

solute size between the Mobile Guard and insurgent samples, a glance at the simple rank orderings reveals the same sort of general convergence observed in earlier comparisons. There are, to be sure, notable discrepancies. Two of these occur in the sectors dealing with "Leather" goods and "Cooperage,"

Table 2.4
Participation by Sector in the June Days, 1848

Sector	Rate per 10,000 Male Workers		Rank Order (1 = High)	
	Mobile Guardsmen	June Arrestees	Mobile Guardsmen	June Arrestees
Food	104	424	4	2
Construction	101	379	5	3
Furniture	76	200	9	9
Clothing and shoes	78	285	8	6
Thread and textiles	118	248	2	7
Leather	45	325	12	5
Carriage-making	60	123	11	12
Chemicals, ceramics	70	167	10	11
Base metals	102	463	6	1
Precious metals	93	185	7	10
Cooperage, basketry	164	224	1	8
Fancy goods	41	96	13	13
Printing	116	347	3	4

Sources: Archives historiques (Xm); Chambre de Commerce (1851); and raw data from Tilly and Lees (1975: 190).
Note: Reprinted, by permission of the publisher, from Traugott (1980a: 703).

the categories that embrace the smallest numbers of workers and are therefore most subject to purely statistical variation. Another involves "Thread and textiles" workers, of particular interest because this most proletarianized of all sectors of the Parisian economy contributed—Marx notwithstanding—proportionately more participants to the repression than to the insurrection.[55] In general, however, trades that were overrepresented in one camp were also overrepresented in the other, and inversely, suggesting that insofar as occupational characteristics were important, they created differential probabilities of participation that were not specific to either side of the conflict.

To give added weight to this conclusion, it is useful to

Table 2.5
Correlations with Rate of Participation in the Mobile Guard

Characteristics of Occupational groups (Chambre de Commerce 1851)	June Rate of Participation	
	Pearson's Coefficient*	Significance Level
Percentage of male workers	0.023	0.403
Average salary	0.031	0.369
Percentage of literate workers	0.127	0.086
Percentage of workers living *en garni*	−0.134	0.076
Average number of workers per *patron*	−0.149	0.054
Rate of unemployment	0.209	0.012

Note: Reprinted, by permission of the publisher, from Traugott (1980a: 704).
* $N = 116$ or 117 in all cases.

examine the correlates of rates of June participation. This is possible because the Chamber of Commerce inquiry organized its findings not only according to thirteen broad sectoral categories but also according to 345 finely divided "occupational groups," providing for each a rich variety of sociological and economic information.[56] For each of these groups it was therefore possible to derive a rate of participation expressed as the number of Mobile Guard volunteers active in June per 10,000 adult males working in that trade.[57]

Table 2.5 presents the first-order correlations of Mobile Guard rates of participation with the relevant sociological and economic variables. Its first line shows that the percentage of male workers in an occupational group bore no relation to the likelihood of taking part in the repression. This contrasts with Tilly and Lees's report that among June *arrestees*, trades with a high male/female ratio were the most active (1975: 193). The discrepancy is, however, more apparent than real and probably does *not* reflect a difference between insurgents and repressors. The alleged tendency of predominantly male trades to furnish most arrestees is merely an artifact, under

74

the method employed by Tilly and Lees, of the large number of female workers in the denominator of the rate of participation in certain sectors. Given this alternative explanation of the apparent relation and recalling the consistency with which Mobile Guardsmen and insurgents have been shown to resemble each other in virtually every occupational characteristic, it seems more reasonable to accept the lack of relation between occupational sex ratios and participation in the case of the Mobile Guard and, indeed, to suggest that, once purely technical issues have been set aside, the same will be shown to hold true of the insurgents.[58]

Similarly, the second line of Table 2.5 reveals a lack of relation between the level of wages in an occupational group and its representation in the Mobile Guard, reinforcing the view that the trades from which volunteers were recruited represented the full range of variations in status and skill levels among the working population of Paris.

Literacy and the percentage living *en garni* are two highly revealing sociological indicators, and here it is precisely the *lack* of correlation with Mobile Guard participation that is highly significant as a test of the lumpenproletariat thesis.[59] Insofar as one would accept illiterates and residents of transient hotels as representatives of the lumpenproletariat, the observed levels of association contradict theories according to which the Mobile Guard constituted a *déclassé* fragment of the lower class by demonstrating a very weak tendency for Mobile Guardsmen to be drawn from occupational groups in which such workers were common.

The data also show that there exists no significant association between Mobile Guard participation and shop size. To the extent that a pattern can be discerned at all, it is for men from small shops to be slightly overrepresented among the June repressors.[60] Indeed, the single correlation that achieves the level of statistical significance is that which relates participation in the Mobile Guard with occupational groups with elevated rates of unemployment, a finding interesting in its very ambiguity. On the one hand, it might seem unsurprising to uncover an overrepresentation of the jobless in an organization formed in part to alleviate an unemployment crisis. Yet this same result could also be read as an indication that the Mobile Guard tended to attract marginal, maladapted individuals or those whose flaws of character rendered them incapable of holding down a steady job—in short, a lumpenproletariat. The latter interpretation, however, is hardly tenable in the context of the economic depression of 1848 where, according to the Chamber of Commerce, fully 54.4 percent of the entire labor force was out of work. In these circumstances, one can hardly claim that the unemployed represented a small and isolated minority of misfits; rather they constituted a majority of the working population of Paris and, incidentally, the quasi-totality of those enrolled in the National Workshops, which supplied a substantial share of the June insurgents. It seems more plausible to interpret the observed correlation as indicating a selective responsiveness among Mobile Guardsmen to environing economic conditions and to reject the inference that the presence of many unemployed reflects lumpen origins on the part of the Mobile Guard any more than it does on the part of the insurgents.

In short, what one learns from the painstaking examination of Mobile Guard enlistment records is to be wary of facile generalizations. Nonetheless, if this attempt to apply systematic methods presents a genuine advantage over the impressionistic views of contemporary observers, it is to permit the cautious extraction of a few well-substantiated conclusions. First, if self-reported occupations tell us anything at all, the Mobile Guard consisted in the main of workers in artisanal trades requiring relatively high levels of skill and training. This is not to deny the presence of a scattering of occupations that fit descriptions of the lumpenproletariat. If, unsurprisingly, no Mobile Guardsman listed his previous occupation as pimp, beggar, or thief, one does find listed a handful of itinerant peddlers, a single ragpicker, several street musicians, a magician, a mountebank, and a number for whom "no profession" is specified. But even if one were to adopt a broad definition of lumpenproletarian status that included tinkers, scrap-metal dealers, market porters, and literati of all kinds, one could come up with only eighty-three such individuals or 3.0 percent of the total sample. In such trivial proportions, the presence of these individuals seems to do no more than confirm the fact that the Mobile Guard constituted a fairly representative cross-section of the Parisian population. Certainly it provides no support for the contention that the Mobile Guard consisted *predominantly* of lumpenproletarians. Indeed, their share of the total is almost precisely equal to the 2.6 percent of arrested insurgents categorized as lumpenproletarians by Price, who concluded that "Marx is thus wrong to identify these demi-world figures with the forces of reaction."[61]

One might, of course, object that self-reported occupation is an imperfect, perhaps even fatally flawed, indicator of class position or maintain that the distribution of Mobile Guard occupations reported here is the result of recruits' wholesale inflation of their status. Although contentions of this type might conceivably impugn the validity of these data, they could never serve to rescue a class explanation of political orientation in the June Days, for they inevitably apply with greater reason to the insurgents. If some form of occupational self-aggrandizement took place among Mobile Guardsmen, the incentives to dissimulate must have been yet more powerful among those arrested for participation in the rebellion. One would still have to explain why the occupational origins of these two groups conform so closely. Is it plausible that individuals' widespread misrepresentation of their occupational status miraculously reproduced among Mobile Guardsmen a pattern virtually identical to that based on what our imaginary critic might presume to be the purely factual reports of June arrestees? It seems more reasonable to conclude that this convergence in occupational distributions reflects an underlying reality and that the explanation of their divergent stance in June must be sought elsewhere.

The Cohort Hypothesis

Although class origin per se has proved to be an inadequate predictor of political orientation in the June Days, this hardly exhausts the explanatory alternatives that might be based on the sociological and economic characteristics of participants. Consistent with the suggestive comments of Gossez (1956b), Caspard has constructed a "cohort hypothesis" of Mobile Guard behavior from his empirical study of its members. His point of departure is the observation that by far the most striking difference between Mobile Guardsmen and June arrestees is one of age. According to his figures (1974: 88, 89), the average insurgent was thirty-four years old at the time of the rebellion, the average Mobile Guardsman just twenty-one and one-half.

Of course, the meaning of this substantial disparity is open to a variety of interpretations.[62] Caspard rejected as simplistic the notion that youth may be equated with a lack of work experience, developed economic interests, and therefore political consciousness. Working with the detailed records available on Mobile Guard deserters arrested for participation on the side of the June insurgents, he was able to ascertain that at the age of twenty or even eighteen years, most of these young men had already acquired several years of occupational experience. Instead, Caspard emphasized that the younger age of Mobile Guardsmen translated into a relatively humble status within the same artisanal hierarchy of which insurgents represented a more senior cohort. He speculated that the former's lack of seniority left them especially vulnerable to the massive layoffs occasioned by the economic crisis. To such jobless individuals, the Mobile Guard offered the modest but respectable pay of 1 franc 50 centimes per day, supplemented with free lodging and clothing and the promise of medical and other benefits.[63] It was thus the relative insecurity of their status in the private economy—and, by contrast, the relative security they enjoyed as Mobile Guardsmen—that set this younger cohort apart from the somewhat older segment of the working class that built and defended the June barricades.

The cohort hypothesis represents a considerable gain in sophistication over strict class explanations. Marx's rather rigid insistence on the opposition of a sharply defined and mutually exclusive bourgeoisie and proletariat forced him to deal with the ostensibly anomalous behavior of the Mobile Guard by developing an empirically ungrounded lumpenproletariat thesis. Caspard argues, on the contrary, that

> The cleavage between insurgents and Mobile Guardsmen does not separate the industrial proletariat from the lumpenproletariat. It passes right through the former, leaving on one side the older workers more deeply rooted in their trade and in their city, and on the other younger workers, consequently less impregnated with the traditions, ideology, and doctrines of the workers' movement. (1974: 105-106)

This argument has the ring of plausibility. Stealing a march on contemporaries of the Mobile Guard who never tired of stressing the extreme youthfulness of its members,[64] the cohort hypothesis raises the primary aggregate difference between June contenders to the level of an explanatory principle. Data based on the six-battalion sample used in the present study appear to confirm Caspard's description by showing that the average Mobile Guardsman was 22.1 years of age at the time of recruitment, whereas Tilly and Lees have established 33.4 years as the age of arrestees at the time of the June insurrection.[65] When all other criteria of comparison have revealed these groups to be so nearly identical, so sharp a contrast in age naturally seems to offer powerful explanatory leverage.

But before accepting the cohort hypothesis at face value, it is important to ask whether this contrast might not signify something else altogether. In actuality, the difference in age, and therefore cohort, that is alleged to account for the divergent political orientation of repressors and insurgents may be no more than an artifact of the organizational constraints imposed upon the Mobile Guard recruitment process. In effect, the decree providing for the creation of the corps called for volunteers between the ages of sixteen and thirty. In other words, the youthfulness of the Mobile Guard was ensured by a statutory bar against the admission of older participants, which quite clearly did not apply in the case of the insurgents.[66]

In addition to age limitations proper, further formal restrictions as well as the conditions of service in the corps reinforced the tendency toward youthfulness. Some (though not all) Mobile Guard recruiting posters prescribed that volunteers be unmarried. Although no systematic information on the marital status of recruits was gathered at the time of enlistment, it is possible to reconstruct the situation from the applications for pensions paid to the survivors of those killed in the June fighting. These show that only one among the thirty listed members of the fifth battalion was married.[67] The proportion of June arrestees who were married was 59.4 percent. This dramatic difference is more readily understood, quite apart from formal regulations, when one recalls that Mobile Guardsmen lived in barracks, were allowed limited leaves of absence, and could be assigned to various parts of the capital and its outskirts (or even to provincial towns) at the whim of the authorities.[68]

The cohort hypothesis is thus neither the only nor the simplest explanation of the age distinction between the Mobile Guard and the group of arrested insurgents. It argues that the former attracted a body of men differentiated from the June arrestees by their youth, not their class origins, and that it is the socioeconomic characteristics associated with age that separated repressors from insurgents. The alternative view is that the difference in age (like that in marital status) resulted from a combination of statutory constraints and self-selection, and since these and related secondary characteristics can be accounted for solely in these terms, they bear no necessary relation to the political alignments observed in June. The latter interpretation suggests that the explanation of the opposition of Mobile Guardsmen and insurgents should be sought not in the traits of individual members but in the collective identities of these groups once they coalesced.

To draw the contrast more clearly still, the cohort hypothesis rests on individual differences that predated the creation of the Mobile Guard; the alternative to be advanced here, although not denying that age-related differences may have explanatory power, assumes the revolutionary situation to be essentially open-ended and concedes the possibility that non-etiological factors may have intervened to shape the evolution of the political equation between February and June. Such a view, emphasizing the initial lack of differences between the Mobile Guard and the rest of the Parisian lower class, is consistent with the fact that Mobile Guardsmen were openly recruited from the February barricades and that Parisian leftists resolutely expected the Mobile Guard to join them in an eventual insurrection.

There is, moreover, one available statistical index that is of use in weighing the two alternatives. After the June Days, about 1 percent of Mobile Guardsmen were arrested on suspicion of having participated in the fighting on the side of the insurgents.[69] It is possible to identify them in the lists of arrestees and, by retracing their records in the Mobile Guard registers, establish their ages at the time of enlistment. If the cohort hypothesis explains the greater part of the difference in June orientation, one might expect that arrested Mobile Guardsmen would tend more nearly to resemble insurgents in age and related characteristics than loyal Mobile Guardsmen. If, on the other hand, the lower age of Mobile Guardsmen is largely the result of recruitment criteria and unrelated to political orientation, one would anticipate that the age of arrested Mobile Guardsmen would approximate that of their fellow militiamen and be substantially lower than that of the insurgents with whom they allegedly sided. An examination of the judicial files of June arrestees shows that the average age of "disloyal" Mobile Guardsmen was 22.8 years. This compares, the reader will recall, with 22.1 years for loyal Mobile Guardsmen and 33.4 years for all insurgents.[70]

Caspard (1974) computed roughly similar figures.[71] He focused on the fact that disloyal Mobile Guardsmen were somewhat older than their loyal comrades-in-arms and concluded that age, not occupation, determined the contours of the political cleavage within as well as outside the Mobile Guard. It seems more appropriate to remark that although the average age of disloyal Mobile Guardsmen was slightly higher than that of their loyal confreres (by 0.7 years according to the figures reported here), it was at the same time substantially lower than that of all June insurgents (by more than ten years, in fact).

Since this is likely to be the nearest approximation to a critical test between the approaches based on individual versus collective characteristics of June participants, it seems worth restating: the average age of Mobile Guardsmen arrested for participation in the insurrection is intermediate between those of comparison groups representing the forces of revolution and reaction. The fact that it is far closer to the average age of other Mobile Guardsmen, however, indicates that age differences were primarily an artifact of recruitment criteria and self-selection. This suggests that the cohort effects were of limited causal significance and can bear relatively little of the explanatory weight.

But if this is true, and if neither the class nor the cohort hypothesis can adequately account for differences in political orientation at the time of the June Days, what alternative squares better with what is known of participants in the insurrection? The next chapter explores an explanatory framework that assumes that June combatants from both sides of the barricades had been as close in political orientation as they were in occupational origins at the time of the February Days. This "organizational hypothesis" asserts that the crucial differences evolved over the period *between* February and June and that, in the case of the repressors, the principal determinants can be traced back to the specific, collective experiences of Mobile Guard recruits as members of that corps.

THREE

An Organizational Analysis of Mobile Guard Political Orientation

THUS FAR this inquiry has achieved the largely negative end of pointing out the shortcomings of previous explanations of the Mobile Guard's June behavior. The virtual identity of occupational origins between insurgents and Mobile Guardsmen revealed the simple class hypothesis to be untenable. Proponents of the cohort hypothesis have argued in turn that the aggregate difference in age that most clearly distinguished the opposing camps, in interaction with economic factors, produced divergent political orientations. But this age differential is most readily explained as the result of the Mobile Guard's selective criteria of recruitment. The evidence linking age to the political behavior of this militia is indirect at best.

There exists, on the other hand, strong though circumstantial evidence to indicate that the February barricades actually furnished a disproportionate share of *both* June repressors and insurgents. If so, then the point of political divergence between the two sides in that historic confrontation must have occurred in the period separating the popular uprisings of February and June. The present chapter elaborates upon elements of the narrative history already outlined in an effort to isolate the collective experience of the Mobile Guard under the early Second Republic and relate it to political behavior. For the purpose of such an analysis, the case of the Mobile Guard seems ideally suited. Not only did it play a pivotal role in June but, since its creation coincided precisely with the onset of the period in question, it can be studied apart from the complications that might otherwise arise from prior history or organizational legacies. At the same time, there exists a relative abundance of primary evidence that clearly documents the process by which the regime in power secured the loyalty of its members.

In undertaking this explanatory task, we are fortunate to possess an invaluable bit of theoretical guidance. The factors contributing to the loyalty or disloyalty of a military formation to a political regime in times of revolutionary upheaval have been analyzed by Chorley in *Armies and the Art of Revolution* (1943: especially 175, 181, 242-48). From her study of a wide assortment of historical cases in the modern era, she has distilled the following conclusions:

1. No popular insurrection can succeed against the energetic opposition of trained troops, united in their purpose.

2. Except at the unsuccessful conclusion of a protracted, large-scale war, the rank and file will invariably obey a unified corps of officers. Properly socialized officers will, in turn, normally support a status quo regime.

3. Even where the officer corps is divided or uncertain in its loyalties, the rank and file is likely to be won over to a revolutionary movement only to the extent that the following conditions are met: the average length of service is short; the mechanisms ensuring collective isolation from the civilian population break down; members possess practical grievances that are both salient and generalized and that are allowed to persist without redress.

These generalizations will serve to structure the subsequent discussion of the circumstances that influenced the political orientation of the Mobile Guard.

Of course, a proper test of Chorley's axioms could never be based on the isolated instance of Mobile Guard behavior in the Parisian insurrection of June 1848. To be sure, events appear to bear out the first rule she has formulated: the Mobile Guard's June conduct was remarkably energetic and, because it helped to galvanize the remaining forces of repression, played an ultimately decisive role in the victory of the repression. But it is impossible to provide a meaningful operationalization of the concept of "energetic" opposition or to identify what might constitute properly "trained" troops or genuine "unity of purpose" on the basis of a single case. Similarly, the experience of the Mobile Guard can offer no positive evidence concerning the effects of foreign war or length of service since these conditions were inapplicable or invariant in this instance. Chorley's second and third propositions, however, direct attention to the determining influence upon Mobile Guard behavior of a cluster of crucial variables: the recruitment, socialization, and unity of the officer corps; and the conditions of service, isolation, and grievances of the rank and file.

A Mobile Guardsman Carried in Triumph by His Comrades
(*l'Illustration* 1848: 224)

The results of an analysis conceived in this way will assume their full significance only when later projected alongside the parallel case of the Mobile Guard's "opposite number," the National Workshops, for such a strategy of paired comparison will reintroduce variations in crucial organizational characteristics and thus permit us to place in relief their causal impact. Yet the more immediate benefit to be realized from the application of Chorley's generalizations, themselves distillations of a great many empirical cases, is to order and to focus the following discussion of Mobile Guard political orientation.

The Constitution of the Mobile Guard Officer Corps

Chalmin (1948) has provided the only extensive treatment of the formation of the Mobile Guard officer corps. Because my conclusions differ from his in important respects, it will first be necessary to summarize his arguments in some detail. In general, Chalmin arrived at a negative assessment of the military qualifications and internal morale of Mobile Guard cadres and therefore of their ability to instill discipline in their subordinates. He attributed these shortcomings to the process whereby officers were selected. In order to oversee the organization and training of the mass of raw recruits enrolled in early March, officers were initially detached to the Mobile Guard from regular army units. According to Chalmin (1948: 51), the commanding officers of the units called upon to supply the necessary manpower seized this opportunity to rid themselves of their least desirable elements. Thus, the Mobile Guard began its career under the leadership of a staff of rejects who set an unfortunate tone for the new formation. Chalmin noted, moreover, that the elections of late March allowed these men to gain a permanent foothold in the Mobile Guard. He cited cases of transferred officers with extensive records of misconduct, their offenses ranging from insubordination to theft and embezzlement. He also pointed to the Mobile

Guard's spotty record for discipline among the rank and file (1948: 49, 51). The connection appeared to him self-evident.

This interpretation is, however, open to question on several grounds. First, Chalmin's assessment of the level of internal discipline adopted as its implicit standard of comparison the conditions that obtain in regular army units in times of political stability, not those characteristic of paramilitary organizations in revolutionary periods. Second, examples of indiscipline in the ranks of the Mobile Guard, though widespread, were almost exclusively confined to the nonmilitary behavior of individual members, and their relevance to the collective political behavior of the corps was never demonstrated. Third and most important, Chalmin's evidence was drawn from the earliest phase of Mobile Guard mobilization and thus failed to consider the crucial process whereby the officer corps was first purged and then consolidated as a bulwark of order. It is therefore essential to reexamine the evolution of the Mobile Guard over the first four months of its existence in order to arrive at an accurate assessment of its organizational effectiveness.

That indiscipline was rampant in the ranks of the Mobile Guard is amply documented. The enlistment records show that even before the June Days arrived, one Mobile Guardsman in twelve had either been ejected from or deserted the corps. This statistic, furthermore, takes no account of the many others who were brought before disciplinary councils for lesser offenses or who returned voluntarily from unauthorized absences and were accepted back into their units. Caussidière, who in his official capacity as Prefect of Police had frequent dealings with individual Mobile Guardsmen, complained that their "attitude left much to be desired as to order and neatness."[1]

The impression of slackened discipline is contradicted in part by both contemporary observers and subsequent analysts who stressed the enormous progress achieved in this sphere in so short a time (Normanby 1857: 89-90; Doumenc 1948: 258). In fact, the Guard's disciplinary problems actually reflected the state of disarray of French politics in general, and roughly similar difficulties were encountered in every police and military body in the wake of the February Days.[2] The infractions of Mobile Guard volunteers were for the most part limited to their off-duty behavior. An example is the complaint, originated by the proprietress of a house of prostitution, that a party of Mobile Guardsmen had initiated a fist fight with the madame's two sons (Archives historiques Xm 32, 29 March). In the same vein, a letter from Prefect Caussidière to General Duvivier implicated nearly fifty Mobile Guardsmen in a disturbance resulting from the rejection of their demand that the owner of a dance hall discount the price of admission, drinks, and dances (Archives historiques Xm 32, 7 April). The commander of the Ecole militaire, portions of which were being used to quarter battalions of the Mobile Guard, reported that certain of these men were piercing holes in the roofs of their barracks in order to permit them to slip out during the night. Corrective measures failed to remedy the problem because "the garrison is so young, so wild, so thoughtless that it almost always happens that a hole closed up today is reopened tomorrow."[3] Other typical offenses involved Mobile Guardsmen bathing nude in the Seine (Archives historiques Xm 32, 14 May) and an incident in which two Mobile Guardsmen were arrested for having made a public spectacle of themselves by traversing the city in a carriage with two prostitutes, exchanging their uniforms for the latter's clothing, and hurling invectives at shocked passersby (Archives historiques Xm 32, 16 May).

There is proof, in short, that rowdiness and misconduct were nearly daily occurrences. Incidents of a political nature were, however, relatively rare. We do find occasional instances of politically tinged behavior, as when three young Mobile Guardsmen, having drunk more than their fill, made a nuisance of themselves on the Place du Châtelet by responding to shouts of "Long Live the Assembly!" with their own cry of "Long Live the Democratic Republic!" (Archives historiques Xm 32, 22 May). Similarly, some two weeks later, as many as 500 Mobile Guardsmen were reported to have gathered on the Champs Elysées to listen to "reprehensible speeches" demanding that Mobile Guard officers renew their oaths of loyalty.[4]

In short, a great deal of impropriety and misconduct is known to have occurred, most of it the work of scattered individuals, but this is matched by a virtual absence of concerted acts of political disloyalty. Caspard (1974: 100-101) has offered the useful distinction between the level of Mobile Guard discipline, which he rated low, and the level of *esprit de corps* in the organization as a whole, which he defined as "respect for officers, pride in the military, and unconditional concern with the maintenance of order" and rated high. Chorley's analysis indicated that the collective decision of a military formation as to its role in civil conflict depends primarily on the latter, and thus the Mobile Guard, despite its frequently tumultuous behavior, seemed predisposed on this ground to loyalty in June.[5]

Still, an explanation of Mobile Guard political orientation requires that one reach beyond unsystematic impressions based on the behavior of isolated individuals and colored in the light of the political exigencies of the moment. To take just one individual example, delegates assigned to the Mobile Guard by the "revolutionary committee" of the Club des clubs, the central council that attempted to coordinate the action of the democratic clubs, wrote of Thunot, commander of the 4th battalion, that he had been an invaluable aid in their mobilizing efforts. They assured their superiors that he could speak for the adherence of his men to the radical cause in any collision with the government.[6] But among the personal papers of General Duvivier, a note signed by this same Thunot pledged his unqualified allegiance to the commander under whom he had already served, nine years earlier (Archives historiques F1 2, dossier for March). Moreover, this officer's individual records show that in June he in fact assumed an important role in the repression.

The above case is not atypical. Moderates and radicals alike were prone to such misreadings of Mobile Guard intentions. We have previously noted that even in retrospect Tocqueville's acknowledgment of the role of Mobile Guard cadres in turning the revolutionary tide was almost grudging. The radical Lefrançais (1902: 52), for his part, characterized its leaders as a collection of "reactionaries of the first water," and Ménard (1904: 188), while neglecting to cite the basis for his judgment, claimed that most officers came from "rich families" and could presumably be expected to side with the forces of order. In short, the most varied constructions of the political orientation of Mobile Guard cadres all seemed plausible at the time, and the spurious assurance of opinions expressed after the fact and based on unsubstantiated assumptions regarding officers' political or economic origins deserves our skepticism. If we are to arrive at a balanced, empirically grounded assessment of the composition of the Mobile Guard officer corps, it will be necessary to reconstruct the process whereby its members were initially recruited and subsequently transformed into a force for order.[7]

If the formal regulations governing the constitution of the Mobile Guard officer corps are any indication, it might have been expected to prove as volatile and unreliable as that of the National Guard. The founding statutes prescribed that all officers, with the exception of the commanding general and his skeletal general staff, be chosen by the rank and file. At the outset and on a strictly provisional basis, half of the noncommissioned officers were to be detached from the regular army,[8] but these were to be replaced once battalions reached half-strength through elections for all positions of responsibility. In fact, this arrangement, intended to ensure the democratic character of this revolutionary militia, was systematically subverted.

It was, moreover, on the initiative of the rank and file that these formal provisions were undermined. Beginning around mid-March, as the first Mobile Guard battalions attained half-strength, General Duvivier designated civilians from the offices of ward mayors to supervise the selection of officers. The report filed by the deputy-mayor of the 11th ward on the elections held on 20 March in the 21st and 22d battalions provided details on the mechanics of this process. Much to the annoyance of this official, his explanation of the ground rules for election degenerated into a heated discussion among those present, many of whom objected to the exclusion of their preferred candidate for battalion commander, a captain detached from the 55th regiment of the line. Just when the deputy-mayor had succeeded in calming the men and convincing them of the futility of their protests, the word that detached officers had been ruled ineligible reached the 22d battalion, waiting its turn in the courtyard outside, and renewed disorders broke out. Efforts to dissuade these Mobile Guardsmen from marching forthwith to the seat of the Provisional Government to overturn this restriction ended in failure, and the deputy-mayor was obliged to suspend operations and burn the few ballots that had already been cast (Archives historiques Xm 32, 20 March).

When much the same difficulties were encountered in other Mobile Guard units, it became clear that the actions of Duvivier were partly responsible for the conflicting interpretations of the electoral statutes. The commanding general seemed torn between his desire to guarantee the internally democratic character of the new militia and at the same time to assert firm control over this important pillar of the moderate republic's program. The deputy-mayor of the 11th ward reported that Duvivier had instructed him on the eve of the elections described above to observe scrupulously the terms of the government's original decree, thus denying consideration to detached officers. But this same informant also regretted that a statement made by the general at that morning's assembly had assured the troops that these men were eligible.[9]

By 25 March, Duvivier had worked out the compromise solution that was ultimately adopted by the Provisional Government. Citing numerous instances in which the rank and file had insisted on electing detached officers and where morale and respect for authority had suffered as a consequence of his refusal on statutory grounds to honor those results, he proposed an alternative system that would permit the selection of experienced officers on whom the troops could count for leadership and the government could count for loyalty. Under the terms of a new decree (Archives historiques Xm 32, 27 March), the election of a detached officer was to be considered as a nomination subject to the approval of the Minister of War, based on the recommendation of the commanding general of the Mobile Guard. When a review of the nominee's dossier proved unsatisfactory, his election would be annulled and he would be immediately returned to the regular army unit from which he derived. When, however, the result of the review process was a favorable judgment, the nominee would assume his new rank in the Mobile Guard and be protected from recall by his former unit.[10]

This compromise proved acceptable to all parties. The rank and file were pleased to have their electoral decisions upheld in the majority of cases. Detached officers thus benefited from much more rapid advancement than they could expect in the army of the line. Above all, the Mobile Guard administration profited by this opportunity to handpick its cadres. The officer corps was open to men of experience and military socialization whose authority was legitimated by election, yet whose obe-

Table 3.1
Previous Military Experience of Mobile Guard Officers

Rank	N	Detached Officers	Volunteers With Prior Military Experience	Volunteers With No Prior Military Experience	Percentage With Prior Military Experience
Battalion commander	23	13	10	0	100
Captain	188	34	110	43	77
Lieutenant	184	15	94	75	59
Second lieutenant	187	11	77	99	47

Source: Archives historiques (Xm).

dience was virtually guaranteed by what amounted to administrative appointment. Continuity and hierarchical integration were enhanced by regularizing the status of the officers who had supervised the training of the new recruits even as the discipline of the Mobile Guard was safeguarded by the commanding officer's prerogative to revoke their commission and expel them from the corps at any time.

The general staff did not hesitate to exercise its right of selection to the full. The number of *destitutions* was high, a fact that has sometimes been interpreted as a measure of the poor quality of the officer corps; but most of these dismissals were the direct result of the intensive process of sifting and sorting among available personnel that by June had resulted in an officer corps consisting for the most part of veterans specially chosen for their loyalty and obedience.[11] Even those officers selected from among volunteers tended strongly to be older men who had previously served in the armed forces.[12] Data compiled from the three special registers devoted to Mobile Guard officers and displayed in Table 3.1 show that the percentage of cadres who possessed previous military experience was substantial in all categories and tended to increase with rank. Veteran's status was, in fact, the single best predictor of obtaining a commission in the new militia. In thus securing the allegiance and reliability of the officer corps, Duvivier evolved a winning strategy in the battle for the loyalty of his unruly troops. He was able to turn the most dangerously democratic aspect of the Mobile Guard's organizational structure to his advantage by using it to weed out refractory elements and to promote those who possessed the requisite military instruction, discipline, and devotion to duty.

Practical Grievances

These measures helped ensure the loyalty of the officer corps and thus fulfilled the most important precondition of unified command. Still, practical grievances, allowed to fester, might have provided the wedge necessary to drive those cadres and the rank and file apart. According to McKay (1933: 45), "uniforms, good pay, and barrack-life contributed to the rapid development of *esprit de corps* and to the weaning of this group from its proletarian sympathies." Yet this retrospective judgment ignored the very real conflicts that for a time sapped morale and nearly turned the Mobile Guard against the government that had created it.

Delays in meeting the Mobile Guard payroll were an early source of friction. The difficulties arose in part from the bureaucratically anomalous structure of the Mobile Guard: funds deriving from the Ministry of the Interior (and not the Ministry of War) were channeled through the mayor of Paris and the twelve ward mayors before delivery to the paymasters of the twenty-four Mobile Guard battalions. In crossing the boundaries between civilian and military authorities as well as between national and municipal administrative structures, they were subject to substantial delays and frequent jurisdictional disputes. The resulting misunderstandings tried the patience of volunteers, many of whom, attracted by the premium wage offered in this militia, were anxious to collect and spend their pay (Archives historiques Xm 32, letters of 26 and 28 February to the Minister of the Interior). Many of them were so nearly destitute that in the first several weeks of their service, local authorities were obliged to feed them by requisition (Archives historiques Xm 32, 28 February). Through the first days of March, the mayor of the 7th ward managed only by temporarily appropriating the donations intended to aid the victims of the February Days (Archives historiques Xm 32). Other ward mayors complained about the noisy crowds assembling before the *mairies* to demand their pay. This threat to public order reinforced Duvivier's efforts to impress upon higher authorities the urgent need to regularize the situation, and this particular problem appears to have been speedily resolved (Chalmin 1948: 44; Schmidt 1926: 21).

The quality of the Mobile Guard mess gave cause for sporadic complaint. Some initial ambiguity existed as to who would bear the cost of food, the call to recruits having specified only that the public would arm, house, and equip volunteers. When the mayor of the 3d ward inquired as to the deduction to be made from the daily pay of Mobile Guardsmen to cover the cost of the bread, meat, and soup being provided, Duvivier replied that in view of volunteers' wage of 1 franc 50 centimes, there was no need either to make deductions or to supply foodstuffs (Archives historiques Xm 32, 28 February). Once public subsidies for meals had ended, some form of voluntary deduction seems to have become the usual practice, for on 23 April (Archives historiques Xm 32) the 120 soldiers of the 6th company of the 10th battalion drew up a petition concerning the 65 centimes they were paying daily into the company mess. They complained of the limited quantity and poor quality of rations that left many of them indisposed for their military duties, reluctantly concluding that this regrettable state of affairs could only be attributed to the "negligence which our leaders bring to our interests." When the appointment of a commission of inquiry failed to produce concrete results, they addressed themselves directly to Duvivier, signing their appeal, "Your children." The general's paternal attentions seem to have resolved the situation to their satisfaction, for no further complaints were registered by this unit.

In the first days after the Mobile Guard's creation, the government's commitment to provide housing for new recruits ran up against the difficulty that none had been specifically provided for that purpose. The obvious solution was to make use of the barracks left vacant by the disbanding of the Garde municipale. It was first necessary, however, to evict the remnants of that corps and their horses, both still occupying their former quarters, and to repair the considerable damage incurred during and after the February Days (Chalmin 1948: 45). Moreover, the Mobile Guard was forced to compete for these facilities with other organizations created by the republican regime, notably the Garde du peuple or Montagnards, providing the occasion for another bureaucratic skirmish between Duvivier and Caussidière. Though a few units were left without accommodations for the better part of a month (Archives historiques Xm 32, 18 March), the dispute was eventually resolved in favor of the Mobile Guard, so grievances arising from housing remained relatively short-lived.

Armament was a further source of contention. The Provisional Government's policy of providing arms to the 100,000 new members of the democratized National Guard created a demand for rifles that was impossible to fulfill. Only by "borrowing" from the allocation to that corps was the Mobile Guard able to make even token distributions. On 18 March, for example, a total of sixty-two rifles were handed out to members of the 13th and 14th battalions, then at a troop strength of some 600 to 700 men each (Archives historiques Xm 32). Meanwhile, arms recuperated from regular army units and intended for the use of the Mobile Guard had been shipped off to the armory at Vincennes for lack of the appropriate administrative signature, so that on 28 March, Duvivier was still addressing urgent requests to the Ministry of War for immediate delivery of the 4,000 rifles he had been promised (Archives historiques Xd 385). When, at last, arms began to arrive in appreciable numbers, most turned out to be antiquated flintlocks. It was in response to this situation that the 5 April meeting of the Club de la Garde nationale mobile promulgated a unanimous resolution calling for the replacement of these arms with percussion rifles (Archives nationales C 930, No. 570). As it happened, late-model arms were acquired in quantity in late March and early April, at just about the time the Provisional Government began to make regular use of the Mobile Guard for purposes of social control.[13]

Although all these situations had the potential to generate dissension in the ranks, they proved to be without serious consequence largely because they occurred early and were handled with dispatch. Although the events of 16 and 17 March found the Mobile Guard militarily unprepared, and although some units remained unhoused, ill-fed, or underequipped, the potential for Mobile Guard disloyalty never was realized. Indeed, since the Provisional Government did not call upon its services in those first chaotic days of the corps' existence, all the grievances previously mentioned proved to be of limited import or duration: disruptions in the payroll were short-lived; food and housing complaints were never sufficiently generalized to unite the troops in discontent; and the delivery of arms, though slow and piecemeal, had necessarily been attended to by the time Mobile Guardsmen were committed to police actions. Thus, despite occasional expressions of disaffection, no systematic decline in morale could be attributed to these causes. The deputy-mayor of the 7th ward attested to this fact in a letter complaining of the lack of proper housing and armament by concluding that the spirit of the two battalions attached to his ward nonetheless remained excellent and that the municipality would not hesitate to make use of them in case of need (Archives historiques Xm 32, 18 March).

There was one issue, however, sufficiently enduring and widespread in its impact to place the allegiance of the rank and file at risk. To understand why delays in the delivery of Mobile Guard uniforms carried the potential for alienating the loyalties of volunteers, one must bear in mind the enormous symbolic significance that uniforms and official dress of all kinds possessed in the French Revolution of 1848.[14] In addition, the purely practical importance of clothing to men recruited off the streets should not be underestimated. According to the decree of 26 February, members of the Mobile Guard were to be outfitted with the uniforms in use in the sedentary National Guard to which distinguishing accessories and trim were to be added. The Ministry of War informed General Duvivier on 28 February that it had 6,000 to 7,000 uniforms on hand and would quickly establish a half dozen workshops of civilian tailors who, under the supervision of the army's master tailors, would provide the balance with only a "brief delay." These arrangements were confirmed in a memo composed the following day, specifying that the number of workshops had been increased to ten and that they

Proposed Uniforms, Equipment, and Armament of
the Mobile Guard (*l'Illustration* 1848: 28)

would complete the work in twenty to twenty-five days (Archives historiques F1 2).

Twenty days later, no uniforms had been delivered and arrangements for the tailors' workshops were still being discussed. The secretary-general of the Provisional Government invited Duvivier to draw cloth from military stores and contract for the necessary labor on the open market (Archives historiques Xm 32, 20 March). A week later, however, the general wrote to the Minister of War that he had not yet received any of the promised yard goods:

Everyone is asking, "Why hasn't General Duvivier armed and dressed his volunteers?" My answer is simple: it is because, since 8 March, General Duvivier has not obtained the least response to the simple and indispensable requests which he has addressed to the various ministers. (Archives historiques Xd 385, 28 March)

By 9 April, raw materials still had not arrived. Disturbing signs of insubordination accompanied the protests now raised among the rank and file, and the commander of the 13th battalion attributed the erosion of his officers' authority to their inability to respond to increasingly insistent demands for uniforms on the part of their men (Archives historiques Xm 35). Delegates from every company of the 12th battalion jointly petitioned Duvivier in these terms:

Discouragement is spreading in our ranks, our men are refusing their duties, which they were already accomplishing very poorly, because they see that they are not being cared for in an active way. Most of the men in the battalion are dressed in tatters and are obliged to do their duty in the inclemency of the harshest weather. When a man has but a single shirt and pants in poor condition and must do two hours of guard duty in such weather, he would have to be made of iron in order not to catch cold. (Archives historiques Xm 35, n.d.)

An anonymous, handwritten poster, apparently torn from the wall of a Mobile Guard barracks, indicated that the common soldier was ready to pass from words to deeds:

Citizens of the Mobile Guard:

Yesterday we read in a newspaper that the citizens of Paris were pleased to see us mounting the guard of at least the principal posts in the city. Well then, citizens, let us interest all Parisians in the question of our uniforms by refusing—but by refusing in an energetic manner, in a manner which authorizes those in charge of this undertaking to accede to our just demands—by refusing, as

I was saying, to perform this service that they are so happy to see us accomplish. Let us not neglect our training, but as for patrols outside the barracks without tunics, let us refuse them. Let us demonstrate that along with our patriotism, we possess a firm will.

And Long Live the Republic![15]

The Prefect of Rouen, where part of the 5th battalion had been detached in April to help quell the civil disturbances resulting from the outcome of the legislative elections, addressed this troubled plea to military authorities:

> In the name of humanity, send some clothing to that miserable battalion of Mobile Guardsmen that you assigned us. They are without shirts or shoes, they sleep on straw, and are dressed in their workers' blouses and canvas pants. . . . I have just sent one company on detached duty to Eu and Tréport and the poor devils left completely nude. . . .
>
> I am still waiting for a half battalion. Do not let them leave [Paris] without clothing. (Archives historiques Xm 32, n.d.)

By 21 April, matters had come to a head in several Mobile Guard units. The commander of the 8th battalion wrote that even at that late date

> We have received nothing. A few agitators had convinced the men that since other battalions had been issued clothes and we had nothing, we should not participate in yesterday's review. (Archives historiques Xm 34)

That same day, the deputy-mayor of the 7th ward wrote Duvivier to say that the 13th battalion had arrived en masse that morning to register complaints not only about the failure to grant them a battalion flag but also about the inordinate delays encountered in obtaining uniforms. He assessed the situation in these terms: "linen are lacking, shirts and jackets are torn, pants are in shreds" (Archives historiques Xm 32).

Of course, the men of the Mobile Guard were quite capable of expressing their own dissatisfaction. They did so, for example, in the petition sent to the commander of the 4th battalion, by appending to this document a half-page of their signatures. Their language evoked their inner struggle, hesitating between displays of deference and a tone of outright disrespect:

> In yesterday's standing order, General Duvivier said that the National Mobile Guard differed from the sedentary only in that it could be ordered to march as far as the borders and that we therefore needed to drill. In our opinion it also differs from the sedentary in that it is neither clothed nor armed nor equipped. Before leaving we must be dressed; before drilling we must be armed. In '93 we fought a war without shoes, but in '93 we were in a foreign country. It is shameful, Commander, to see, in this capital of civilization, soldiers who have nothing to shelter their devotion but devotion itself.
>
> We wanted to refuse to drill and even to mount guard duty because we did not want to make a spectacle of ourselves, [to appear to be] beggars shouldering soldiers' arms; but a degree of discipline which we shall always observe under your command had prevented us from taking this course up to now. Would you, Commander, be so kind as to show the general this request, to which all our signatures have been affixed, so that he may see it as a demonstration to the one who calls himself our father. (Archives historiques Xm 34, 4th battalion, n.d.)

These and many other bits of evidence of smoldering discontent testify to the surprising potential that the issue of Mobile Guard uniforms possessed for uniting the rank and file in opposition to their officers and general staff. The surviving records show that by late April this disruptive potential was rapidly being realized in increasingly strident protests and calls to disobedience.[16]

As Chorley has pointed out, however, the great weakness of such practical grievances as a spur to disaffection is that, once recognized, they can be quickly remedied by concerned and vigilant authorities. Duvivier, with the paternalism that characterized his personal style, was already attending to the problem with all the means at his disposal. At an assembly of his troops on the day following the *journée* of 16 April, he took care not only to congratulate his men on their loyal and soldier-like conduct but also to reiterate the promise that the long-awaited uniforms would arrive presently. The general was as good as his word. Deliveries began on 19 April, and though the initial flow amounted to a mere trickle, it immediately had the desired effect on Mobile Guard morale. The agent whom Duvivier employed to monitor sentiment among the troops filed a 20 April report that read in part:

> Yesterday the larger part of the Mobile Guard engaged in no other pleasure than that of cleaning their rifles and discussing the question as to whether, yes or no, they would be clothed. At 5 P.M., shirts and pants were distributed in the courtyard of the Ecole [militaire]. [Shouts of] "Long Live the Republic!" and "Long Live General Duvivier!" were heard. (Archives historiques F1 6)

Through 24 April, the limited number of tunics and pants were used to deal with cases of particularly dire need. Official tallies show that by that date an average of seventy-five to 100 complete uniforms had been delivered to battalions then operating with complements of over 500 men (Archives nationales F9 1150). Only in the two weeks following did supply begin to catch up with Mobile Guard demand. Commander Couchot of the 8th battalion, who ten days previous had warned of an impending disaster, now wrote that, "the hostile demonstrations which had occurred because of [the lack of] clothing have quieted down as a result of the distributions" (Archives historiques Xm 34). By early May, dissension in the ranks of Mobile Guardsmen had declined abruptly, and the

Workshop of the Fraternal Association of Tailors
(*l'Illustration* 1848: 230)

threat of mass insubordination evaporated even more quickly
than it had appeared.

Furthermore, the residue of ill feelings on the part of the
rank and file as a result of this episode was directed not at
the officers and general staff of the Mobile Guard nor even
at the government but at the workers of the Fraternal Association of Tailors. At the initiative of Louis Blanc, a cooperative association of some 2,000 unemployed tailors had been
established in the former prison at Clichy, abandoned as the
result of the Provisional Government's decree abolishing imprisonment for debt. As an experiment in the organization of
labor, this group was awarded an exclusive contract from the
city of Paris for the provision of 100,000 military frocks for
the members of the expanded National Guard. After lengthy
negotiations, the contract for the bulk of the uniforms destined
for the Mobile Guard was likewise accorded to these workers.
Their association obtained the capital for tools and raw materials through a loan of 11,000 francs from the association

of master tailors. Though not fully realizing the ideals of Blanc's *Organisation du Travail*, in part because the state proved unwilling to underwrite the initial expense of setting up the workshop, it did operate according to many of his principles (Blanc 1858: 157-68; see also Caspard 1974: 101, and Renard 1907: 35). All positions of authority were filled by election, and the member tailors "adopted the system of equal wages and equal profits." Blanc himself reported that the results achieved were "in every respect remarkable": the association's contractual obligations were scrupulously fulfilled, the orders received were completed "in due time," and the loan was promptly repaid, leaving a small surplus.

Those for whom the uniforms were intended, however, arrived at a quite different assessment of this experiment in workers' democracy. According to Stern, the disillusionment of Mobile Guard volunteers began when, frustrated at the continual delays, they attempted to pay visits to their brother workers:

> At the time of which I am speaking, the majority were still half nude; many lacked shirts and shoes. Irritated by the slowness involved in clothing them, they went several times to the workshops in Clichy to demand their uniforms. This became the occasion for very lively quarrels between them and the tailors and was the beginning of the split which occurred between these children of the proletarians and the proletarians themselves, between the people in work frocks and the people in uniform, a split which not long after appeared in an as yet passive and almost unacknowledged form in the *journée* of 16 April and which burst forth two months later in a mortal combat. (1862: II, 165)

What particularly annoyed the Mobile Guardsmen were the additional delays occasioned by the association's maneuvers to block the hiring of more tailors. The Clichy workers sought to gain exclusive control of the contract and thus protect themselves against the competition of outsiders willing to work for substandard wages rather than not work at all.[17] The men of the Mobile Guard understood only that this most radical and ideologically aware fraction of the Parisian working class was obstructing efforts to expedite delivery of their long-awaited uniforms. When a show of concern by the Mobile Guard administration was shortly followed by the arrival of the goods, the spirit of discontent that had welled up against authorities within the corps in March and April was redirected. It left behind only a rankling antagonism toward radicals and socialists that would resurface in May and June. In this way, practical grievances that might otherwise have played a role in splitting the rank and file of the new militia from the moderate republic were effectively neutralized and even turned to account in cementing Mobile Guard loyalty to the regime in power.

MOBILE GUARD ISOLATION

Chorley's review of the historical record suggests that the armed forces' will to fight in situations of civil conflict quickly dissolves once insurgents with whom soldiers share common social origins and outlook are able to present direct appeals. In the case of a popular militia such as the Mobile Guard, recruited from the lower classes of the very city in which they were expected to maintain order, the task of isolating the rank and file from contact with civilians became at once more formidable and more essential. Previous analysts have stressed the partial failure of attempts to quarantine this force from external political influences. Chalmin (1948: 97-98) concluded that, "the living conditions of Mobile Guardsmen after enlistment never allowed an impenetrable barrier to be established between them and the Parisian population from which they came." Schmidt (1926: 21-22) remarked that without uniforms Mobile Guardsmen could hardly be distinguished from the workers whose demonstrations they were asked to police.

In early June, the commander of the 7th battalion alerted

his superiors to *symptômes facheux* observed within the ranks, attributing them to "mysterious agents [who] seek to capture the minds of the volunteers" (Archives historiques Xm 34, 7 June). Reports filed by the Prefect of Police occasionally detailed the activities of Mobile Guardsmen observed to meet with known radicals.[18] On 6 June, soldiers of the 6th battalion, quartered in the fort at Noisy-le-sec, briefly refused to obey their officers. This breach of discipline was ascribed to "persons foreign to the locale who came to give money to these soldiers."[19] Incidents of this type not only aroused the concern of the Mobile Guard administration but fed the popular expectation that the rank and file would side with an eventual insurrection.

Yet despite the inclination and opportunity of the rank and file to mingle with the populace, Mobile Guard authorities, constantly alert to such dangers, managed to maintain a remarkable and increasing degree of insulation, especially as the polarization of the political situation became more acute. The bulk of the available evidence indicates that lapses in the isolation of Mobile Guard recruits were a less important source of contamination than has sometimes been suggested.

In many ways, the formal conditions of service in the Mobile Guard left its members accessible to civilians to a degree intermediate between that of soldiers in the regular army on the one hand and of volunteers in the National Guard, traditional bellwether of the success or failure of popular insurrection, on the other. In order to assess the net result of this situation, it will prove helpful to begin with an inventory of the mechanisms employed by the authorities in establishing a *cordon sanitaire* around the men of the Mobile Guard.

First, Mobile Guardsmen were isolated by a studied organization of their daily schedule. In contrast to the citizen-volunteers of the National Guard, Mobile Guardsmen were full-time soldiers subject to a structured military existence. From 6 A.M. to 9 P.M., their time was rigidly apportioned between assembly and inspection, instruction and drill.[20] Whereas the National Guardsman left work and family only for a weekly training session or on the beating of the *rappel*, thus remaining firmly embedded in his networks of nonmilitary social relations, the Mobile Guardsman passed his entire day in the company of his comrades-in-arms.

Even during off-duty hours, the conditions of barracks' life kept the Mobile Guard recruit somewhat apart from the civilian population.[21] Although originally recruited by ward, the assignment of specific battalions to quarters of the city depended primarily on the availability of facilities and does not appear to have followed any definite pattern at first. Files of correspondence covering the initial weeks of the corps' existence provide the example of a lieutenant in the 24th battalion complaining because his unit had been stationed in the Babylon barracks of the 6th ward rather than in its home territory of the 12th. He cited two reasons in explanation of delays in the collection and transmission of important information requested by his superiors:

> The first is that we are really too far away from our ward, that communications are too slow and even problematic, that this distance hampers many of the men who need to finish up business at home.
>
> The second is that we are suspect in the 6th ward, which views us askance.

The lieutenant went on to make the suggestion, never acted upon by the higher authorities, that an exchange of accommodations take place between his battalion and the 55th regiment of the line, then quartered in the 12th ward (Archives historiques Xm 32, 17 March, No. 1670).

Just the opposite complaint was registered by the commander of the 17th battalion. It was originally assigned to the Ave Maria barracks in the heart of the 9th ward, the very one from which its volunteers had been recruited. The commander stated that

> This location, which could be suitable for organized and disciplined troops, presents, given the current state of the

corps, almost insurmountable obstacles to a proper and prompt organization. Situated in the center of the 9th ward, a very populous quarter which furnished the battalion with the greater part of its forces, closed in and offering in the immediate vicinity all the temptations to be feared for young men who up to now have enjoyed an almost unlimited freedom of action, this barracks, in my opinion, is not suitable as a residence for men who must bend little by little to discipline, however gentle it may be. (Archives historiques Xm 35, 17th battalion)

He therefore requested the battalion's transfer out of the 9th ward.

This apparent lack of system in the assignment of quarters could not be immediately overcome, given the constraints that Duvivier faced in the early days of Mobile Guard organization. In a letter to the mayor of the 3d ward, he pointed out that not only was the distribution of barracks uneven over the city but that the total space available was insufficient to house his forces (Archives historiques Xm 49, p. 1). With time, this difficulty was resolved by following the recommendation of the commander of the 17th battalion to use the forts situated on the outskirts of the capital. Beginning in mid-May, a number of battalions were relocated in Vanves, Nogent, Reuil, Courbevoie, Romainville, and Rosny.[22] Caspard's estimate of "six or seven battalions thus distanced from Paris" is slightly low, and his conclusion that such movements were of "little importance" seems unwarranted. Eight battalions, fully one-third of the Mobile Guard total, were affected by this measure. In addition, if one counts the units temporarily detached to Amiens and Rouen and those that had already been quartered in the barracks at Montreuil and Aubervilliers, beyond the city limits, then 68.9 percent of all Mobile Guardsmen who can be definitely placed had been posted outside Paris proper. Indeed, by the time of the June Days only the 1,126 men of the 7th and 17th battalions or 10.6 percent of all those who could be categorized were still living in barracks located in the ward from which they had been recruited.

This manipulation of the geographical distribution of Mobile Guard forces, which Renard (1907: 58) and Gossez (1956b: 447) acknowledged to have been the self-conscious policy of the government, would prove to be of enormous significance in protecting individual members from direct confrontations with friends or relatives. The prospect of brother fighting brother (literally as well as figuratively) weighed heavily on the popular imagination. In at least two individual cases there exist purported accounts of incidents that raised this issue, though neither produced the result that both conservative and radical observers had anticipated. Balleydier (1848: 92) cited the case of a young volunteer from the 12th battalion, questioned by a group of insurgents as to how he could fire upon his brothers. "You, my brothers!" he is reported to have replied. "Do you take my mother for a no-account?" Pardigon (1852: 162) related the story of an insurgent who, though wounded and taken prisoner by the Mobile Guard, continued to hurl invectives at his captors. "Me, I have a son in the Mobile Guard," he supposedly cried. "It should be my son who has to kill me, the monster. It's up to him. Do you hear me, over there, you assassin?" And, if we are to credit this account, the son, who indeed was among the sentinels on duty, responded by threatening to do just that. To be sure, this kind of anecdotal evidence is virtually worthless for analytical purposes, though it does suggest how salient the concern over Mobile Guard loyalties must have been.[23] But it was precisely to prevent such situations from arising that the general staff systematized its efforts to separate recruits from their home territory by assigning battalions to distant quarters.

The constraints of barracks life remained, of course, an imperfect insulating barrier. The radical opponents of the moderate republic found that access to whole units of the Mobile Guard was difficult but exploited opportunities to approach small groups of volunteers on leave in the city. It is known, for example, that the presence of several noncommissioned officers and soldiers of the Mobile Guard at tumultuous gatherings at the Porte St. Denis and Porte St. Martin prompted the Minister of the Interior to write to Duvivier, requesting that the latter issue orders prohibiting the participation of his men in such assemblies (Archives historiques Xm 32, 2 June). A wave of proselytic activity accompanied the June organizing drive for the "twenty-five-cent banquet," initiated in conscious imitation of the campaign that had precipitated the February Days. A police report of 4 June remarked that a number of Mobile Guardsmen were among the 15,000 who had already subscribed (France, Assemblé nationale 1848: II, 198). Another, filed some five days later, quoted a speaker at the Club Blanqui on the attitude of the rank and file as perceived by the radicals:

> As for the Mobile Guard, we can count on its assistance. It will come to the banquet whatever happens and will break down the doors of the barracks rather than miss the rendezvous. (Archives historiques Xm 32, 9 June)

Had that banquet actually taken place, it is quite possible that no less drastic a reaction would have proved necessary, for, in an effort to curb the rise in fraternization, Mobile Guard authorities had begun to confine their men to quarters (cf. Archives historiques F1 15, 15 May; Xm 34, 3d battalion). When the Mobile Guard was mobilized on 22 June to put down the growing rebellion, the Executive Commission employed the same tactic of confinement not only to maintain this force in a state of constant readiness but also to minimize contamination from the insurgents.[24] In this way, the radical workers' attempts to win the sympathies of these lower class agents of social control were limited to raising cries of "Long Live the Mobile Guard!" through the fortified walls of barracks dispersed throughout the city or across the barricades already scattered through the Parisian streets.[25]

Thus, in the weeks preceding the June confrontation, fraternization between workers and Mobile Guardsmen was increasingly difficult and infrequent. Meanwhile, contact between the Mobile Guard and other troops was openly tolerated or even encouraged by the authorities. These relations dated from the period of improved morale that followed the Mobile Guard's successful intervention in the *journée* of 16 April. The commander of the 8th battalion related how, after 150 *cuirassiers* had been moved into the Mobile Guard's Orsay barracks, soldiers from both corps were excused from drill in order to celebrate with their new-found friends.[26] Duvivier's confidential informant described in telegraphic style a similarly warm relationship that had grown up between Mobile Guardsmen and regular army units in mid-May:

> Courtyard of Vincennes: some National Guardsmen, Mobile Guardsmen, and troops of the line fraternized to cries of "Long Live the Republic!" The greatest harmony appeared to reign between the Mobile Guard and the troops of the line.[27]

Best documented are the efforts of bourgeois units of the National Guard to strike an alliance with the Mobile Guard. Tocqueville described how "the wealthy legions of the National Guard gave banquets for the army and the Mobile Guard at which they mutually urged each other to unite for the common defense" (1971: 164; see also Renard 1907: 58). Whereas contact with politically suspect civilians was being actively repressed through Mobile Guard councils of discipline, public displays of solidarity with other social control forces were just as actively fostered.[28] Thus, both the extent and character of the rank and file's outside contacts were artfully managed so as to inhibit the contaminating influence of Parisian leftists and reinforce the Mobile Guard's commitment to the party of order.

Conclusion

This outline of the organizational structure and experience of the Mobile Guard has shown that although it was impossible to seal off hermetically its members from the Parisian population from which they had so recently been recruited, they were effectively restrained from fraternization by the corps' quality as a full-time militia and by the conditions of barracks life. Mobile Guard authorities were also careful to restrict interactions that might weaken the corps' loyalty to the republican government but were permissive with respect to contact with the National Guard and army.

In the period immediately following the Mobile Guard's constitution, there existed a number of practical grievances that, left unattended, might have undermined the morale and loyalty of the rank and file. Some of these, however, lacked the generalized nature necessary to produce widespread disaffection, and others were resolved in relatively short order. By retracing in detail the evolution of the single most serious of these issues—the delay in the delivery of Mobile Guard uniforms—it has been possible to illustrate not only the potential that such grievances have for setting officers and men at odds, but also how quickly discontent can be dissipated by the prompt attention of the authorities.

Control over the officer corps, that most crucial determinant of the loyalty of the rank and file, was likewise the result of a dynamic process. The original provision that Mobile Guard cadres be elected from among its volunteers might well have led to political unreliability had it been meticulously observed. In fact, however, the terms of the decree were subverted in such a way as to permit the higher administration of the Mobile Guard to exercise a veto based on case-by-case reviews of nominees and thus to select a pliant group consisting almost entirely of military veterans.

Of course, an analysis based on organizational characteristics of the Mobile Guard will prove convincing only to the extent that the factors emphasized here are seen as central in the determination of political orientation at crucial junctures in the early history of this corps. Fortunately, in arguing for the salience of just these variables, we are not limited to the experience of the Mobile Guard alone. There exists another case, drawn from this same historical context, that offers substantial parallels as well as an instructive contrast with that of the Mobile Guard. The National Workshops—created in February, recruited from this same Parisian lower class, shaped by a nearly identical set of economic and social forces, but diametrically opposed in its political role in June—provides us with an ideal basis of comparison. To test the conclusions reached in our investigation of the determinants of Mobile Guard political orientation, we therefore turn in the next chapter to consideration of the paired case of the Parisian National Workshops.

FOUR

The Transformation of the National Workshops from Instrument of Cooptation to Insurrectionary Core

THE PRECEDING two chapters have advanced the view that the collective characteristics of the Mobile Guard, and not simply the aggregated characteristics of its individual members, best explain its central role in the June repression. In associating political orientation with organizational experience, however, the argument has thus far concentrated on just one side of the June configuration of forces. Although Chorley's emphasis on the importance of authority relations, practical grievances, and isolation were derived from the study of regular *military* formations, their aptness in the case of a militia like the Mobile Guard suggests that they may also be of value in explaining the political orientation of *insurgent* groups where these satisfy minimal criteria of longevity and organizational definition.

The present chapter attempts to test these hypotheses with respect to the insurgent camp. It begins by establishing the comparability of the National Workshops with the Mobile Guard, first in descriptive terms, as a quasi-military body recruited from the same strata of society, and second in terms of their historical role in the June insurrection. After examining in detail the social composition of the workshops, it next retraces the evolution of this institution between late February and June with two purposes in mind: to indicate the level and orientation of political activity and insurgency at major junctures; and to identify the principal events to which variations in the level and orientation of that activity correspond. Finally, it focuses attention on those collective attributes of the National Workshops that explain the patterns observed and seeks to test the organizational hypotheses derived from the study of the Mobile Guard.

THE NATIONAL WORKSHOPS AS A COMPARATIVE CASE

The National Workshops were set up as a volunteer, civilian corps of the Parisian unemployed. The Provisional Government's reasons for creating them were identical to those that led it to found the Mobile Guard. On the one hand, it feared that, unless it assumed the initiative, the large number of idle workers, still exuberant from their participation in the overthrow of the July Monarchy, could prove to be a destabilizing influence that might threaten the young Republic. It hoped, on the other hand, to win the good will and political support of these workers by prompt action to provide relief from unemployment. Thus, the creation of this institution represented a bold and optimistic political gamble on the part of members of the Provisional Government.

At the same time, however, the intervention of the revolutionary crowd was directly responsible for the declaration of the "right to work" and the founding of the National Workshops. On 25 February, less than twenty-four hours after the Provisional Government had been formed, some 5,000 to 6,000 workers assembled outside the Hôtel de Ville (Barrot 1875: 55). A representative drawn from their midst was allowed to enter, interrupting the deliberations of the government to present the popular demands. Garnier-Pagès (n.d.: I, 324) described this dramatic confrontation in these terms:

> The worker Marche, a vigorous man, drawing on the authority of his status as delegate and aided by his physical force, managed to open a path [through the crowd]. He presented himself alone before the Provisional Gov-

ernment, excited by the tumult, by his recent exertion, by what he was doing. Fire in his eye, his voice raised, striking the floor with the butt of his rifle, he delivered a petition and shouted: "Citizens, the organization of work, the right to work in one hour! That is the will of the People. We are waiting! . . ." Then, concluding his speech in a mute language more expressive even than his words, he pointed his finger to the square before the Hôtel de Ville where the clamor redoubled and announced the boiling over of passions.

The redundant language of the official response reflects the haste with which it was prepared. Penned by Blanc, approved with virtually no serious discussion, it was read forthwith to the crowd.

The Provisional Government of the French Republic commits itself to guarantee the worker's existence through work;

It commits itself to guarantee work to all citizens;

It recognizes that workers must associate themselves to enjoy the fruits of their labor. . . . (Blanc 1850: 31; France, Comité national du centenaire de 1848, 1950: 9)

This public pledge constituted the first concrete step in the direction of social reform.

But a statement of intent, extracted from the government's moderate majority under duress, was one thing; its institutional translation quite another. The announcement recognized the right to work and the right of association; it avoided mention of the *organization* of work and carefully remained at the level of abstract principle.

A first attempt at implementation was made on 26 February. On the same day that the first volunteers were being inducted into the Mobile Guard, the Provisional Government decreed the immediate establishment of workshops under the administrative control of the Ministry of Public Works. These were to be *National* Workshops, as distinct from the *social* workshops that Louis Blanc had proposed in his *Organisation du travail*.[1] The immediate precedent appears in fact to have been the *ateliers de secours*, which as recently as 1830-1831 had been used as a response to lower class agitation.[2] Barrot (1875: 58), implying that members of the government had this earlier experiment clearly in mind, referred to this form of unemployment relief as "something which recurs each time society needs to reestablish calm, to avoid aggravating the danger of political fanaticism arising from the hopelessness of hunger."

Marie, saddled with responsibility for the workshops' organization, attempted to deal with the crush of applicants through a cumbersome decentralized structure, operating through the twelve ward *mairies* and a couple of clearinghouses. Fortuitously, one of the latter was located directly opposite the residence of Emile Thomas. Thomas, a former student of the Ecole centrale des arts et manufactures, thus had ample opportunity to observe the unruly gatherings of would-be members. He also obtained an insider's view of the workshops' state of institutional chaos from the students of his alma mater who had been pressed into administrative service.[3] Quick to grasp the political as well as the practical dilemma, he drew up a proposal to restructure the workshops, and with the help of family acquaintances was granted an audience with Marie.[4]

From the first, it was the workshops' potential for disturbing public order that attracted Thomas's attention. He criticized the existing administration for having no clear lines of command, no standardized system of organization, no control of elementary logistics, and no coordination of work projects. According to him, the "most complete disorder" reigned, and the *rue Bondy* witnessed a "permanent riot" each morning from five o'clock on, as workshops' members gathered (Thomas 1848: 32; see also Garnier-Pagès n.d.: II, 25-26).

The alternative that he presented to the Minister of Public Works envisioned a centralized structure that would classify workers by occupation and distribute them among agencies where they could be usefully employed (Thomas 1848: 35).

To accomplish this, he had two tools at his disposal. The first was organizational, for he proposed to give a quasi-military structure to the workshops.[5] The second consisted in the "moral influence" that he and students of the Ecole centrale would acquire through intimate daily contact with the membership.

Marie's response was enthusiastic, as was that of Garnier-Pagès, then mayor of Paris, when called in to hear Thomas repeat his suggestions. Thomas was sent off to commit his proposal to paper and to begin the search for suitable administrative headquarters.

On 5 March, at an assembly of notables including the twelve ward mayors of Paris, the Thomas plan received final and unanimous approval (Cherest 1873: 193). As set down from memory, Thomas's introductory speech pointed out to his audience the "terrible opportunities for disorder and anarchy" and criticized in the existing regime the very abuses—laxity in the verification of credentials for admission, double and triple inscriptions, and lack of useful work—for which his own administration would later come under fire.[6] The only serious question raised about the proffered corrective measures was how quickly they could be instituted. It was agreed that five days should be allowed for the necessary preparations and that the new administration would assume control on 9 March. The broad outlines of this agreement were published in the Ministry of Public Works decree of 6 March (Thomas 1848: 56-57), which named Thomas, then twenty-six years old, Director of the central bureau of the National Workshops with the title of Commissar of the Republic.

Like the Mobile Guard, the National Workshops were meant from the first to serve two distinct and potentially contradictory objectives of the Provisional Government. The first was economic and humanitarian and could be publicly proclaimed: to blunt the worst consequences of the depression by providing relief to the unemployed. The second was political and self-interested, and consequently remained covert: to pacify the mob or perhaps even secure its adherence. Although this second objective never figured in official statements of policy, it was voiced privately or after the fact by key participants. For example, Lamartine wrote of the workshops that "they were merely an expedient for preserving order, a rude auxiliary summoned on the morrow of the Revolution by the necessity of feeding the people, and not feeding them idle, in order to avoid the disorders of idleness" (Lamartine 1849, quoted in Blanc 1858: 204). Thomas reported that on 23 March, Marie took him aside to ask if his workers could be counted on. Thomas replied that he thought so, but that the rapid growth in their numbers made it difficult to maintain the sort of direct contact that might guarantee their loyalty.

> The Minister [then] said to me, "Don't worry about the number; if you can hold them in line, it can never be too large. But find a means of attaching them to you sincerely. Don't worry about money; if need be, we can grant you secret funds."
>
> "I don't think I'll need them," [Thomas reports that he replied], "and they might later be a source of difficulties. But to what end, other than that of public tranquillity, are you making these recommendations?"
>
> "For the purpose of public welfare. Do you think you can establish complete control over your men? The day is perhaps not distant when we will have to send them into the streets."[7]

Thus, Thomas found himself the commanding general of an irregular army of the poor. In this capacity, he was obliged to fight daily battles to maintain the morale and retain the loyalty of his men.

But if Thomas's role in this campaign was that of tactician, Marie appears to have been the strategist responsible for the implementation of the government's overall program of social peace through social welfare, of pitting the workshops against the radical influence of the Luxembourg Commission, and, failing all else, of preparing for the eventualities of civil war.

Lamartine described his influence on the workshops in the following terms:

> For four months he made them not a force at the mercy of socialists and insurrectionists but a praetorian army (admittedly idle) in the hands of the regime. Commanded, directed, and supported by officers who shared the secret thought of the anti-socialist faction of the government, the workshops counterbalanced the sectarian workers of the Luxembourg and the seditious workers of the Clubs until the arrival of the National Assembly. In the eyes of Paris, their size and the uselessness of their labors were a scandal, but unbeknownst to Paris they protected and saved it several times. (Lamartine 1849: II, 120)

This army grew far beyond the expectations of its creators. In promulgating the National Workshops' organization, the Provisional Government had anticipated that enrollments would peak at a maximum of 10,000 to 12,000 (Cherest 1873: 198). At the 5 March planning session, despite indications that 14,000 to 17,000 workers were *already* besieging the ward *mairies*, the authorities clung to the belief that this number would remain stable.[8] Table 4.1[9] shows that, far from tapering off, enrollments rose without a break. The enormous increase in

Table 4.1
Bimonthly Membership in the National Workshops

Date	Number enrolled
March 15	14,000
March 31	28,350
April 15	64,870
April 30	99,400
May 15	113,010
May 31	116,110
June 15	117,310

the month of April was fueled by the continued deterioration of the Parisian economy in the face of political uncertainty. The growth in May was held to 17,000 only because admissions were suspended on the 12th. The peak nominal enrollment approached 120,000 and although this figure may include as many as 20,000 fraudulent inscriptions, it does not count the 50,000 workers said to have been seeking entry on the eve of the June Days (Normanby 1857: II, 15; McKay 1933: 130, citing Faucher).

THE WORKSHOPS' ROLE IN THE
JUNE INSURRECTION

It is all too easy to conclude, with the benefit of hindsight, that the Provisional Government miscalculated badly in creating in February an army of the unemployed that in June would fight on the side of the insurgents. To be sure, the workshops' role behind the barricades proved to be no less central than that played by the Mobile Guard on the side of the repression. If one ignores the effective cooptation of the workshops through May and considers the events of June alone, the evidence indeed appears conclusive. Over the weeks immediately preceding the insurrection, workshops' members had actively negotiated a leftist alliance with club groups and craft unions (Amann 1960). They used the preexisting workshops' networks to promote the populist "twenty-five-cent banquet" and tried to develop sympathetic relations with units of the National and Mobile Guards through fraternization efforts. Lower echelon officers worked to stiffen the resolve of the rank and file.[10] On 22 June, a delegation from the National Workshops met with Marie in a confrontation that, according to Cherest (1873: 253), marked "the first symptom of insurrection." Later that same day, delegates from the workshops and the disbanded Luxembourg Commission met to plan further joint action (Cherest 1873: 254). These initiatives were possible because the formal authority of work-

General Lamoricière Parleying with the Insurgents
(*l'Illustration* 1848: 189)

shops' officers and delegates made them natural focal points for mobilization efforts.

As the principal preexisting, large-scale popular institution, the workshops constituted the best available organizational base for insurrection. Their role was not limited to the preparatory stages. In the absence of the most visible and militant leftists, arrested after the 15 May debacle, it was the workshops (and to a lesser extent the National Guard) that supplied the leaders of the insurrection. Amann called them "the one element which was to be most intimately associated with the June insurrection" (1960: 444). Members took the initiative in the construction of the first barricades (Schmidt 1926: 39-40). Their banners and insignia were prominently displayed at the preliminary demonstrations and at the scenes of the fiercest fighting (Archives historiques AA, note of an anonymous agent, *dossier* Pujol; Barrot 1875: 257; Normanby 1857:

II, 30; Renard 1907: 78; Molok 1952: 84). Loyal and disloyal workshops' cadres alike conceded that whole units of the rank and file fought on the barricades and persuaded or compelled their officers to join them (Delessard 1900: 28; Lefrançais 1902: 55). The Commission of Inquiry on the June Days concluded that

> The documents which we have analyzed establish that the insurrection found in the national workshops a paid army. . . . The brigadiers and paymasters of the national workshops must have served as the cashiers of the uprising. (France, Assemblé nationale 1848: I, 42)

Quentin-Bauchart, the Commission's *rapporteur*, spoke of the "twenty-five to thirty thousand workers of the national workshops who comprised the most active battalions of the insurrection" (1901: I, 203).

Of course, the National Workshops cannot be any more completely identified with the insurgent forces of June than the Mobile Guard with the repression. The data available on participation show that the situation is more complex. As noted in Chapter One, contemporary estimates of insurgent strength ranged from 12,000 to 50,000. Even if one accepted the inflated upper estimate and assumed that all insurgents were enrolled in the National Workshops, it would immediately be clear that only a minority of the nearly 120,000 members took part.

In fact, there is a basis for more accurate calculations. Records of arrests made after the June insurrection establish that roughly 40 percent to 50 percent of all those detained were members of the National Workshops.[11] Prorating on the basis of estimates of total insurgent strength, we can determine that between 5,000 and 25,000 workshops' members manned the June barricades.[12]

Thus, the situation can be viewed from two quite different angles: on the one hand, only a relatively modest share of the membership—perhaps as little as 10 percent to 15 percent—actively joined in the rebellion. On the other hand, this workshops' contingent constituted a very substantial share—perhaps half—of all insurgents. Although the greater part of those enrolled sat out the June Days, the organizational experience acquired over the previous three months seems to have prepared their more committed brethren to exert a disproportionate influence on the course of events.

SOCIAL COMPOSITION OF THE
NATIONAL WORKSHOPS

It has been established that a remarkable similarity exists in the occupational distribution of insurgents, Mobile Guardsmen, and the general Parisian population. What remains to be seen is whether the social composition of the National Workshops, the organization from which a significant portion of the June insurgents was recruited, conforms to a similar pattern. It would be ingenuous to rely solely on the unsystematic impressions of contemporary observers, for they are too often in flagrant contradiction. In general, public opinion was as sharply divided in its view of the National Workshops as in the case of the Mobile Guard. Conservatives were quick to credit any derogatory insinuation, for instance that a substantial proportion of members were ex-convicts.[13] The government itself was alarmed at the number of foreigners and French provincials who, it believed, were pouring into the capital to join the workshops.[14] The Minister of Public Works gave his view of the workshops' composition in a speech before the National Assembly on 30 May that distinguished between the minority of agitators, misguided souls, and malefactors and the great majority of well-meaning individuals for whom he reserved the team "real workers."[15] It is hardly surprising to learn of a "right-wing" representative who decried the fact that the National Workshops were making "lazzaroni out of honest and industrious workers" (Garnier-Pagès 1872: X, 102, 105). But even the socialist historian Renard referred to the membership as a "veritable army of mercenaries in the pay of the bourgeoisie" and portrayed the workshops in terms reminiscent of the lumpenproletariat thesis.[16] Indeed, it sometimes seems that the rarest of historical documents of the period are assessments of the makeup of the National Workshops unclouded by ideological presuppositions. Perhaps the nearest approximation is this summary sketch from the pen of an observer of the acknowledged probity of the Comtesse d'Agoult:

> The proletarians who rebelled in June did not form, as party prejudice dared to assert, the refuse of the human race. They were not 100,000 madmen suddenly, in an access of brutal cupidity, throwing themselves on the rich to slaughter them. Moreover, nowhere to my knowledge did one see *those wretches in the pay of factions* pointed to by a poisoned press, according to which they were paid, at so much per hour, the wages of murder, rape, and arson. If it had been that way, such a band of malefactors, even supposing it more numerous still, could not have held out a single day, exposed as they were, against the skill and discipline of an army, against the horror and execration of the entire population. (Stern 1862: II, 369-70, author's emphasis)

Unfortunately, none of the conflicting claims concerning the workshops' social composition are ever likely to be put to the test of statistical verification. One of the consistent criticisms of Thomas's administration was that it had failed to maintain proper records of its charges. Moreover, the time-consuming and politically sensitive census of the membership that became the raison d'être of the Lalanne administration in June appears to have been completely lost.[17]

There is, however, one source that permits us to effect a comparison of the social origins of workshops' members with those of relevant reference groups. From an early date (Cherest 1873: 233), Thomas had been under pressure to conduct a census within his organization for the purpose of justifying expenditures and facilitating the allocation of work. He appended to his history of the workshops a classification of members by occupation carried out on 19 May (1848: 376–78). Table 4.2 reports the results, recoded into the Tilly and Lees categories to permit direct comparison with the insurgents and with the present study's sample of Mobile Guardsmen. These data reveal a gross correspondence in the distri-

Table 4.2

Occupational Distribution by Sector: June Arrestees, Mobile Guard, and National Workshops
(Percentage)

Sector (Tilly and Lees)	June Arrestees	Mobile Guard	National Workshops
Food	4.0	3.7	0.9
Construction	18.2	15.0	24.1
Furniture	6.9	8.1	10.0
Clothing and shoes	10.3	8.7	5.1
Thread and textiles	3.3	4.9	4.7
Leather	1.6	0.7	0.7
Carriage-making	1.6	2.4	1.4
Chemicals, ceramics	1.3	1.7	0.6
Base metals	12.2	8.0	12.0
Precious metals	2.4	3.7	4.3
Cooperage, basketry	1.1	2.4	3.8
Fancy goods	2.0	2.5	1.5
Printing	4.5	4.7	3.2
Transport	4.1	2.0	1.1
Services and others	13.1	14.1	25.3
Liberal professions	2.8	2.2	0.1
Commerce	7.6	6.6	1.2
Military	3.0	8.5	0.1
TOTAL	100.0	99.9	100.1
(N)	(8,371)	(2,696)	(87,913)

Sources: Raw data from Tilly and Lees (1975); Archives historiques (Xm); Thomas (1848).

Note: The format of Table 4.2 resembles that of a table published in Traugott (1980b: 37). The percentages by sector reported here for June arrestees differ, however, because they are based exclusively on Parisians who reported an occupation.

bution of National Workshops' occupations, not nearly so exact as that between opposing sides in the actual fighting yet clear enough to refute claims that the workshops drew upon a sharply differentiated population.[18]

The lack of suitable data precludes any detailed investigation of the correlates of National Workshops' participation.[19] What can be said with confidence about the workshops' composition is simple. It is, first, certain that their membership was essentially working-class. Indeed, the workshops' ultimate size was so large in proportion to the Parisian labor force (and to the city's male population) that this was almost inevitably true. But beyond this, an extremely thin evidential base allows us to assert only that members' occupational status bore a loose resemblance to that of the insurgent population.

This essential similarity hardly seems surprising in view of the fact that roughly half of all insurgents were members of the National Workshops. But more important than sheer numbers was the disproportionate role these men assumed as leaders and organizers of the insurrection. This was possible because the workshops had from the first been conceived as an organizational weapon and given a military structure, though one that could be mobilized as readily against as for the government that had created them.

CHANGING POLITICAL ORIENTATION,
FEBRUARY TO JUNE

Since the timing and purpose of the creation of the National Workshops as well as their social composition were so nearly identical to those of the Mobile Guard, a purely etiological explanation might reasonably predict a general correspondence in the political orientation of both groups. In fact, alignment in the June fighting was dramatically different in the two cases. In order to come to terms with this apparent discrepancy, it will prove helpful to review the stages of the workshops' political evolution, assessing the state of members' loyalty and morale in each of the four periods associated with a major popular intervention.[20]

We have seen that Thomas's original plan for restructuring the National Workshops was motivated by concern over their potential for disorder. Prior to the installation of the new administration on 9 March, complaints had been registered about the rowdy behavior of those who gathered at their ward *mairies*, clamoring for admission. This agitation, however, remained sporadic, uncoordinated, and largely apolitical. Through mid-March, most of the organization's efforts had been focused on admitting members, and only 1,000 men had actually been assigned to work projects.[21]

March 17 was the date of the first, largest, and most successful *journée* of the early Second Republic. Members of the National Workshops were, however, conspicuous by their absence. Though organized on short notice, the public nature of the event gave Thomas sufficient forewarning to lay his plans. Though he had no useful way of occupying 13,000 of the 14,000 men then enrolled, he resolved, "cost what it might," to summon them all at 6 A.M. and send them off to worksites on the outskirts of the city (1848: 95). Only 3,000 remained at the staging area when, at 11 A.M., the arrival and immediate confiscation of enormous red posters proclaiming the objectives of the demonstration sparked "a veritable riot." Workers, rightly suspicious of the administration's sudden insistence that they be kept busy to the last man, saw this maneuver as a preparation for a coup by conservative forces.

Thomas quickly set in motion a strategy that he would repeatedly employ in the months to come. He instructed his subordinate officers to circulate among the rank and file and engage them in discussion. The object was to allay members' fears and convince them that their interests would best be served by departing for work and thus demonstrating their good will toward and confidence in the republican government. Despite their sympathy for the demonstrators, workshops' members drew the line at open insubordination. By taking up their tools and reporting for work, they were able to "establish their alibis" (Thomas 1848: 95-98). Thomas, in defending himself before the Commission of Inquiry, could later claim that "thanks to my influence, not a single worker participated in the demonstration of 16 March [sic]."[22]

In the second phase of the workshops' political evolution, Thomas moved to consolidate his control over the membership. His first tactic was to provide for the election of lower level cadres. Superior officers, at least as far down as company commanders, were drawn exclusively from the roster of students of the Ecole centrale. This arrangement seems to have enjoyed the general support of the rank and file, though some objected to the appointment of these nonworkers to head their fifty-five-man brigades and ten-man squads.[23] Thomas proposed to Marie that elections be held to fill these lower level posts in the belief that this would enhance the legitimacy of workshops' cadres. With the Minister's approval, these elections were set for 26 March, the administration reserving the right to review the results and to remove for cause those elected as officers (Thomas 1848: 147-52).

The second organizational innovation was the creation of the Réunion centrale des Ateliers nationaux. Within a month of their founding, the workshops had grown so large as to preclude the kind of face-to-face contact between cadres and workers that Thomas deemed essential to the maintenance of the proper *esprit de corps*. Seizing upon the suggestion of a worker,[24] Thomas argued for the creation of a representative body in which, with the help of Ecole centrale students, invited ex officio, he could influence the most active of the workers and, through them, control the membership at large. Thomas succeeded in convincing Marie of the immense value of

a barometer which would indicate from moment to moment the emotional state of the workers, revealing the schemings and insinuations of the party of anarchy and permitting me to combat them in the light of day. (Thomas 1848: 157)

At the first meeting of this body on 2 April, Thomas asked delegates to help in formulating and transmitting workshops' policy, thus assuring the efficient delivery of services and the maintenance of internal order.[25]

The effectiveness of this strategy was demonstrated at the public rally of 16 April. Twelve to 15,000 workshops' members turned out on the Champ de Mars to support demands that the Provisional Government proceed with the "organization of work." But, at the direction of Thomas, workshops' cadres were also present to challenge the abstract propositions of radical leaders and dissuade members from rash action that, they claimed, might jeopardize the sole institution that was seeing to the practical welfare of the unemployed. Their efforts met with success. When the *rappel* sounded, summoning National Guardsmen to police the march, "nearly all" the workers under workshops' authority withdrew to join their units. That members should sympathize with the radical cause was neither surprising nor new. More remarkable was the fact that only a scattering of the 60,000 men then enrolled persevered in the march on the Hôtel de Ville and that the bulk of the initial workshops' contingent ended by participating in the *journée* as loyal members of the social control forces rather than as demonstrators.[26] Again, the timely intervention of the administration had prevented favorably disposed workers from joining in antigovernmental action.

Numerous sources support Thomas's assertion of National Workshops' nonparticipation, though they also tend to play down the actual degree of members' sympathy with the aims of the demonstration. Cherest, for example, concluded that

> Incontestably, the National Workshops, despite the instigations originating in the Luxembourg, refused to cooperate in the revolutionary manifestation of 16 April. [The men] remained at their worksites or left them only to join the National Guard companies to which they belonged. By their attitude, they facilitated the victory of the party of order.[27]

The antagonism existing between the leadership of the National Workshops and Luxembourg sheds further light on the political stance adopted by the former in this period. It was given public expression in the byplay surrounding the Fête de la Fraternité on 20 April. Given that the parade of troops—their rifles decorated with flowers in token of the spirit of peace and fraternity they were celebrating—lasted fourteen hours, one can well imagine that the question of seating arrangements assumed considerable importance. The delegation from the workshops, headed by Thomas, happened or contrived to sit in the portion of the reviewing stands reserved for the representatives of the Luxembourg Commission. When they refused to be displaced, members of the two delegations mingled. The leaders of the two factions actively vied for the attention of those assembled even as members of the Provisional Government were making a ceremonial joint presentation of a banner to these two previously hostile groups (Thomas 1848: 210-12).

The immediate object of all this jostling, as of the *fête* itself, had been to garner workers' votes in the elections scheduled for 23 April. Unfortunately for the leftists, their role in the demonstration of 16 April and their efforts during the subsequent week were seen by many as an attempt at intimidation and produced the opposite of their intended effect (Barrot 1875: 139; Cherest 1873: 238). Moderates and conservatives, especially those who could assume republican coloration, were swept into office throughout France. Even in Paris, the capital of revolution, the radicals fared poorly. In the struggle for control of the Constituent Assembly, Thomas, despite his earlier appeal to workshops' delegates to set political considerations aside, did not hesitate to press his men into the service of moderate candidates.[28]

Electoral defeat and, soon thereafter, the revelation of the Assembly's unwillingness to compromise, quickly closed off reformist avenues of change to the Parisian left. For the first time, open calls to insurrection were heard among its more extreme spokesmen. According to Thomas, the period of his directorship between 23 April and 15 May marked the high point of popular agitation. He graphically described the late-night planning sessions inspired by ministerial warnings of new threats to order; the departure at all hours of cadres sent forth on horseback to quell incipient unrest; and the verbal skirmishes in which he was embroiled with increasing frequency in the council of workshops' delegates (1848: 244-45).

But as tempestuous as activists' sentiments had grown, within the workshops a high degree of restraint and discipline appears to have been the rule. It is instructive to note, for example, that in the unincorporated suburbs of the capital where the spirit of rebellion was especially widespread, insurgence ceased at once when the mayor of Paris and the Minister of Public Works agreed to extend the organization and benefits of the National Workshops beyond the strict limits of the city. When late in April the workers of Rouen rose in defiance of the moderate republic, a delegation from the National Workshops actually offered its services to help put down the rebels.[29] When approached by the organizers of a 12 May demonstration, Thomas not only rejected out of hand their request that he authorize his men to take part but also, by immediately deploying his company commanders, was able to prevent even unauthorized participation.[30] And although in the routine review of the assembled membership on 13 May, the Director had to brave jeers and threats to his person from a growing number of dissidents, he was nonetheless able ultimately to rally the vast majority of workers to his defense (1848: 253-56).

Thus, the consistent pattern of late April and early May was of initiatives on the part of radicals to win over workshops' members, effectively countered by prompt executive action. Yet one key event overshadowed all others in this period, for it was the 15 May invasion of the Constituent Assembly that intensified the reaction and ultimately convinced public opinion of the need to do away with the National Workshops. Because the role of workshops' members was generally misunderstood by contemporaries, and because this erroneous view would prove to be of great consequence, it will be treated here in considerable detail. The essential distinction that most observers failed to grasp was that the activities of that fateful day comprised two phases, each with its own objectives, rallying cries, and constituencies. At 10 A.M., a crowd of 15,000 to 25,000[31] attended a widely publicized, pacific gathering in favor of the democratic movement in Poland, held on the Place de la Bastille. Later in the day, some 2,000 to 3,000 of those individuals forced the gates of the Assembly. Accounts of 15 May have sometimes confused the presence of substantial numbers of workshops' members at the peaceful rally with participation in the violation of the assembly chamber, of which that group was innocent.[32]

Days before, Thomas had been made aware that a rally was to take place for the purpose of signing petitions in support of Poland. He took no advance precautions other than a last-minute appeal against participation that went unheeded by perhaps as many as 14,000 workshops' members.[33] In thus expressing their solidarity with Polish freedom fighters, these workers hardly saw themselves as challenging the legitimacy of republican government in France. Indeed, their shouts of "Long Live the Republic! Long Live Poland! Long Live the National Assembly!" suggested just the opposite.[34] Although no concerted effort had originally been made to prevent members from attending the demonstration, upon hearing that they had turned out in such numbers—rallying, moreover, around their company banners—Thomas dispatched his lieutenants to the Place de la Concorde to intercept the column that had set out on the march to the Assembly. Company commanders warned their men of the belligerent turn that events might take. Their arguments were apparently convincing, for when the columns of marchers encountered the National and Mobile Guardsmen massed on the bridge commanding the approach to the Assembly and the nonpacific intentions of the leaders were gradually revealed, workshops' members quickly reconsidered the implications of their presence. Though the

troops obeyed General Courtais's order to sheathe their bayonets, the group of activists that was thus allowed to pass was
only a small fraction of those who had begun the march.
According to Thomas, the entire workshops' contingent was
to be found among the defectors.

What lends credibility to the account Thomas rendered in
his memoirs is a message from him to workshops' members
dated 16 May and therefore written before the thought of
creatively reconstructing events is likely to have occurred to
him.[35] In it he deplored the attempt by the organizers of the
demonstration to exploit the noble sentiments of workers "in
the name of an oppressed people" and congratulated his men
for remaining loyal to the government once the true designs
of "the anarchists" were disclosed. Still, Thomas's version
(1848: 260-61) might be suspect, were it not supported by
others, notably Stern (1862: II, 269-70). Even antagonistic
commentators like Renard confirm the essential point by remarking that of the National Workshops' banners so much
in evidence earlier, not a single one was to be seen in the
assembly chamber.[36] For his part, Barrot, whose activities in
the Constituent Assembly showed him to be no friend of the
National Workshops, has provided a succinct summary of this
dilemma of historical interpretation:

> The National Workshops had remained basically foreign
> to the invasion of the Assembly, yet they formed, if not
> the totality, at least a great part of the army which fought
> in June. (1875: 285; see also 234)

The problem of specifying just when, within a period of a few
weeks, the change in workshops' loyalty occurred may at first
glance seem of minor interest. Yet, fixing the approximate
moment is actually of the greatest significance, for in order
correctly to associate the shift in allegiance with the political
events that motivated it, one must establish its timing with
relative precision. For this reason, evidence of members' political sentiments will be examined in as much detail as the
historical record makes possible.[37]

From the surviving documents, it can be established that even before 15 May, the moderates had privately resolved to move against the workshops. Just two days previous, the government had closed admissions and voted a measure (neither published nor implemented for more than a month) providing for the diversion of the youngest members into the army (France, Assemblé nationale 1848: II, 161). On that same date, in a consultation with Thomas, Trélat, the newly appointed minister responsible for the workshops, referred to them as "a permanent hotbed of insurrection" that had to be eliminated at the earliest opportunity (Thomas 1848: 263). But it was the invasion of the Assembly that served as pretext for an all-out, public offensive against that institution.[38]

On 15 May, the membership of the National Workshops paraded its liberal sympathies in the streets; it nonetheless stopped short of overt disloyalty to the formally legitimated parliamentary organ of the French people. According to Picattier (1899: 110), "this was the last time that the laborers from the worksites resisted the revolutionary agitation and joined with the party of order." Yet, nearly a week later, at a march arranged for 21 May, National Workshops' units maintained an obstinate silence rather than respond to radicals who shouted slogans in favor of the social republic.[39] McKay, the twentieth-century analyst who has given us the fullest treatment of National Workshops' history, concluded that their political orientation remained essentially unchanged nearly to the end of the month:

> The great majority of the members of the National Workshops were still loyal to the cause of order on 15 May. And in the ten days following, despite concerted attacks on the institution by newspapers of the right and menacing declarations of Trélat before the assembly, there was little indication of serious disaffection. (McKay 1933: 70)

Caussidière (1849: II, 214-15) and Barrot (1875: II, 239-40), two contemporary observers of very different political persuasions, concurred in the observation that Thomas's dismissal on 26 May prompted a burst of agitation in the workshops. And Delessard, himself an officer in the National Workshops, stated categorically that the increase in "effervescence" among the rank and file as well as the rapprochement with the Luxembourg Commission dated from what he called the "abduction of Emile Thomas" (1900: 22-27). Indeed, the bulk of the available evidence points to 26 May as the precise date and to the government's dismissal of Thomas as the crucial determinant of the realignment of workshops' loyalties.

Workshops' members correctly perceived Thomas's removal as a first step in a comprehensive program designed to do away with the organization altogether. The link is unambiguous. On 24 May, Thomas received a report on the morale of the rank and file informing him that "the disposition of the men is good in all respects."[40] This was the last date on which such a statement could be made, for on that same day, Thomas received a set of written instructions from Trélat encapsulating the government's plan for the effective disbanding of the workshops (Thomas 1848: 271-73). These included the following provisions, all slated for execution "with the greatest possible speed":

1. The long-awaited census of workshops' members was to be completed immediately. It would verify the individual credentials only loosely scrutinized in the original admission process, permitting the administration to exclude from the lists multiple inscriptions and those unable to demonstrate six months' prior residence in Paris. It would also provide the information necessary for the implementation of the measures listed below.

2. Unmarried workers from 18 to 25 years of age were to enlist in the army. Refusal to comply was to result in the individual's dismissal from the workshops.

3. Using the data compiled by the census of workers' occupations, a newly established placement center would seek to fill employers' hiring requests. Refusal to accept such positions was again to result in dismissal from the workshops.

4. Workshops' members were to be regrouped for transfer to public works projects in the provinces. Once again, refusal to comply was to result in dismissal.

5. The restricted number of members expected to remain on the enrollment lists (and now explicitly classified as "temporary") was thenceforth to be paid according to a strict piece-rate system rather than on the basis of a daily allocation.

In the eyes of the members, the government was reneging on the assurances made after the February Revolution. Workers were being forced to choose among four bleak alternatives: conscription, unchecked economic exploitation, deportation from the capital, or starvation. The Assembly's strategy was clearly to reduce the burden on the treasury and the political pressure in the capital by shifting responsibility for the workers' subsistence to the army or the private sector and by exiling from Paris as large a share as possible of the unemployed working class.

In the event, it was Director Thomas who was the first to be exiled. Upon reading these instructions, he hastened to an interview with the Minister of Public Works. He protested that these directives were not only illegal, in that they were inconsistent with the government's guarantee of the right to work, but also impolitic, for they would surely lead to the breakdown of public order. According to Thomas, Trélat feigned acceptance of these arguments and promised a respite of twenty-four hours in which to obtain further counsel (1848: 273-75). In fact, Trélat used this time to obtain the permission of Garnier-Pagès, now a member of the Executive Commission, to force Thomas's removal.[41] Thomas was summoned to the

Minister's office on the morning of 26 May and unceremoniously asked for his resignation.[42]

Aware that Trélat had resolved to "take measures for which I did not wish to assume responsibility," Thomas proceeded to direct at the minister one of those appeals to reason and moderation that had succeeded so well and so often with the workers. His basic argument was that "moral influence" remained the most efficacious lever upon the opinion and action of the people. But Thomas's appeal fell on the deaf ears of a minister who believed that the moment for policies premised on moral considerations had passed.

Even then, Thomas showed himself willing to compromise his position in the interest of public order. He composed a letter of resignation, himself devising the pretext—the appointment of a supervisory council, restricting his power as director—that would provide the government with an acceptable explanation for his departure (1848: 287). No sooner was this task concluded than Thomas, to his complete surprise, was informed of his appointment to a "new mission" that required his instant departure from Paris.[43] After forbidding him to communicate with his co-workers and friends, Trélat peremptorily announced that Thomas would leave within the hour for Bordeaux in a closed carriage, accompanied by two armed guards.

Thomas's abduction, which contemporaries freely compared to the *lettres de cachet* of the sixteenth century, shattered the calm that had recently been established in the capital. In his daily report, the Prefect of Police had informed the government that from the evening of 25 May through the day of 26 May, "Paris reveled in the most complete tranquillity" and that public assemblies were continuing to become less frequent, less well attended, and more peaceful. Early on the morning of the 27th, he was pleased to announce that "no disorder, no serious incident" had been brought to his attention. And at 8 A.M., workers arriving at the headquarters of the National Workshops at the Parc Monceaux appear still to have been serenely unaware of the events of the previous evening (Archives nationales C 932A, Nos. 1674, 1693, 1696). Only the assistant directors had reason to believe that something was amiss, having learned that at 11:30 P.M. on the 26th Boulage had delivered an enigmatic three-sentence note from Thomas to his mother. Soon, however, rumors were sweeping through the organizational structure from top to bottom, provoking a vigorous reaction against the authorities and ultimately a resurgence of unrest in the capital that would grow in scope and intensity until it erupted in the conflagration of June.

To a barrage of questions, Boulage replied only that he would return with the minister to clarify the situation. Trélat arrived soon thereafter to confront an excited crowd of 200 to 300 people. When he failed to provide a satisfactory explanation for Thomas's unexpected absence, the five assistant directors promptly tendered their resignations. Trélat retired from the scene but sent emissaries to plead with the higher officers of the workshops to "continue to fulfill their functions, to maintain order and calm among the workers." They agreed to do so on condition that Thomas be exonerated of any imputation of wrongdoing and that they be relieved of their responsibilities as soon as possible, "since they did not desire to be part of a new organization in which the conditions of influence and authority that they had previously exercised would be attenuated by the perhaps irreparable act that had occurred."[44]

The immediate response of the rank and file was one of anger (Delessard 1900: 24). The membership was quick to seize upon even the most implausible explanations—for example, that Blanc was responsible for Thomas's arrest. At first it was suggested that the workers proceed en masse to demand that the Executive Commission provide an explanation for their leader's detention or exile. Members were overheard muttering that they possessed arms and munitions and would overthrow the government if it suppressed the workshops (Archives nationales C 932A, No. 1696, and France, Assemblé nationale 1848: II, 186). Late on the morning of 27 May,

Buchez, President of the Constituent Assembly, sent an anxious note to the Prefect of Police, signaling the disappearance of the Director of the National Workshops and the massing of crowds around the assembly chambers (Archives nationales C 932A, No. 1690).

At 3 P.M. on the 27th, Trélat presented himself to the assembly of workshops' delegates. His evasive replies to pointed questions "aroused a veritable tempest" (Delessard 1900: 25). Feeling was running so high that he might not have escaped the wrath of the crowd without the help of a handful of Ecole centrale students who managed to spirit him out the back door. One should not conclude, however, that the higher echelons of the workshops were in sympathy with the Minister; on the contrary, they seem to have taken the lead in mobilizing the rank and file. According to the reports of the agent Falaiseau de Beauplan, there were at that very moment "secret committees being organized under the leadership of several of the superior officers of the National Workshops" (Archives nationales BB30 313, 2d *liasse, dossier* 445). He informed the government that "Not one of the chiefs of the workshops did his duty, all are guilty."[45] Warrants were issued for the arrest of assistant directors Jaime and Pierre Thomas. In addition, the concentration of troops (two battalions of Mobile Guardsmen among them) was increased around the headquarters of the National Workshops (Archives nationales C 932A, No. 1755).

By the morning of the 28th, petitions were circulating among workshops' members demanding that the National Assembly restore Thomas to his post (Archives nationales C 932A, No. 1746). Throughout that day and the one that followed, assemblies were called at points scattered through the capital and its suburbs to keep workers apprised of recent developments (see, e.g., Archives nationales C 932A, Nos. 1764 and 1765). From 27 May onward, the unmistakable impression conveyed by the reports of police spies, military commanders, the newly appointed Director of the National Workshops, and a variety of contemporary chroniclers was of a suddenly mounting level of ferment in the capital, centered in the National Workshops. Members' activities ranged from peaceful informational meetings to boisterous, threatening mob scenes (Archives nationales C 930, No. 698). Overnight, they initiated campaigns to increase fraternization witth the Luxembourg delegates on the one hand and with the Mobile Guard on the other (France, Assemblé nationale 1848: II, 193; Archives nationales BB30 313, 2d *liasse, dossier* 445). Members engaged in angry confrontations with social control forces including the exchange of insults and mutual jostling with units of the National Guard (France, Assemblé nationale 1848: II, 192-93). It was, in sum, the government's attack on the director of the workshops—the very individual most responsible for the erstwhile cooptation of the membership—that accomplished the sudden unification and radicalization of the Parisian working class.[46]

The significance of the timing of this rise in insurgence did not escape the notice of the more perceptive contemporary observers. Boulage, who, despite his bureaucratic dependence on Trélat, seems to have preserved his political candor, testified before the Commission of Inquiry "that after the departure of Emile Thomas agitation grew within the National Workshops" (France, Assemblé nationale 1848: I, 242). Barrot (1875: 240) spoke of the "lively irritation" caused by a "*lettre de cachet en pleine république.*" Nearly the same words were employed by Marie (Cherest 1873: 230-31), who added that he gave the order to surround the Parc Monceaux with troops because of the threat of riot. On 1 June, the British ambassador gave the following description of the situation in Paris:

> For several days, groups have been formed each evening in the neighborhood of the Porte St. Denis and the Porte St. Martin. I have seen them myself, when I have been returning from some of the more distant boulevards; and on each successive occasion they have seemed to extend over a wider space. They have hitherto had the character

only of debating clubs in the open air and have dispersed whenever summoned to do so by the patrols, but have soon formed again. They discuss different topics of the hour with much animation, and not always with much courtesy; but they have not proceeded to *des voies de fait*. (Normanby 1857: I, 431)

When the Assembly adopted its Labor Committee's proposal for the dissolution of the workshops and began discussion of decrees intended to divert members from the capital, the turmoil set in motion by Thomas's removal was given a new focus and redoubled in intensity.

At this point the members and supporters of the National Workshops might well have followed the example of the insurgents of May by rushing headlong into premature direct action. Had they done so, the result would almost surely have been another brief episode of isolated, piecemeal resistance, met with instant repression. What they did instead was to direct their efforts to the broadening of their base of support, building upon preexisting organizational networks. Internally, members made use of the lines of communication established by the system of brigade-level delegates. The latter held almost daily meetings, usually on a small scale, to pass along information to the rank and file and maintain the level of grassroots mobilization. The resignation or political neutralization of higher officers allowed a stratum of junior-level cadres, whose activism had previously been held in check, to come to the fore. These new leaders, spontaneously chosen by the workers in the elections of the preceding two months, initiated a campaign for external support on three fronts. Their first offensive involved a rapprochement with the radical delegates of the now disbanded Luxembourg Commission and the democratic clubs. The joint efforts of these groups in the elections of 4 June produced a notable improvement over the dismal results achieved in the April vote. The second target was the social control forces of the republican regime. Not only had representatives of the Mobile and Republican Guards been included in the electoral coalition of early June, but police reports of that same period indicated that efforts to divide the ranks of the National and Mobile Guards by winning over their lower class members were begun immediately and intensified as the June Days approached.[47] A third front in the June offensive centered on a projected banquet "at 25 centimes." The Parisian left, and notably the Luxembourg Commission and the National Workshops, undertook this campaign in late May as a show of unity and strength and as a self-conscious effort to broaden the base of radical support (Amann 1960: 1968).

The links forged in these cooperative efforts—all of which originated in the days immediately following the change of directors—were to become an invaluable basis of mobilization in the coming weeks. As late as 6 and 7 June, unruly gatherings of up to 6,000 men were being attributed to Thomas's 26 May disappearance. The republican government decided to press for a law banning public assembly. The measure produced the opposite of its intended effect.[48] Though the new workshops' administration had recently congratulated itself on completing the first wave of an internal census without serious incident, this appearance of calm was illusory. The political activities of the members had merely been redirected outward. The fate of the workshops had become the central preoccupation of all parties, inexorably driving forward the process of progressive polarization.

The government's mounting fear of disorder trapped it in a vicious circle. The institution of new repressive policies served only to fuel popular discontent, which hastened, in turn, the trend toward reaction. To the decree limiting the right of assembly was added a law restricting freedom of the press and measures directed at specific democratic clubs. With this change in the political climate, the workers became convinced of the hopelessness of reformist change within the framework created by the moderate Assembly. They resorted with increasing frequency to the now illegal alternative of direct mass action. Conservative legislators like Falloux, a member of the special subcommittee on the National Workshops, exploited the continuing agitation among the rank and file to maneuver the Assembly into an intransigent stand for early dissolution.[49] Members of the National Workshops reacted with particular vehemence. The Assembly's aggressive response left them embittered at what they could only see as a repudiation of the promises made to the Parisian working class after the February Days. They were at the same time anxious because they faced the immediate prospect of forced separation from family and friends. Above all, they were desperate because the sudden elimination of the workshops would reduce most of them to utter destitution.

Members' worst fears were realized on 21 and 22 June when the first contingent of Parisian workers was transported to the provinces and the order requiring younger members to enroll in the army was published. This news provoked a flurry of activity. Of the many meetings convened in lower class quarters of the city, the one held in the faubourg St. Marceau on the 21st has generally been recognized as the immediate antecedent of the June insurrection (McKay 1933: 136-40). There and at a massive torchlight parade that evening the slogans most in evidence were "We Won't Go!" and "Bread or Lead!" A variety of maledictions were heaped upon the National Assembly, the Executive Commission, Lamartine, and Marie. The crowd's approval was reserved for the unlikely combination of the National Workshops, Barbès, and Louis Napoleon.

The conflict had reached the point where virtually all thought of conciliation had been abandoned. When a delegation of five members of the National Workshops was admitted to the office of Marie, even the semblance of decorum was lost. The same man who, as Minister of Public Works, had supervised the creation of the workshops now seemed bent on their destruction. To the demands of the workers he gave only this blunt reply:

If the workers don't want to leave for the provinces, we will constrain them to go by force. . . . Do you hear? By force! (Stern 1862: II, 367)

Needless to say, this unconditional ultimatum did nothing to calm the passions of the workers.

By 6 A.M. on 23 June, the crowd had reconvened before the Pantheon. Its leader was Pujol, a lieutenant in the National Workshops whose prominent role in many of the events of this period had earned him a reputation as a rabble-rouser.[50] Most of those in attendance were drawn up in quasi-military formation behind the banners of their workshops' companies. They set out for the northeast corner of the city, answering the exhortations of their brigadiers with cries of "Liberty or Death!" It was this column, dominated by workshops' members, that, upon arriving in the rue St. Denis, crossed the final boundary separating peaceful protest from overt insurrection. Shouting "To the Barricades!" they began amassing the impromptu materials from which Parisian revolutionaries fabricate the structures symbolic of their characteristic form of urban warfare.

The events leading to the June insurrection reflected no great credit on the integrity of the authorities. Yet even more damning than the ease with which they went back on the promise of "the right to work" was the lack of foresight displayed in disbanding the National Workshops.[51] From late February through mid-May, this institution had consistently functioned as a force for order and a source of working-class support for the moderate republic. This is not to deny recurrent signs of latent sympathy on the part of workshops' members for the program of reforms subsumed under the label of the "social republic." But at every crucial juncture prior to the June Days and notably in the three great preliminary *journées*, the workshops' organization managed to restrain members from joining the radical cause. It is precisely this combination of members' underlying sympathy with the aspirations of the left and their consistent abstention from acts against the government that suggests the self-destructive nature of the Assembly's decision to do away with its most efficacious instrument of control over the working class.

The last date on which it is possible to document the membership's active sense of loyalty to the democratic republic is 21 May. The last date on which the Thomas administration can be said to have exercised effective command over the National Workshops was 24 May. Beginning on 27 May, the level of discontent among members would rapidly escalate from spontaneous protest to acts of civil disobedience and finally to mobilization for armed insurrection. The government had made a self-fulfilling prophecy of its fear that the workshops would turn against it.

This is not to imply that Thomas's removal was merely an elite miscalculation that can be ascribed to the obtuseness of a few key figures and abstracted from the analysis of the developing political situation. Thomas was dismissed for cause. His demonstrated reluctance to cooperate with the Executive Commission in betraying the promises made to the workers in combination with his acknowledged achievements in giving them organizational coherence made him a supremely dangerous individual. He had become as much of an obstacle to the government's plans to destroy the political effectiveness of the working class as he had been for months to the leftists' hopes of radicalizing it. To the members of the National Workshops, his forced resignation was a symbolic act. But, contrary to the calculations of that institution's opponents, the organizational structure that Thomas had set in place survived his departure, and soon its potential for concerting the activities of Parisian workers was being mobilized to new ends.

This interpretation of events, far from being an end in itself, is merely a preliminary to a proper analysis and cannot stand without the help of further documentation. The next chapter purports to show (1) that through the creation of a core of loyal cadres the Thomas administration was able to impose a degree of quasi-military discipline and effectively coopt the workers through late May; (2) that with the disintegration of this organizational framework, members' relative isolation from outside political influences was ended, along with the government's control over their behavior; and (3) that the practical grievances of workshops' members, the chief of which was the threat to the institution's very survival, were systematically ignored if not exacerbated by government action until a workers' insurrection became a foregone conclusion.

FIVE

Organizational Determinants of National Workshops' Political Orientation

In REVIEWING the history of the National Workshops, the previous chapter uncovered important parallels with the Mobile Guard. The two institutions were roughly similar in social composition in the sense that both represented a broad cross-section of the Parisian working class. They also assumed strategically similar, if diametrically opposite, roles as the organizational centers of the contending forces in the June insurrection. The attempt to explain the workshops' political orientation, however, revealed a more complex pattern: although in the first three months of their existence the workshops remained as staunchly loyal to the moderate republican government as had the Mobile Guard, they subsequently underwent an abrupt political reorientation toward the end of May. This shift in allegiance naturally draws the analyst's attention, because, given the size and internal structure of the National Workshops, it was a crucial precondition of the outbreak of rebellion in late June.

In the earlier treatment of the Mobile Guard, it proved possible to use organizational characteristics to explain how the loyalty of the rank and file was secured for the moderate camp. The question that inevitably arises in the case of the National Workshops is whether these same organizational characteristics can also account for their less straightforward pattern of political orientation and behavior. The present chapter explores this possibility by examining in turn the practical grievances, officer corps, and degree of isolation of the National Workshops and their specific connection to the record of members' participation in the principal events of the period.

PRACTICAL GRIEVANCES

Throughout the brief four-month existence of the National Workshops, members complained about the lack of useful work and the continued insecurity of their status. Always a sensitive gauge of the only half-conscious sentiments of his men, Thomas, in undertaking the reconstruction of the workshops in early March, expressed his apprehension over the consequences that might flow if the need for work were not satisfied:

> I cannot hide from you the fear that such an organization should inspire. A powerful lever for doing good, it can be powerful for evil as well; for it is not very different in its form of radiating organization from the cells of secret societies. If sufficient work does not daily permit us to distribute the greater part of the idle workers among various worksites, controlling them will become extremely difficult, if not perilous, and incalculable disorders could result.[1]

Despite this warning, the average number of workers usefully employed on workshops' projects never exceeded 14,000.[2] This meant that once the full complement had been enrolled, as much as 90 percent of the membership was without work on any given day. Congregations of unassigned workers could be observed in scattered corners of the city, whiling away the hours until they could draw the reduced pay to which they were entitled. These gatherings gave rise to citizens' frequent complaints about the card-playing, drinking, and womanizing carried on in public view and at public expense.

This enforced indolence was in part an outgrowth of the initial conception of the National Workshops. Intended largely as a preventative measure against the risk of popular unrest, they never confronted the need to introduce changes in the

The National Workshops on the Champ de Mars*

structure of the Parisian economy. On the contrary, it would be fairer to say, along with Blanc, that the government established them in part to forestall proposals for the "organization of work." Moreover, the growth of the membership was so unexpectedly rapid that it was never possible to plan beyond the exigencies of the moment. Swamped in March with the task of enrolling the backlog of indigent workers, the administration found that the number seeking admission only increased in April and May. The additional burden of paperwork resulting from payroll, accounting, and the provision of assistance-in-kind was staggering. Finally, the inertia or outright obstructionism of the public engineers whose job it was

* *Note*: The caption is from the original, found in Garnier-Pagès (n.d.: II, 121). In order not to perpetuate a common error, it should be pointed out that this particular workshop of about 5,000 men was originally under the authority of the Ministry of War and was made part of the National Workshops only after 16 May. Thomas contrasted its reputation for disorderliness with that of his own workshops (Thomas 1848: 208-209; see also Delessard 1900: 20, though the latter's dates are confused).

to devise suitable work projects could not be overcome.[3] In combination, these factors resulted in a lack of work that frustrated the administration and infuriated the opponents of the workshops. The latter pointed out that the enormous expense of supporting over one-third of the Parisian labor force with public funds was not compensated by the slightest worthwhile result.

More to the point, perhaps, the lack of work was deeply corrosive of the morale of the rank and file. Members of the National Workshops were not ashamed, in principle, of receiving assistance from a state to which, in better times, they would willingly contribute their fair share of revenue. They had in fact a proprietary attitude toward a republican regime that owed its existence to their support in February and that had, as one of its first official acts, declared the "right to work." Cheated of the chance to justify their meager pay with an honest day's labor, however, even these nominal wages assumed the character of a demeaning dole.

> We are not asking for charity. The Republic promised to provide its children with a livelihood. Give us work which permits us to live as free men should live and you will see, you self-satisfied critics, if we are lazzaroni asking no better than to live off public funds.[4]

Not just the scarcity but also the quality of the available work was a source of frustration. The few substantial projects actually undertaken involved earthworks, the repaving of roadways, and the shoring up of quays and ramparts. The highly skilled artisans who constituted the bulk of the membership were not only inexperienced at this sort of manual labor but considered it wholly inappropriate (Cherest 1873: 216).

> It is not our work that lacks good will, but rather our arms that lack useful work suited to our occupations. We desire it, we call for it with all our hearts.[5]

Given the sterility of these make-work projects, and with the private sector at a virtual standstill, Thomas soon concluded that stimulation of commerce and industry with massive doses of public money was the most promising alternative.

In a report delivered to Marie on 20 March, Thomas suggested that the government provide subsidies to entrepreneurs in the hope of creating jobs.[6] In a report of 10 April, he pleaded with the minister to take the funds then being squandered on make-work projects that merely encouraged habits of laziness in the workers and devote them instead to some great enterprise that might have long-term value for France and might, in the short run, capture people's imagination.[7] In May, Thomas became convinced that the only viable solution was to create "specialized workshops" that would bring together workers in a single trade. The associations of wheelwrights, shoemakers, and tailors that, beginning in April, he had instituted within the existing organizational framework had convinced him that these workshops "were the only ones which produced suitable results" (1848: 234). By May, he was projecting the creation of others employing founders, weavers, skin-dressers, painters, and sculptors (1848: 188-89).

In the early experiments with this new form of organization, raw materials purchased with workshops' money were made into shoes and clothing and sold to members at cost (Thomas 1848: 198). The enlarged system of specialized workshops envisaged by Thomas would have provided for sales to outsiders at minimal profit. Such a scheme had already been put into effect in the women's workshops with great success.[8] Thomas was careful to stress that under his plan the state would not replace the capitalist but would merely guarantee loans advanced to a syndicate composed of workers and employers in equal proportions (1848: 240). This attempt to differentiate his proposal from the ideas of Louis Blanc was apparently a failure, and Renard (1907: 65-66) claimed that the government's suspicion that Thomas had assimilated too many socialist ideas was a major factor in the decision to remove him from office.

To members, the lack of work was demeaning, and the government's rejection of alternatives exasperating. But only with Thomas's dismissal and the launching of a full-scale campaign against the workshops did the full extent of their indignation become apparent.

> You who don't know what poverty is, you reproach us for the 23 sous per day that we are given by the state. We don't earn them, you say. Well, by God, we know that as well as you, and that is what leads us to despair. For you don't know, you rich, what it costs us honest workers, used to earning our living through work, to spend the whole day in the burning sun and then to accept the price of labor we haven't done. But we have to eat and have to feed our families, and hunger, that terrible enemy of the poor, chains us to this humiliation until such time as we can return to our respective jobs.[9]

In the workers' view, they were being punished for the government's failure: the idleness imposed upon them was being used as an excuse to do away with the very institution created to alleviate the effects of massive unemployment.

In late February the workers had pledged three months of patient suffering in the name of the Republic. In March and April, with the government seemingly committed to the workshops' preservation for the duration of the economic crisis, morale was relatively high and Thomas was even able to reduce members' pay by one-third—from 12 to 8 francs weekly—without provoking serious protest. In May the general political climate tended toward reaction, and the advocates of political and social revolution parted company for good. Grumbling was heard among the workers, and Thomas noted a sharp upsurge in indicators of discontent.

But it was only in June, after Thomas's departure, that the fate of the National Workshops became the leading issue of the day, overshadowing all others. The government and the new workshops' administration initiated a series of what McKay (1933: 133) labeled "provocative measures": the firm stand taken against further admissions; the attempt to remove non-Parisians from the rolls; the suppression of assistance-in-kind and of the medical dispensary; and the proposal to remove members to the provinces or divert them into the army. First rumors, then the publication of parliamentary debates, and finally the promulgation of official decrees resolved any lingering doubts as to the government's intentions. Soon members were marching to shouts of "We won't go!" They vigorously protested against their exile to the notoriously unhealthy swamps of Sologne to undertake drainage projects. They refused to be separated from wives and children, cut off from friends and neighbors, removed from their place of residence and work. They vowed to resist the government's plans to undo its commitment to the right to work. Faced with the loss of those few gains they had extracted from the young republic, their pleas to the Assembly became progressively more strident and embittered.

> You have just pronounced, through the voice of one of your viziers, a law of proscription which affects 20,000 proletarians, and you add to the injury of exile the insult of throwing them a beggar's crust. . . . Is this really the same people that you used to call the liberator of the human race? (Lavisse 1921: 100)

The workers were disillusioned to find that at the end of the three months of sacrifice they had pledged to the government, they were unceremoniously to be thrown upon their own resources. Protest among the members of the National Workshops rose directly in proportion to their perception that the survival of the institution was endangered. All subsidiary complaints were subsumed under the threat of dissolution and the obliteration of that slim measure of security that the workshops provided. When, late in June, members' worst fears were realized, barricades reappeared in the streets of Paris. The link between this most practical of grievances and the change in members' political orientation was unmistakable.[10]

COHERENCE OF THE OFFICER CORPS

Maintaining clear and orderly lines of authority presented the workshops' administration with seemingly insuperable difficulties due in large part to the phenomenally rapid growth of the membership. Initially, Thomas's intention was to rely on a small and tight-knit cadre composed of students and alumni of the Ecole centrale. This seemed feasible when enrollments were expected to peak at 10,000; it clearly was not, two months later, when admissions exceeded the initial estimate by a factor of ten. Yet Thomas demonstrated a flair for managing a difficult political situation that many found surprising in an untried youth of twenty-six. He succeeded in building a command structure that effectively secured the political adherence of workshops' members. By first retracing the process whereby this staunchly loyal corps of officers was created, the contrast offered by its disintegration after the change of administration will be easier to understand.

It is important to appreciate the motivation of Marie, who, as Minister of Public Works, presided over the first two-and-one-half months of the workshops' existence. Though he would later favor the workshops' dissolution, at the outset he identified strongly with the new institution. The reader will recall that he advocated its formation as a counterweight to the Luxembourg Commission and even hoped that through it workers could be persuaded to lend armed support to the cause of the moderate republic. Thus, all but the last two weeks of Thomas's tenure in office were served under a minister who had a personal investment in the survival and success of the National Workshops.

In the constitution of an officer corps, Thomas's natural inclinations proved to be sound. His decision to rely on his former classmates and fellow alumni provided him with a relatively homogeneous, primary group whose members were linked by preexisting bonds of solidarity.[11] In his tiny five-man command unit, those ties were reinforced by bonds of friendship, propinquity, and blood. Like Thomas, the four assistant directors, one of them his brother, lived at the Parc Monceaux. They worked together by day and dined at Thomas's table each evening (Thomas 1848: 75, 110-15). Their identification with the Director was so complete that upon hearing of the latter's dismissal, they promptly tendered their own resignations. At this level, then, Thomas relied on intense ties of personal loyalty, cemented by a daily life shared in all its aspects.

The remainder of what could be called the "high administration" consisted likewise of young men who through their association with the Ecole centrale possessed a common socialization and outlook. The positions of ward, service, and company commanders were filled primarily by second- and third-year students whose studies had been interrupted by the outbreak of revolution. It was to them that Thomas gave the charge

> to mix as much as possible with the workers, to speak to them, enlighten them, communicate to them by words as well as affectionate and sympathetic deeds the love of order and the rejection of any caste distinction. . . . (Thomas 1848: 78)

From the first, Thomas recognized that "this cadre of already formed officers," perhaps 150 strong, could exercise the desired "moral influence" only if they entered into regular contact with men who knew them on a fairly intimate basis.[12] When the ranks swelled, the consequent dilution of officers' authority brought about an organizational crisis.

Thomas's threefold response was typically astute. He resolved to preserve the homogeneity and strict loyalty of the high administration at all costs by continuing to reserve these positions for students of the Ecole centrale. To provide the supervisory staff necessary to handle the burgeoning membership, however, he created a new, middle-level rank, the lieutenancy. Prior to appointment, candidates submitted credentials—including "certificates of morality"—and underwent a series of examinations to guarantee their competence and loyalty; after appointment, these officers were subject to review procedures that allowed the administration to remove them for cause on short notice (Thomas 1848: 72, 122, 164-68; Picattier 1899: 81-83).

This screening process was instituted in concert with a change in what can be termed the "low-level" administration, consisting of brigadiers and squad leaders. These lower echelons had originally been staffed with men whose names were suggested by ward mayors, usually without any serious, substantive review.[13] As the pace of workshops' admissions accelerated in April, this already unsatisfactory mechanism became entirely unworkable. At full complement, the workshops employed nearly 2,000 brigadiers and approximately 10,000 squad leaders. Thomas's solution to the dual problems of selecting this vast number of low-level officers and holding them in line was, on the one hand, to have them elected by their men and, on the other, to intensify administrative surveillance of their conduct in office (1848: 147-52).[14] As he explicitly noted, he hoped in this way to add to the legitimacy of the entire officer corps and thus help to secure the allegiance of the rank and file.

From the beginning, Thomas recognized the danger that such a plan created. *After* the events of June, he was roundly criticized for instituting a procedure that allegedly allowed dishonest and disorderly elements to gain positions of authority (Garnier-Pagès n.d.: II, 276; Cherest 1873: 233-34; France, Assemblé nationale 1848: II, 147-48). The rank of brigadier was singled out as the locus of discontent because these officers were often selected by the very men whom they had themselves recruited into the National Workshops.[15] Even before Thomas's ouster, this arrangement had required modification, due primarily to the election as workshops' officers of a number of members of the Luxembourg Commission. Thomas took steps to purge the lower echelons by calling for new elections late in April in which any individual serving as a delegate of any other organization was ruled ineligible (Thomas 1848: 227-28). Thanks to Thomas's unerring sense of timing, this maneuver appears to have been successful in reducing, if not entirely excluding, the influence of the Luxembourg Commission.[16]

Although the evidence indicates that even the most refractory brigadiers and squad leaders were effectively kept in line through early May, Thomas appears to have shared some of the apprehensions of outside observers concerning the political role of these cadres. Not content with the safeguards already outlined, he foresaw the need to reinforce administrative control at the lower levels of the workshops. The organizational form created for this purpose was the Réunion centrale des délégués, usually referred to as the Club of Delegates. Here, too, he used the electoral process to legitimate an assembly of potential activists, initially one from each of the then-existing companies, whom he then proceeded to disarm politically.[17] Their meetings were convened in the presence of the entire body of *centraliens* in the hopes of concentrating the full moderating influence at the Director's disposal upon this group of visible and vocal delegates.[18] He hoped thus to compensate for the rapid influx of lower level officers over whom his control was less direct. He clearly considered the Club of Delegates the most favorable terrain on which to fight a battle for the hearts and minds of his men, a battle that, due to the growth of the membership, could no longer be won in the workshops themselves. Later, moderates and conservatives would complain of the potentially (Garnier-Pagès n.d.: II, 126) or actually (Barrot 1875: 60, 233) pernicious influence exercised by this organization. The record, however, supports Thomas's claim that under his control it was a highly effective device for implementing administrative policy as well as a weapon against disorder. Through this body, Thomas introduced the reduction in workshops' pay, the regulations concerning infractions of discipline, and a host of other reforms that were thus presented to the rank and file with the stamp of approval of their elected representatives. Thomas himself asserted that it was "thanks to this assembly . . . that I was able to prevent the 15th of May from assuming the proportions of the 22nd of June, by using delegates to restore to prudent attitudes those workers who had been led astray by bad advice" (Thomas 1848: 157).

A consistent pattern emerges from this review of the Thomas

administration's policies, and one that offers both parallels and contrasts with the situation in the Mobile Guard. Both organizations placed a premium on regimenting the outlook and identification of the administrative staff. Yet, whereas in the Mobile Guard the legal mandate for the election of all officers up through battalion commanders was gradually undermined, in the National Workshops the evolution appears at first to have been the reverse, with the workshops moving from sole reliance on appointment to the controlled use of elections. In fact, the two organizations converged from different directions on much the same solution: each administration was ultimately able to enhance the legitimacy of its officer corps through the use of elections for low-level positions at the same time that it ensured discipline and loyalty by instituting bureaucratic review of the candidates selected. Thomas, however, appears to have stolen a march on Duvivier in bringing the representative body of workshops' delegates under his authority and effective control; the Club of Delegates produced no such inflammatory statements as those emanating from the independently organized Club de la Garde Mobile and was generally an aid in the accomplishment of the administration's objectives.

Indeed it appears that 100 years before sociologists invented the concept of "cooptation,"[19] Thomas had mastered many of its more subtle variations. Both his words and deeds demonstrated a purposeful desire to involve the rank and file in the operation of the institution of which they were members in order to shape and control their behavior. Thomas understood not only how to set up cooptive mechanisms but also how to guarantee their smoothly regulated operation. He clearly limited the realm of participatory decision-making to the election of low-level officers and the discussion and transmission of directives that, however, it remained the prerogative of the high administration to initiate. Just as important, he went to great lengths to protect those higher echelons from any contamination or dilution.

For all its elegance and effectiveness, the edifice Thomas

had methodically built up collapsed quickly in his absence. His departure triggered a breakdown in the normal functioning of the institution that his successor was unable to correct. The new director, Lalanne, had been picked as much for his formal credentials and pliant attitude as for his political or organizational expertise.[20] He obediently accomplished the task of dismantling the workshops' structure. He suppressed virtually every welfare agency previously set up under the workshops' umbrella: the bureau of assistance-in-kind, the medical bureau, the voluntary placement bureau, and the services in "moralization" and "charity" (Thomas 1848: 338-43). He increased by 50 percent the price to members of goods produced in the specialized workshops (Thomas 1848: 343) and substituted piece rates for daily wages for their employees (Lalanne 1848: VI). His disbanding or reorganization of those brigades with reputations for belligerence was naturally seen as a provocation by many workers (Delessard 1900: 27). According to his own testimony before the Commission of Inquiry (France, Assemblé nationale 1848: I, 302), he proposed to proceed with a wholesale turnover of personnel in the rank of brigadier.

From the organizational point of view, however, his most destructive acts were to disrupt the high and middle levels of the officer corps, thus allowing the radicalism of its lower echelons free rein; and to drive the Club of Delegates out of the administration's embrace and into the arms of the Luxembourg's supporters. The circumstances of Thomas's removal had already prompted the resignation of the four assistant directors.[21] Although a substantial number of Ecole centrale students in mid-level positions appear to have stayed on (Delessard 1900: 26-30), Lalanne introduced a stratum of new cadres with credentials from the rival Ecole polytechnique (McKay 1933: 118; Lavisse 1921: II, 93). These changes demoralized the formerly unified and strongly progovernment officer corps. They released the repressed radicalism of lower level cadres from institutionally imposed constraints. The most striking individual case is that of Pujol, the lieutenant in the

National Workshops who rose to prominence in the final hours before the June Days and personally delivered a sizable contingent of members to the insurgent cause.[22] But Pujol was merely representative of the substantial number of brigadiers and squad leaders who, similarly estranged from their superiors, ended by taking their stand on the barricades along with their men.[23]

The suppression of the Club of Delegates was probably the most serious organizational error committed by the new administration. Lalanne considered it a "dangerous" and "menacing organization" (France, Assemblé nationale 1848: I, 301; Lalanne 1848: VI). Unlike Thomas, he was blind to "the marvelous influence it possessed over the totality of workers."[24] In eliminating it he not only deprived himself of an invaluable weapon but appreciably strengthened the opposition. Though Lalanne claimed that the Club of Delegates entirely ceased meeting (Lalanne 1848: VI), it is clear that his efforts to eradicate a source of potential subversion were a miserable failure. Delegates continued not merely to meet and maintain their networks of influence among the rank and file but became the principal link through which an alliance was forged between the workshops and the Luxembourg Commission (Thomas 1848: 339; McKay 1933: 118). Indeed, the primary consequence of the Club's supposed elimination seems to have been to allow it to escape from any form of official regulation and to facilitate its conversion into "a sort of authority independent of the administration" (France, Assemblé nationale 1848: II, 143). Left to its own devices, the Réunion centrale immediately strengthened its own internal organization, founded a newspaper, and began to post placards authorized in concert with the Luxembourg delegates (Thomas 1848: 343).

In brief, the period following the change of administration was characterized by the rapid deterioration of workshops' morale and the systematic dismantling of all those collective means of social influence and control that had previously inhibited antigovernment behavior. Thomas would later write of Lalanne, with evident bitterness, that "he suppressed every one of those levers of action that he didn't understand and by virtue of which I had kept the workers in line and gained their perfect obedience" (1848: 168). It was precisely this combination of growing discontent at the bottom and diminishing legitimacy and effectiveness at the top that drew the National Workshops out of their state of political insulation.

The Abrupt End to Workshops Isolation

The most formidable task confronted by the Thomas administration was to isolate an unruly mass of 100,000 unemployed workers from the radicalizing influence of Parisian politics. A similar feat had been accomplished in the Mobile Guard, but there it involved just 16,000 men, most of them quite young and unmarried and therefore possessing fewer ties to the community and who, moreover, could be segregated in barracks under conditions of military discipline. In the workshops, the problem of sheer numbers was compounded by the fact that members returned home each evening and thus remained embedded in the social networks based in their extended families, neighborhoods, and places of work.[25] Despite the quasi-military structure of the workshops, discipline was never so strict nor the jurisdiction of officers' authority so broad as in a proper militia. For lack of constructive projects, workers lay about most days, readily accessible to every sort of outside influence.

But although the inherent difficulties of a policy of isolation were much greater than in the Mobile Guard, the Thomas administration devised a number of measures intended to place a cordon around the membership. One was to build the greatest possible degree of structure into daily workshops' activities. Members were to be formed into their squad units promptly at 6:30 each morning and marched off, if not to worksites at least to areas of the city where their presence would be minimally disruptive. They remained on call for twelve hours. To help ensure compliant behavior, pay was distributed daily, but only at the end of the afternoon. In addition, Thomas gave strict orders to his assistants "to keep the workers dispersed and never, in case of nonactivity, to assemble more than 10 at a time."[26]

Furthermore, brigades were formed and assigned to staging grounds or worksites in such a way as to prevent the spread and mutual reinforcement of grievances. From the beginning, Thomas had insisted on a geographical rather than occupational system of organization in the workshops. Thus, most ten-man squads had a mixed composition, every brigade and company contained workers in a wide variety of trades, and each service and ward unit constituted an occupational microcosm of the city as a whole. Thomas purposely dispersed the members of each trade "in order to avoid contact and, consequently, coalitions among workers in the same occupation, which, for certain of these occupations, could lead to serious disadvantages or even dangers" (1848: 52-53). This at least was Thomas's position at the outset when he believed that the need for political calm outweighed economic considerations and therefore chose to fragment the potential constituencies of professional associations rather than undertake risky experiments with the organization of labor. Only later did he acknowledge the sterility of this policy, which, by failing to confront the imperatives of the economic crisis, led inexorably toward the very instability it was intended to circumvent.

Isolation, as well as obedience, was likewise the implicit object of the preoccupation with the ideological purity of workshops' personnel. Thomas required evidence of moral as well as professional competence on the part of those seeking positions of authority. "Moral" appears to have meant in part a willingness to bend to the dictates of the higher administration. Thus, in April Thomas was able to forbid electoral agitation of any kind within workers' brigades yet use workshops' resources to assist moderate candidates.[27] And, as noted previously, when Luxembourg delegates appeared to be gaining a foothold in the workshops by standing for election as low-level officers and delegates to the Réunion centrale, Thomas called for new elections under rules specifically barring them from running. By his own admission, he conducted a concerted campaign to expunge the influence of the Luxembourg Commission from the workshops. He had won Marie's approval for the creation of the Réunion centrale by arguing that to prevent the infiltration of radical ideas there was an

> immense advantage in creating an altar against that of the Luxembourg from which my exhortations could counterbalance the latter's pernicious influence. [The Club of Delegates] would thus give me a barometer which would indicate from moment to moment the emotional state of the workers, reveal to me the agitations and insinuations of the party of anarchy, and permit me to fight them in the light of day. (Thomas 1848: 157)

At the inaugural session of this council, Thomas sought to protect it from contamination by calling upon members "to exclude from our discussions any political or social topic whatsoever" (1848: 176). He then proceeded to use this representative body as a sounding board for his own ideas, combating doctrines he thought harmful in the most favorable institutional context he could design.

Despite the obvious vulnerability of the workshops' membership to leftist mobilization, these efforts on the part of the administration would have to be judged a qualified success. The most telling evidence, of course, is the fact that in the great *journées* of March, April, and May, members participated in limited numbers, if at all. Additional proof is provided by the initially antagonistic attitude toward the Luxembourg delegation adopted by workshops' members attending the 20 April review; by the workshops' rebuff of the organizers' invitation to participate in the leftist demonstration of 12 May; by the stolid refusal of the assembled workshops' membership to respond to the radicals' chanted slogans in favor of the social republic at the march of 21 May; and by the unsolicited offer on the part of workshops' members to help put down a rising of workers in Rouen.

Thomas's dismissal can be directly linked to the termination of this virtual state of political quarantine and to the efforts of workshops' members to effect a reconciliation with the Parisian left. When the Club of Delegates issued a poster protesting the government's high-handed treatment of the director, the remnants of the Luxembourg organization, in the form of the Comité centrale des corporations, wrote to suggest that the two groups coordinate their efforts in the future (Gossez 1967: 301-302). This overture led to the meetings of 28 and 29 May at which representatives of both institutions, along with the presidents of the democratic clubs and representatives of the Mobile and Republican Guards, mapped a coordinated strategy for the by-elections of 4 June (McKay 1933: 102-103). Opinion in the workshops and in the working class more generally had shifted significantly since the April elections; still, the crucial difference was organizational. Whereas then the popular vote had been extremely fragmented, in June the major lower class organizations collaborated in presenting a common slate of radical candidates including the names of such prominent leftists as Cabet, Proudhon, and Raspail. Though turnout was light, four of the eleven names on that list were elected, a notable improvement over the disaster that had occurred just six weeks earlier.

Significantly, the union between the workshops' delegates and those of the *corporations* was effected only after both groups had been institutionally cut adrift.[28] The alliance was, somewhat surprisingly, helped along by no less a personage than Lamartine, who assembled representatives of the two organizations at his home on 11 June in the hope of mobilizing them against the growing Napoleonic threat. Despite the fact that this gathering resulted in a poster addressed to all workers and warning of "the pretensions attributed to Louis Bonaparte," this budding coalition inspired hesitation on the part of many Luxembourg delegates. The latter were unable to shake off the memory of the unreliable, even counterrevolutionary political attitude the workshops had previously adopted or the fear that in a true test of strength they would defect to the party of order. Joint meetings continued through the early weeks of June with varying degrees of success, but it was only as the breech with the government widened and insurrection seemed increasingly immanent that these two dominant working-class organizations closed ranks (McKay 1933: 102-103; France, Assemblé nationale 1848: II, 207; Archives nationales C 932B, No. 2239).

A further context for the politics of conciliation was provided by the campaign to promote the great "banquet of the people" originally scheduled for early June.[29] With the cost of admission set at the modest price of 25 centimes, the organizers of this event sought to attract the broadest possible representation of the working class in a display of liberal sentiment. Neither they nor the members of the government lost sight of the precedent of February, when Louis Philippe's attempt to prevent a similar function had brought the monarchy crashing down. The announced intention of the promoters was to draw in the entire membership of the National Workshops.[30] They also hoped to make use of workshops' cadres, if we are to judge by a poster issued by the organizers in which brigadiers were "invited to collect subscriptions."[31] Director Lalanne, disturbed by rumors that the entire workshops' membership had signed up, was just as determined to discourage participation by all means short of an explicit order.[32] Despite his opposition and the fact that the banquet never actually took place, a substantial share of the workshops' membership was involved in the new grass-roots leftist alliance through the planning, organizing, and publicizing of this event.

In short, the context for the decisive shift in National Workshops' orientation was provided by the convergence of two interrelated crises, one external and one internal to that organization. The invasion of the National Assembly on 15 May provoked a powerful reaction not only on the part of the constituted authorities but also among the general population of Paris and the nation at large. Over the succeeding weeks, this attack on the principal formally legitimated institution of government in France resulted in the severance of the radical party from the still vast reservoir of amorphous republican support. It also spelled an end to social reform.

This initially external set of events helped precipitate the crisis within the National Workshops. For reasons that were both practical and symbolic, the fate of the workshops had become the most highly charged of political issues. With their elimination, the Assembly sought not only to relieve an over-burdened treasury and to remove the threat posed by an armed and organized body of 100,000 men but also to set a new tone and direction for the policies of the Second Republic.

It was precisely this new, repressive tone that mobilized workshops' members. The attempt to disband an institution that had become the sole source of livelihood for one-third of the Parisian labor force was a potent grievance. The removal of the Director not only signified a repudiation of social welfare policies but brusquely decapitated a corps of officers that had contained the political activities of the rank and file with amazing success. Workshops' members first mingled with, soon joined, and ultimately led the radical opposition from which they had previously stayed aloof.

The organizational hypothesis thus helps to complete the explanation of workshops' participation in the June Days, much as it did in the case of the Mobile Guard. It ties political orientation to the collective experiences of the historical actors directly and concretely. But the full value of these two case studies emerges only when their findings are integrated, assessed comparatively against competing perspectives, and probed for implications that reach beyond the year 1848, a set of considerations that constitutes the agenda of the concluding chapter.

SIX

The Organizational Analysis of
the June Days

IN JUNE 1848, two irregular armies of the urban poor fought a four-day battle in the streets of Paris. Its outcome would not only help decide the fate of the pan-European revolutionary movement of that year but also, through the writings of observers like Marx and Tocqueville, leave its lasting imprint on social scientists' conception of the generative process of social movements. Through the critical examination of the surviving records, this study has tried to assess how well the received interpretations of the June Days match up against the available empirical evidence. Because its argument challenges those interpretations at many points, it is important to make its logic as explicit as possible. Having, in brief, conducted the reader through these roughly charted regions, it is now time to attempt a general survey of the terrain covered, to map out the key decision points that have fixed us in our path, and to draw out those principles that might guide us in future explorations.

In this excursion, the concept of the anomaly has proved to be an indispensable orienting device. Following Kuhn's (1970) analysis of the natural sciences, Gouldner (1980) has called attention to the crucial role of anomalies in the process leading to theoretical advance in the social sciences. With this term he designated discrepancies between the assumptions and conclusions that a theorist uses to explain a specific case and those that might be expected to follow from that theorist's general theory or "primary paradigm."

Anomalies have special heuristic value for several reasons. First, they reveal the limits of a theory's claim to generality.

Second, they encourage renewed contact between theory and the body of relevant evidence that might establish the extent of its validity. Third, they help free us from the restrictive influence of our intellectual inheritance. Finally, they alert us to the possibility of creatively recasting the theory by opening up new avenues of inquiry and explanation that potentially add to its power.

The argument laid out in the previous chapters can be seen as an attempt to disentangle a series of nested anomalies. It was the apparent discrepancy between Marx and Engels's general theory of the class determination of political behavior and their exceptionalist treatment of the June Days that first aroused my curiosity about the case of 1848 in France. It was, moreover, the anomalous parallel between the riffraff and lumpenproletariat theses—typically the products of "conservative" and "radical" ideologies, respectively—that prompted an empirical investigation into the social origins of the June insurgents and repressors. The finding that the social compositions of these groups were virtually identical led to the conclusion that this type of etiological explanation was inadequate in accounting for the June alignment of forces.

The failure of strict class explanations led me to ask what alternative might be set in their place. My attention shifted to those institutional entities, the Mobile Guard and the National Workshops, that could be most directly linked to the warring factions in the June Days. I was then forced to confront in still more concrete terms the apparent anomaly that two organizations whose social compositions and early histories seemed to have destined them to identical roles in the revolutionary drama were in fact the main protagonists on opposite sides of the barricades.

Taking my cue from Chorley, I attempted to resolve the seeming contradiction through a close examination of the collective experiences of Mobile Guardsmen and members of the National Workshops between February and June. The elements of an explanation were provided by the contrasts between

(1) the relative coherence and continuity of authority relations in the Mobile Guard throughout the period and the sudden rupture of the workshops' structure after Director Thomas's dismissal;

(2) the relative isolation that could be impbsed between Mobile Guardsmen and the most radical segment of the Parisian working class as opposed to the latter's comparatively easy access to members of the National Workshops, especially after late May; and

(3) the purposeful if sometimes tardy response to Mobile Guard discontents and the unrelieved accumulation of grievances within the National Workshops, culminating in May and June with the government's efforts to disband that organization.

As the assault on each successive layer of anomaly proceeded, the focus of my argument appeared to become increasingly specific to circumstances of time and place. Yet it also developed into a strategy of research with implications for the study of social movements generally, one that can be defined more sharply by juxtaposing my interpretation with competing explanations of these same events.

Explanations from Economic Factors

The classic economic explanation of the June Days derives directly from the writings of Marx and Engels. Subsequent research has shown their analysis to be empirically inaccurate and theoretically unsatisfactory. The characterization of the June insurgents as "a class-conscious proletariat" is simply untenable, at least if one is to attribute to those words any meaning more specific than "a discontented minority of an amorphous working class." To interpret the phrase in that way would, moreover, mock the materialist premise that ties social conflict to concrete economic structures and thus corrupt what is most essential in the Marxist system.

Just as indefensible is the contention that the June repression was carried out by "an armed lumpenproletariat." If the term is to constitute anything more than a convenient label for groups that obstinately refuse to act as the general theory predicts, it must also be attached to specifiable material conditions. But there is no satisfactory evidence to justify the view that members of the Mobile Guard were economic or social marginals. Quite the contrary, their self-reported occupations have demonstrated that these young recruits were drawn from the highly skilled trades that predominated among workers in the French capital.

Indeed, it was the virtual identity between the occupational origins of insurgents and Mobile Guardsmen—to say nothing of the general Parisian population—that showed Marx and Engels's juxtaposition of the proletariat and lumpenproletariat to be not merely imprecise but analytically futile. It is impossible to explain the diametrically opposite political orientations of the two key groups by their class position alone when those positions fail to differ in any significant respect. Add to this conceptual difficulty the fact that the strict class hypothesis denies virtually any independent causal influence to political and organizational factors—precisely those that this inquiry has shown to be of crucial significance—and the inadequacy of this explanatory alternative is made even more apparent.

The implications of this study's findings are more equivocal when used as a test of the major revisionist line advanced by social historians who stress the theme of artisanal activism. A growing body of recent research has consistently demonstrated that participants in popular movements during France's long nineteenth century of revolutionary turbulence were predominantly drawn from the ranks of skilled workers. From this perspective, the events of 1848 appear to conform to a pattern now well established for 1789 (Rudé 1973; Lefebvre 1976; Soboul 1980), 1830 (Pinkney 1964, 1972; Newman 1975), and 1871 (Rougerie 1964; Zeldin 1973).[1] This pattern is the more impressive since it holds not only for Paris but also for Lyon in 1834 (Bezucha 1972 and 1974); the Drôme in 1851 (Margadant 1975); Toulouse through much of the nineteenth century (Aminzade 1981); and the region of the Loire on into the twentieth century (Hanagan 1980). It extends, moreover, well beyond the borders of France. Much the same configuration of popular urban forces has been observed in the case of English Chartism (Thompson 1963; Calhoun 1982), Germany in 1848 (Hamerow 1958; Noyes 1966; Langer 1966; Moore 1978), Russia in both 1905 and 1917 (Bonnell 1983), and in comparative assessments of nineteenth-century movements across Europe (Tilly, Tilly, and Tilly: 1975; Hanagan and Stephenson 1980). In all these cases, artisans provided both the political initiative and the greatest share of the mass following in movements of popular protest.

On the strength of such findings, various authors have argued that the activism of skilled workers results from the autonomy and control that this elite retains in the workplace; from the ease of mobilization that tight-knit occupational and neighborhood communities make possible; or from the radical potential that inheres in the essentially defensive reactions of still potent artisanal groups resisting the advance of industrial capitalism.[2] However these different factors may be weighted, this research has tended to show that the thesis of artisanal activism is of questionable relevance for the case of 1848. For, although both insurgents and repressors were drawn from the ranks of skilled workers in overwhelming proportions, in this respect they merely reflected the composition of the general Parisian working-class population. Given the makeup of the labor force, it would be difficult to imagine a major political confrontation that would *not* inevitably involve a preponderance of artisans. Insofar as it is possible to identify participants recruited from the more proletarianized sectors of the economy, my data indicate no strong tendency for them to participate at appreciably different rates. Thus, although the findings of the present study confirm the predominance of artisans, they leave open the question of whether revolutionism is the consequence of properties specific to skilled workers' social and economic experience or whether it merely corresponds to a critical phase in the development of the capitalist system in which artisans happened to prevail.[3]

Moreover, the observation that skilled workers were numerically predominant, although consistent with the generalization that they invariably assumed a major role in the revolutionary mobilizations of the period, cannot address the central question posed by this study, namely the explanation of political orientation. Here the thesis of artisanal activism founders in the same way and for the same reasons that Marx's original account proved vulnerable: because artisans constituted the core of *both* insurrection and repression. Not only in choosing sides in the June Days but in virtually all its behavior from the February Days onward, the Parisian working class displayed a political indeterminacy that defies simple class analysis. Moreover, this indeterminacy extended well beyond June. Although Louis Napoleon's victory in the presidential election of December 1848 would have been assured solely by the votes of rural France, analysts too often overlook the fact the he enjoyed the support of a substantial majority of Parisian workers (Price 1972: 221-22), in whom vague identifications with socialism and Bonapartism frequently coexisted. On the basis of the June configuration alone, therefore, there are no clear grounds for conclusions about the characteristic levels of activism or the political alignments of artisans as opposed to more proletarianized segments of the working class.

Significantly, explanations of artisanal activism typically argue from the experiences of *employed* workers. But for participants in the Parisian insurrections of 1848, the overriding concern was critically high levels of *unemployment*. Here the scope of the great industrial crisis of 1848—a factor that might be termed "conjunctural" in that it was less an ever-present, structured element of the economic system than a force specific in its magnitude to the immediate situation—assumed a role that etiological analyses fail to capture due in part to their tendency to reduce historical causation to the operation of a few inexorable principles. In the absence of direct data on the

173

employment status of June arrestees, estimates of the extent of joblessness among insurgents must be based on surmise.[4] Tilly and Lees have established that at a time when unemployment averaged more than 50 percent in the city at large, arrests of suspected June insurgents tended to be more frequent in wards and quarters of the capital where joblessness was especially high.[5] Moreover, since roughly half of all arrestees are known to have been members of the National Workshops, one can assert with relative assurance that not less than three-fourths of those defending the June barricades were out of work.[6]

More important than the purely quantitative impact of the unemployment crisis, however, was its qualitative dimension. The popular movement of February had adopted the "right to work" as its rallying cry in preference to the alternative proposed by Blanc, the "organization of work." This fateful choice of what Sewell (1980) would call the "language of labor" permitted the Provisional Government to concentrate its resources on the avowedly apolitical National Workshops instead of the radical program of the Luxembourg Commission. Thanks to the tightly knit organizational structure that Thomas gave them, the workshops in fact functioned as a highly successful cooptive mechanism through the first three months of the Second Republic. Only when, under the intense political pressures generated by the 15 May invasion of the Assembly, the government moved to disband the workshops was the potential of economic exigencies to mobilize the workers actually realized. The activation of predispositional influences of long standing (of which class position and age are the primary examples) depended on a number of temporally specific political, economic, and organizational circumstances that gave workers' grievances a focused expression. In this sense, the June insurrection was not a "necessary" outcome, for most of the possibilities inherent in the situation pointed in directions that differed in varying degrees from the events observed. In searching for valid generalizations, the historical sociologist must examine both long- and short-term sets of forces, but without the a priori assumption that their complex interactions can be summarized as laws that apply without qualification. This study has shown that in the case of 1848, the immediacy of the forces arising out of the evolution of Parisian politics between February and June proved to be a more powerful determinant of the changing terms of social conflict.

The difficulty of capturing this interplay of forces contextually should not be minimized. Too often, the relevant historical evidence is ambiguous, fragmentary, or simply lacking. Ideally, to understand political orientation in the June Days one would want complete job descriptions and job histories for all participants to match with detailed information on their political beliefs and behavior. In the absence of this kind of exhaustive documentation, one might gladly settle for data on the rate of unemployment for discretely defined segments of the Parisian working class along with reliable indications of the rate at which each participated in the events of June. In reality, I count myself extremely fortunate to possess crude aggregate statistics on the Mobile Guard and National Workshops along with the Paris Chamber of Commerce survey's indication of levels of unemployment by sector and occupational group, even if its horizontal classificatory system precludes the most direct test of the class hypothesis. A vertical categorization (i.e., by class or level of skill rather than sector) or greater precision in the definition of categories would, moreover, probably be pointless, given that the self-reports of occupation by Mobile Guardsmen and arrested insurgents are typically not specific enough to link unemployment and political orientation in a definitive manner.

Yet, despite the limitations of the available evidence, it has still been possible to effect a critical assessment of the class hypothesis. In its "strong form," according to which any group clearly defined in class terms should be unequivocally associated with a specific political stance in the June Days, it is obviously disconfirmed by the sweeping similarities uncovered in the social composition of opposing camps. It is, of course, possible to revive the class hypothesis in substantially modified forms more consistent with the observed configuration of social forces. One of the most appealing of these forms, as noted above, is the thesis of artisanal activism. But here the further similarity between both sides of the June insurrection and the general Parisian working-class population makes it impossible to draw any clear-cut conclusions from the prominence of skilled workers in the fighting. All that can be said with confidence is that if an individual's status as an artisan predisposes him to political activity, it exerts no necessary influence on the direction of his political leanings. The question in which this study originated cannot therefore be directly answered on the basis of the class or general economic position of individual participants. The obvious place to turn in search of an alternative explanation is to the single variable that most clearly differentiates between opposing camps in the June Days.

Explanations from Differences in Age

The striking difference in age between insurgents and Mobile Guardsmen, so salient in the minds of their contemporaries, has also been an inspiration for the theoretical speculation of historical analysts. Caspard used it as the basis for what I have called the "cohort hypothesis." According to this view, the younger members of Parisian trades remained incompletely socialized into their occupational communities. Even more important, they possessed less experience and seniority and were therefore the first to be let go as the economic contraction took firm hold. Implicit in the cohort hypothesis is the notion that the political orientation of these younger workers was deeply influenced by gloomy estimates of their immediate material life-chances. As members of the Mobile Guard, it argues, they were particularly susceptible to the government's reactionary influence.

The age differential between Mobile Guardsmen and June arrestees has also served as the basis for an alternative line of analysis recently advanced by Bezucha (1983), which I have elsewhere dubbed the "generational hypothesis" (Traugott 1983a). From this perspective, the twelve years that separated the average age of members of these two groups translate into a sharp contrast in the formative political experiences of successive generations of French workers. The insurgents of June 1848, then entering their mid-thirties, had acquired a first-hand knowledge of workers' struggles under the July Monarchy. The key conflicts of 1832, 1834, and 1839, each of which involved a Parisian insurrection, and the wave of strikes against the encroachments of the *marchandage* system in 1840 had found them already members of an occupational community. Their political outlook was inevitably marked by their identification with the workers' cause and by their sense of betrayal at the hands of a government placed in power by a popular revolution. These lessons in practical politics were not forgotten during the period of relative quiescence that the boom years of the early 1840s ushered in; they would persist in shaping the outlook of older workers when the mass action of 1848 produced another change of regime.

According to Bezucha, the situation was quite different for the youths of the Mobile Guard. With an average age of twenty-two years at the time of the June Days, they had reached a stage of political awareness and been integrated into their occupational communities *after* the wave of labor agitation had passed. Having completed their apprenticeships in the relatively settled 1840s, they were then confronted with an economic crisis of exceptional severity in 1847-1848. It arrived at a point in their careers when, lacking models of collective action on the basis of working-class solidarity or the previous experience of betrayal by the liberal bourgeoisie, their prospects seemed better in alliance with the democratic republic than with an opposition movement whose chances of success were very much in doubt.

If this generational hypothesis has not been previously discussed it is because it exists for the moment only as a body of highly suggestive speculation. Although I do not wish to minimize the difficulties of data collection, it should be possible to gather at least impressionistic information on the history of political involvement and on the attitudes and aspirations of workers of different ages by making use not only of autobiographies and memoirs but also of the often richly documented files of arrested insurgents and Mobile Guardsmen. Only then could one proceed to an empirical assessment of the explanatory power of this perspective in comparison to others. Yet, even if this evidence were now available, this longitudinal version of the argument from differences in age would be subject to many of the same objections that can be addressed to the more cross-sectional view represented by the cohort hypothesis, and these closely parallel analyses will therefore be treated as one in the comments that follow.

Arguments from age, in whatever form, fail to account for the true complexities of the historical record. Levels of unemployment, a crucial link in the presumed causal chain (particularly in the cohort hypothesis), were so high across the board as not to differentiate strongly between the groups in question. Moreover, whatever the variations in rates by sector or by age within the general Parisian labor force, joblessness was, virtually by definition, 100 percent among those who became members of both the Mobile Guard and the National Workshops. Yet the principal difficulty in both the cohort and generational hypotheses resides in the implication that differences between insurgents and repressors derive from characteristics of individuals that, because they correspond to differences in age, long predated the February Revolution and were merely brought out or exacerbated by the deepening economic crisis that led to the February Days. Yet the previous chapters have shown that members of the Mobile Guard and National Workshops alike were recruited from the February barricades, at which point they constituted an undifferentiated mass. Even more revealing, it has been established that through late May both groups were effectively coopted and, despite differences in age, were quite similar in political orientation (just as the workers organized around the Luxembourg Commission, though they can be presumed to be comparable in age to workshops' members, were nonetheless politically distinct). Also remarkable was the relative absence of intergenerational issues in the politics of the early Second Republic, a situation that contrasts sharply with the case of Germany in 1848, where divisions between masters and journeymen were quite salient. Neither form of the argument from age directly addresses the fact that the significant differences in political alignment between the crucial groups developed only in response to events that intervened between the February and June Days and, to be still more specific in the case of the National Workshops, only in the last month of that period.

Thus, a first problem with interpretations based on age differences is that they imperfectly correspond to the flow of events that this study has painstakingly detailed. A second is that they compare unfavorably with alternatives that explain the differences in participation between the major groups more simply and directly. Marital status, for example, is a correlate of age that offers equal or greater leverage in explaining the difference in political loyalties than age itself. Whereas 60 percent of arrestees and three fourths of National Workshops members were married (Tilly and Lees 1975: 189; Schmidt 1948: 28) and a majority of the latter were also said to have children (Audiganne 1854: 197), this research has shown that this was true of virtually none of the Mobile Guardsmen of 1848. To these clear differences might correspond sharp distinctions in the social status, networks of social relations, and views of future prospects of the members of these two organizations. Without sketching the argument in detail, it should be obvious that the rationale for drawing a credible connection between marital status and the determinants of political orientation is no more circumstantial or indirect than in the case of age. The distinctive qualities of life as a single, unattached soldier were in all probability a good deal more important than age itself to the sociological reality experienced daily by the socially isolated members of the Mobile Guard as opposed to their counterparts in the National Workshops who remained more deeply embedded in the community defined by family, friendship, and neighborhood relations.[7]

Even more problematic for the cohort and generational hypotheses is the likelihood, previously discussed, that differences in age (and, by the same token, marital status) were merely an artifact of recruitment requirements, and that the primary determinants of the divergent political orientation of Mobile Guardsmen and members of the National Workshops therefore lie elsewhere. If parsimony is to be our guide, the most satisfying explanation seems to be that, although no more complicated screening device was applied to the insurgents than a willingness to fight and die on the barricades for a just cause (and therefore all categories of age from adolescents to the elderly were represented among arrestees), the criteria for admission to the Mobile Guard specified that only unmarried males between the ages of sixteen and thirty were eligible. Although we know that these recruitment regulations were imperfectly applied, it is readily demonstrated that exceptions to the maximum age limit were relatively rare. This selective recruitment process is sufficient to explain the observed difference in age without recourse to any considerations that might bear on the question of political orientation.

This is not, of course, to deny that the Mobile Guard was much younger on the whole than the group of arrested insurgents; it is merely to point out that due to criteria of enlistment the Mobile Guard was younger than *any* group of comparable political significance, regardless of orientation in June. One can assert with complete assurance, for example, that Mobile Guardsmen were distinctly younger than the group of National Guardsmen who fought with the insurgents *and* that they were younger than those who remained loyal to the government.[8] Only by limiting one's consideration to the single comparison with arrested insurgents can the youth of Mobile Guardsmen be made to appear the primary determinant of their alignment with the repression. In broader perspective, it seems far more likely that the difference in age represented an artifact of the statutes that created the corps than the key to explaining political orientation.

In raising the issue of recruitment criteria, for the first time the explanatory focus shifted from variables representing the aggregation of the characteristics of individual members to variables conceived as the irreducible properties of whole groups. This shift is what alerted me to the advantages of a research design structured in terms of paired comparisons between the groups that assumed decisive roles in the June Days. This microcomparative strategy of analysis allowed me to compensate in part for the limitations of my data, since it relieved me of the need to establish, for example, the social composition of the insurgents and repressors in *absolute* terms, a virtually impossible task given the fragmentary and imprecise nature of the evidence. Instead, I could focus on the question of the *relative* composition of these groups. Sources of sampling or statistical error, distortions of informants' occupational status, the lack of reliability in their informal system of job classification, and a host of other, potentially confounding factors that could reasonably be assumed to apply with equal vigor to both sides could therefore be discounted. When my inquiries revealed extensive similarities in indicators of class composition for Mobile Guardsmen and insurgents (as well as the general Parisian population and the membership of the National Workshops), the causal significance of class in determining the political orientation of June participants could be shown to be quite limited, irrespective of the general criticisms to which the data were subject, simply because such criticisms were equally valid with respect to both terms of the comparison.

The superior explanatory power of a strategy of paired comparisons suggested as its corollary the idea of concentrating my search for an alternative to both class and age-based explanations on organizational entities. In theoretical terms, my conviction that the difference in political orientation between insurgents and repressors postdated the February Days led me to focus on the internal evolution of those institutional structures, the Mobile Guard and the National Workshops, that were best situated to influence the choice of members' political loyalties. Methodologically, the juxtaposition of organizational characteristics that could be assessed in relative terms would again free me from a number of otherwise unresolvable difficulties in analyzing the historical evidence. In this way, my investigation came to focus—pace both Marx and Tocqueville—not on the question of class warfare but on divisions within the working class, an issue whose relevance obviously persists to the present day.

THE ORGANIZATIONAL HYPOTHESIS

The present study has argued that organizational analysis is capable of accounting for both the similarities and the differences in the sociological characteristics of opposing forces in the great insurrection of mid-1848 and in particular for their contrasting political orientations. In contrast to arguments that proceed from the more distant causal influence of class or age, it provides a simpler and more direct explanation that is at the same time consistent with the fluidity and dynamism of the political process observed between February and June.

To support this argument, I have made extensive use of the generalizations that Chorley based on her investigation of the role of armies in insurrectionary situations. But I might just as appropriately have taken as my model the work of Soboul (1980) on the Parisian *sans-culottes* of 1789. His aim was to illuminate the source and character of the popular movement between June 1793 and the year II. In the course of his inquiry, he uncovered a number of determining factors that closely parallel those on which the present study has focused. The *sans-culottes* constituted a loose aggregation of mixed social composition in which artisans and petty entrepreneurs predominated. They possessed no clear sense of class consciousness but were instead united, however briefly, by their antagonism to the old regime and to large-scale capitalists. Their sense of common identity was expressed in forms of dress,

182

language, and a set of political principles that were, moreover, highly ambiguous in their application. The originality of Soboul's analysis derives in large part from its stress on what, with little distortion, could be called the organizational determinants of popular politics: the division of the Parisian population into forty-eight sections; the insistence on the "permanence" and autonomy of sectional assemblies and committees; the material incentive provided by "indemnities" for popular participation in the governmental process; the control of representatives and police by election and recall; the use of voting by roll call and by acclamation; and the "rights" to fraternization, popular intervention in the democratic process, and, as a last resort, insurrection. It is to such factors that he attributed not only the democratic flavor of the popular movement but also, in an essentially Michelsian analysis, the reasons for its ultimate failure. Each of these factors has an equivalent in the analysis I have offered of the determinants of participation in the June insurrection of 1848.

Soboul ended his book with an appeal to researchers "to find out who played the leading role from June 1848 to the Commune of 1871" (1980: 264). He clearly expected such work to make it possible to "chart the decline of [the traditional popular masses] in terms of the triumph of industrialization." Although the present work might be seen as one step in the indicated direction, it is not at all obvious that my findings support the conclusion that Soboul seems to have anticipated. Cobban (1965) has criticized Soboul, among others, for contributing to the "myth of the French Revolution." This myth consists in the view that the Revolution was of bourgeois inspiration, was set in motion by fundamental changes in productive and class relations, and resulted in a further acceleration of these economic trends. For his part, Cobban stressed the degree of diversity among *sans-culottes* and bourgeois alike and rejected interpretations phrased essentially in class terms.

One almost wonders whether in calling for research on 1848 Soboul was not trying to make his strategic retreat from the strict Marxist interpretation of 1789 more hopeful by managing to suggest that economic forces had by the later date reached a stage of sufficient development and polarization to justify a strict social-class interpretation. Unfortunately, this intimation has helped foster a corresponding "myth of the French Revolution of 1848." The notion survives despite work by Price (1972) and others that has clearly shown that even by the middle of the nineteenth century, industrial capitalism had not progressed far enough in France to assure the predominance of a modern proletariat or of an unambiguously revolutionary socialist movement.

Cobban notwithstanding, however, it hardly seems that a return to traditional political or labor history is indicated. The weakness of that style of analysis is that it tended to treat the forms of organization—the union, the party, the occupational association—as if they *were* the class. What is needed is a synthetic approach that conceptualizes class and organization as semi-autonomous determinants of collective action and, if the case of 1848 is any indication, acknowledges that any class-based propensities of actors are conditioned by a set of contingent organizational forces. For this purpose, Soboul's brand of organizational analysis, once shorn of its false optimism concerning evolutionary trends, seems full of promise. Moreover, this promise is already being realized by the best social historians of the current generation. This style of argument is, for example, central to the work of Charles Tilly—who, not incidentally, has trained or inspired a number of those cited above in connection with the thesis of artisanal activism—and has been extended by Skocpol (1979) to explain the revolutionary mobilization of peasants. I have tried to demonstrate the value of this preoccupation with organizational factors in the study of the June Days. My analysis has stressed the importance of measures that ensure the continuity of authority relations in paramilitary groups and pointed out the costs attached to their disruption. It underscored the need for prompt and effective handling of rank-and-file grievances if the loyalty of popular forces is to be maintained. It emphasized that along with authority relations and grievances, the degree of social isolation affects the interactions and identifications of participants and thus the balance of forces in an insurrectionary situation.

The Mobile Guard represents the "positive" case on each of these three variables in the sense that the integrity and morale of the officer corps were preserved intact through several changes of commanding general; the outstanding grievances of the rank and file were redressed before they had a chance to become generalized; and a high degree of isolation was achieved by quartering troops in barracks dispersed throughout the city and its suburbs, generally outside the wards from which the men had been recruited. These measures inhibited the formation of cross-cutting loyalties, and in June the Mobile Guard remained the staunchest supporter of the regime in power.

The situation was more complex in the National Workshops. At least through mid-May, similarities with the Mobile Guard predominated. The workshops' paramilitary structure, the stratagems used to purge and control its officer corps, the handling of the grievances of the rank and file, and the efforts of the administration to isolate members from the Parisian population—all these combined to keep the membership loyal to the moderate Republic. But late in May, with the removal of the director personally responsible for the creation of this organizational structure, the workshops underwent a dramatic transformation that can be gauged in terms of the same three key variables. The higher echelons of the officer corps were left in shambles, the rank and file were drawn into a political alliance with radical workers they had previously shunned, and, when the government confirmed members' longstanding fear that the institution would be disbanded, this most practical of all grievances propelled them into the insurgent camp.

Concluding Remarks

What analytic lessons are to be drawn from this study of the June Days? To what extent can its findings be generalized beyond the case of 1848? Some readers may wonder if it even makes sense to ask such questions of an argument that appears to be specific to the history of the French Second Republic. But despite the fact that this inquiry has increasingly focused on circumstances of time and place, it has made use of a few principles or strategies of analysis that hold some promise of broader relevance. The three points I would offer for the historical sociologist's consideration are the advantages of a collective unit of analysis, the need to restore the sense of historical contingency that etiological explanations too frequently excise, and the decisive role of political and organizational variables in explaining the course and outcome of collective action.

Regnault, reflecting on the loyalty shown by the National Workshops in the events of 16 April, observed that members' behavior was determined "more by discipline than by reasoning" (1850: 300). He thus emphasized that obedience (like organized protest) is a collective achievement, resulting more from the existence of relational bonds than from a calculus of individual interests. Garnier-Pagès expressed a similar insight in contrasting the Mobile Guard in its earliest days with the disciplined militia it would gradually become:

> Not yet outfitted with uniforms, it did not have the *esprit de corps* which tames the soldier; neither did it have the habits which tie the will of the individual to a higher will. (n.d.: II, 110)

Uniformity of dress, the intensification of bonds of solidarity, and the inculcation of behavioral patterns through repetitious drill are the time-honored techniques that military organizations use to submerge the characteristics of individuals beneath a common identity. In attempting to account for the alignment of forces in an insurrectionary situation, it is the "emergent" properties of opposing camps that most directly explain the observed configuration.

The men who joined to form the Mobile Guard and National Workshops respectively can be described, in the aggregate, in terms of sociological characteristics they possessed before the February Days. These descriptions can in turn be used to ground "etiological explanations" that connect preexisting social conditions to forms of political conflict. But although such factors as class or age may exert a predispositional influence, more crucial to an understanding of the outbreak and outcome of the June Days is what these groups *became* in consequence of members' collective experience over the preceding four-month period.

One version of "the myth of the French Revolution of 1848" would have it that the June Days, like those of February, were wholly spontaneous; according to another, they were the ineluctable consequence of blind historical forces. Both points of view oversimplify. Against the first view, it is worth remarking, for example, that the government's eleventh-hour decision to continue temporarily to pay members of the National Workshops after 22 June effectively restrained any "spontaneous" inclination of the majority to join the rebellion. Similarly, the participation of the militant minority can be understood only in terms of a lengthy institutional history that conditioned its response to the government's decision to disestablish the workshops. Yet the course of the June insurrection was neither planned in advance nor narrowly determined in any concrete sense. The sorts of antecedent factors to which subscribers to the second view have pointed merely helped to define a range of possible outcomes. Although the class position of Parisian workers in combination with the insecurity produced by conjunctural economic crisis created a potential for violent social conflict, this constituted but a single plausible eventuality and, in the event, one not realized in most of those affected.

Three key collective actors in the politics of the Second Republic illustrate the variety of possible responses. In the case of the workers associated with the Luxembourg Commission, the determining influence of economics upon political behavior appears to have operated as class analysis might predict. Although little is known of these individuals, their relatively well-elaborated radical beliefs suggest that the salience of ideological position is crucial in completing the connection. For the volunteers of the Mobile Guard, on the contrary, the observed behavior was the reverse of what the class hypothesis would lead one to expect. Here organizational determinants, at odds with the underlying economic predisposition, intervened to block the anticipated translation of class position into militant action. The inherent ambiguity of political discourse made possible a "democratic-republican" orientation antagonistic to the political program of more progressive workers. In the case of the National Workshops, the class hypothesis failed to account for the activities of members through the month of May. But with the collapse of the organizational structure responsible for their previous cooptation, a portion of the membership was drawn into the radical camp and eventual involvement in the June insurrection. Even so, the majority abstained from involvement in the June Days.

These observations illustrate the limitations of a strict class interpretation. In historical analysis, where the outcome of a sequence of events is known in advance, the role of contingent factors is often discounted. This is especially true in the work of the historically oriented social scientist who, in the search for generalizable propositions, all too readily comes to regard the observed outcome as the "predictable" or "inevitable" result of a deterministic process. A similar flaw is common to etiological explanations, which frequently ignore the role of mediating factors that may inflect the causal process. The links between underlying structural conditions and their behavioral consequences are assumed rather than demonstrated. These problems are particularly acute in Marxist class analysis which combines the retrospective bias inherent in a grand historical perspective with a sometimes misplaced emphasis on the determining role of material forces. Although Marx's distinction between classes-in-themselves and classes-for-themselves admits the possibility of their temporary disjuncture, the general theory nonetheless presumes that under the intrinsic logic of the capitalist mode of production, class position translates directly into class action.

The case of 1848 shows that this translation process is by no means historically necessary. Despite the potential predispositional influence of class origin or class-linked vulnerabilities like age—especially when these interact with situationally specific factors like the wave of unemployment that followed the February Days—class-in-itself analysis alone is insufficient. An intervening level of analysis must demonstrate by what mechanisms macrosociological structures are converted into forms of consciousness and the probability of collective action. This study has located the all-important mechanisms in the organizational properties of what would become in June opposing armies of the poor. The Mobile Guard and the National Workshops, conceived as sites of crucial social interactions, exerted a semi-autonomous influence upon the ambiguous mobilizational potential of their respective members.

Moreover, these organizational properties, which are merely a form of micropolitical relations, proved to be every bit as "structural" as their economic counterparts for which the label is customarily reserved. Authority relations between officers and their men, the spread of practical grievances, the opportunity for fraternization—all these constituted patterns or regularities in the behavior of individuals that were shaped and reinforced by supraindividual forces. As such they lent direction, continuity, and increased historical significance to the collective action of participants.

The political forces at work under the early Second Republic were neither more nor less deterministic than the economic. For example, the severity of the 1848 crisis in France (especially when contrasted with the outcome of the initially analogous sequence of economic events in England) was powerfully influenced by political uncertainties resulting from the February Revolution. The Provisional Government's decision to establish the Mobile Guard and the National Workshops was, to be sure, conditioned by the structural realities of widespread unemployment and the dislocations associated with capitalist transformation; but the government was also constrained by the insistent demands of the revolutionary crowd, the lack of reliable social control forces, and its own uncertain legitimacy. Marie's adoption of the Thomas plan for the militarization of the workshops and the positive impetus he initially gave to their growth must be understood not merely as an expedient for the administration of unemployment relief but as a bold political bid to win the allegiance of the Parisian masses. Duvivier's success in instilling discipline among the volunteers of the Mobile Guard—even when its members were committed against their fellow workers—was achieved not just by offering them the security of a daily wage but by nurturing a genuine *esprit de corps*. The use of elections to enhance the legitimacy of officers was a technique carefully manipulated in both the Mobile Guard and the National Workshops so as to favor a moderate stance on the part of members; the choice of the rank and file in both cases fell upon individuals who were seen not just as representatives of class interests but also as possessing such desirable traits as military experience and practical political skills. And the Assembly's resolve to disband the workshops in June was overdetermined both by the massive drain of public funds resulting from the growth in the membership and the widening political gulf between ever more conservative public opinion and ever more radical workshops' sympathies from late May onwards.

Political and economic forces may be convergent, as in this selection of examples from the early Second Republic, or divergent, as illustrated by the failure of the simple class-determinist conception of the role of the Mobile Guard or of the National Workshops under Thomas. What the case of 1848 teaches is that they must be treated as semi-independent causal influences and their association viewed as a contingent outcome to be demonstrated in a concrete historical context. In the attempt to explain collective action, where the adoption of a group unit of analysis helps to reveal the mechanisms that may—or may not—translate predispositional influences into behavior, organizational properties will often prove decisive.

METHODOLOGICAL APPENDIX

Procedures Used to Construct the Mobile Guard Sample

DATA ON the occupations pursued by Mobile Guard volunteers before enlistment were, of all the information at my disposal, at once the most germane and the most problematic. The construction of a systematic sample around this variable was not a simple process. Depending on the conscientiousness of the recording officer appointed in each battalion, the percentage of recruits whose previous employment was known varied from zero to more than 80 percent. To maximize the completeness of occupational data, the Mobile Guard battalion was adopted as the sampling unit and all battalions in which the occupations of fewer than 50 percent of the volunteers were recorded were first excluded on the basis of a cursory examination of each register as reported in column 6 of Table A.1.[1]

At the same time, not all Mobile Guard battalions played an active part in the June Days. Only those that engaged in actual combat were considered. The 6th battalion, for example, had been detached to Rouen some weeks earlier. Although the 3d battalion was present in Paris at the time of the insurrection and stationed near the Pantheon, it neither fired nor was fired upon in the fighting. The number of combat deaths incurred in each battalion, as revealed in the reports of battalion commanders (Archives historiques F1 15), was adopted as the measure of active participation. These figures are displayed in column 7 of Table A.1.

In forming a picture of the sociological makeup of the Mobile Guard, it was obviously crucial to consider the range of socioeconomic variations among volunteers. Here the fact that

Table A.1

Sampling Characteristics of Parisian Wards and Mobile Guard Battalions

1 Ward of Paris	2* Prosperity Measure	3 Prosperity Rank (1 = low)	4 National Guard Loyal (L) or Disloyal (D)	5 Mobile Guard Battalion	6** Percentage of Occupations Indicated	7*** Number Killed in June	8 Number Enrolled by June
1	74.3	12	L	1	50	6	686
				2	0	7	764
2	54.9	11	L	3	60	0	665
				4	0	9	687
3	40.6	9	L	5	80	11	523
				6	30	1	575
4	12.8	1	D	7	0	13	662
				8	80	11	614
5	25.4	7	D	9	15	10	919
				10	0	4	877
6	24.2	6	D	11	0	3	788
				12	60	13	857

7	21.5	3	D	13	0	22	710
				14	20	7	667
8	21.6	4	D	15	0	9	763
				16	60	4	636
9	21.7	5	D	17	40	8	563
				18	60	3	520
10	41.7	10	L	19	60	9	648
				20	0	13	606
11	28.0	8	D	21	50	6	520
				22	40	10	517
12	13.6	2	D	23	60	6	735
				24	40	10	656

Note.

▮ = Sampled wards and battalions.

* Prosperity measure = (% over 1,000F)/(% under 300F) $\times$ 100, based on the distribution of property qualification given in Daumard (1963:55).

** Derived from a 10 percent sample drawn from each of the twenty-four battalion registers (Archives historiques Xm).

*** From battalion reports in Archives historiques (F1 15).

each battalion could be associated with a specific ward of the city made it possible to stratify the sample by including districts characterized by different levels of wealth or poverty. Using data from Daumard (1963), I selected battalions representing the richest and poorest wards of the city as well as four of intermediate prosperity. Data on the relative ranks of the twelve Parisian wards are arrayed in column 3.[2]

A final concern was to guard against any tendency to bias the sample of Mobile Guardsmen due solely to the political characteristics of the wards in which the selected Mobile Guard battalions originated. The first and simpler precaution was to seek an even balance of battalions from each side of the east/west political divide that became so apparent at the time of the June Days. In addition, since the legions of the democratized National Guard were, like the Mobile Guard, drawn from discrete wards of the capital, their sympathies in the June Days could be used as an indicator of the underlying disposition of the general population. It was only necessary to choose Mobile Guard battalions from three wards in which the National Guard remained loyal to the government, and three in which it went over to the insurrection, as shown in column 4.[3]

One could hardly take for granted the feasibility of simultaneously satisfying all these considerations. Yet all the conditions enumerated are met by a sampling frame consisting of the 1st, 5th, 8th, 16th, 19th, and 23d battalions of the Mobile Guard. As indicated in Table A.1, these represented wards ranked 1st, 2d, 4th, 9th, 10th, and 12th on a scale on which higher ranks indicated higher socioeconomic status. In one half of them the bulk of the National Guard fought with the repression in June, in the other half with the insurgents. In only one of these six battalions did the percentage of Mobile Guardsmen for whom occupation was indicated approach the lower limit of 50 percent, whereas in two it was as high as 80 percent. It was ascertained from battalion reports that all of the battalions selected were active in June, and that their aggregate rate of fatalities differed negligibly from that of the corps as a whole.[4] By considering all 3,845 individuals en-rolled in these six battalions before June, it was thus possible to define a sample of a size and composition that captures the full range of occupational as well as demographic and soci-ological variations characteristic of the larger population of Mobile Guardsmen.

The total number of Mobile Guardsmen active in June has been estimated by Caspard (1974: 82) at 14,000 and by Chal-min (1948: 68) at 12,000. My figures show that by 22 June, 14,918 volunteers had signed up in the twenty-two active battalions. Subtracting the 8.4 percent who were absent be-cause they had already been discharged by the onset of the June Days and allowing for those who deserted, changed bat-talions, appeared in more than one register, were reported missing during the fighting, remained inactive, and so on, one arrives at a best estimate that falls between those just cited: approximately 13,000 to 13,500 Mobile Guardsmen actually participated in the June repression.

Of the 3,845 Mobile Guardsmen included in the present study's six-battalion sample, 3,521 were active in June. This compares with the approximately 4,250 individuals from twelve battalions who, according to information generously supplied by Pierre Caspard in a personal communication, were included in his data on Mobile Guard occupations. The principal meth-odological difference is that for any given variable, Caspard used all individuals for whom information was available, dropping others from his calculations. In the absence of any indication of the extent of missing data, it is difficult or im-possible to assess the consequences of this procedure. It would not, for example, have been possible to use those data to establish correlations among variables, as they do not bear on the same population in every case.

Aware of the potential difficulty represented by missing data, Caspard compared the rates of literacy among those retained in his calculation of occupational distributions with those dropped for lack of information. Finding no appreciable disparity, he concluded that systematic bias was absent.

Similarly, in order to verify the representative character of the sample used in the present research, two variables were chosen—age and literacy—for which information was readily available for nearly every Mobile Guard recruit. Next, a 10 percent systematic sample of all twenty-two active, regular battalions was drawn. Its aggregated values for age and literacy were compared with those for the six-battalion sample. The distribution of ages in the 10 percent sample of all battalions yielded a mean of 21.6 and a mode of 18 years; the corresponding figures for the six-battalion sample population were 22.2 and 18 years. The convergence in the case of literacy is still more striking. Although individual battalions displayed appreciable differences in the proportion of illiterates—from 8.6 percent to 18.1 percent—the average rate of illiteracy for the six-battalion sample was 12.8 percent as compared with the 12.4 percent rate found in the case of the 10 percent general sample.

NOTES

Chapter One

1. Although the rising in Berlin was the most notable instance among the German states, riots and rebellion also took place at various junctures in Schleswig, Saxony, Bavaria, and Baden. The principal turmoil in the Italian states occurred in Milan, Venice, Sardinia, Tuscany, Sicily, and the Papal territories, much of it directed against Austrian rule. Note, however, that the rising in Naples *predated* the February Days in France. Minor, unsuccessful, or purely constitutional changes also took place in Denmark, Holland, Switzerland, Poland, Rumania, and Bohemia. For brief overviews of these events, see, for example, Herzen (1871: 225); Stearns (1974); Palmer and Colton (1963); and Kamenka and Smith (1980: 1).

2. Compare McKay's simple and accurate description: "nothing more or less than a professional army recruited from the gamins of Paris" (McKay 1933: 45).

3. Lamartine (1849: II, 120). Louis Blanc, the most radical member of that government, is reported to have referred to the workshops as "the army of hunger" (Cherest 1873: 198). Garnier-Pagès (n.d.: II, 125), a conservative member of the Provisional Government and briefly mayor of Paris, speculated about their political leanings in similar terms: "Organized as a pacifistic army of labor, might these workshops not become a militant army of insurrection?"

4. *Le Constitutionnel* (22 June 1848). Compare also *le Journal des Débats* (29 May 1848): "an army of more than 100,000 unemployed."

5. France, Assemblé nationale (1848: I, 41). Compare also Falloux (1925: 304), one of the members of the Constituent Assembly most directly responsible for the ultimate dissolution of the workshops, who called them "an army of the most dangerous kind of socialism." For similar statements by contemporaries, see also Achard (1872: 132); Tocqueville (1971: 171); Regnault (1850: 345); Ménard (1904: 142); Proudhon (1868: 104); Bonde (1903: 197); and Léon Faucher, cited in Barrot (1875: II, 237).

6. Price (1972: 20) cites figures according to which more than 14,000,000 individuals of a total population of approximately 23,000,000 were directly engaged in agriculture. The rural population was, of course, substantially larger. In 1848, it represented three-fourths of the national total (Mauco 1932: 17), and even in 1872 it accounted for nearly 25,000,000 of a total of 37,000,000 Frenchmen (Price 1972: 10-11). The second half of the nineteenth century was in France a time of substantial economic growth under conditions of demographic stagnation.

7. The term "proletarian," which was just coming into general usage in mid-nineteenth-century France, provides an even clearer example of this ambiguity. When in June 1848 the new Director of the National Workshops announced a plan to assign members to projects in the provinces, workers phrased their protest to the government in these words:

> Through one of your viziers, you have just pronounced a decree of proscription which affects 20,000 proletarians (*prolétaires*), and you heap insult upon the cruelty of exile by throwing them a beggar's crust (cited in Lavisse 1921: II, 100).

At a moment when the writings of Marx and Engels were unknown in France, the term "proletarian" retained its generic sense of "member of the laboring classes." This meaning could be applied with perfect justice to the artisans of Paris (and, as the example shows, was applied by the workers themselves), whereas the more modern and specific sense of the word could not (and would have been vehemently rejected by those same workers).

8. Zeldin (1973: 210). Clapham (1961) has shown that this remained essentially unchanged long after 1848. The rise of factories in France is usually dated from around 1830. Mauco (1932: 17) sets the 1851 ratio of those engaged in small- versus large-scale industry at 4,352,000 to 1,330,000 in the nation as a whole. It should be noted, however, that the standard for "large-scale" industry was typically quite inclusive. The 1848 Chamber of Commerce study, for example, defined its largest category of shop size to embrace all enterprises employing ten or more workers per *patron*.

9. Langer (1966: 91). Though net in-migration actually declined sharply in the years immediately preceding 1848, the drop was due less to a slackening of in-migration in absolute terms than to

an increase of out-migration and, as indicated by Chevalier (1950: 48, 285), the Parisian working class continued to consist to a considerable extent of individuals born elsewhere. According to Bertillon, only half of all Parisians who died in 1833 had been born in the capital; by 1861, the proportion had dropped to 36 percent (cited in Chevalier 1950: 45).

10. The explanation of this geographical distribution in Paris, as in many other European cities, is to be found in the prevailing westerly winds. Those who could afford it avoided noxious industrial fumes by locating in upwind areas that to this day tend to be the more exclusive sections of the city. Chevalier (1950: 120-21) noted that, despite some highly local occupational specialization, residential patterns were otherwise only loosely fixed by class or *département* of origin.

11. In these lodging houses, located primarily in the center and in the east, entire families might live in one cramped room, and single workers often occupied beds in communal dormitories (Chevalier 1958: 278).

12. Potatoes had been a staple of growing importance in the northern regions of France for some time. The yield in 1845 was the lowest since 1832 and fell still further in 1846. The wheat harvest of 1845 was disappointing, but it was only with the enormous shortfall of the following year—the worst France had experienced in a quarter century—that the crisis assumed national proportions. See Labrousse (1956: v, xvi).

13. The Chamber of Commerce survey of the Parisian labor force produced the following estimates of the diminution of personnel employed in each of thirteen production sectors:

Sector	Percent Reduction
Furniture	73
Construction	64
Base metals	58
Precious metals	57
Thread and textiles	53
Fancy goods	52
Clothing and shoes	51
Carriage-making	47
Cooperage, basketry	46

Printing	46
Chemicals, ceramics	46
Leather	40
Food	19
Total	54

These figures are based on 342,530 workers employed in 1847, of whom 186,405 had been laid off by mid-1848 (Chambre de Commerce 1851: 41). See also Audiganne (1849: 993).

14. Although it was sometimes experienced and described as a "crisis of overproduction," this situation should not be confused with an economy of glut. Like preindustrial crises, the decline in demand originated in the scarcity of foodstuffs. Unlike crises of the old regime, however, it was crucially affected by France's growing involvement in the world economy. On the specific interaction effects between the English and French crises, see Traugott (1983b), which considers in greater detail the events briefly recapitulated here.

15. In this section, no sources have been cited for information that can be considered general knowledge or that is available in standard texts. Most of the points that might be considered controversial are discussed and documented in later chapters. For the reader who wishes to acquire more detailed knowledge of this fascinating period, useful English-language secondary sources include the following: Duveau (1967); Price (1972); and Robertson (1967). Among the most valuable contemporary accounts by participants or observers are Blanc (1850 and 1858), Caussidière (1849), Lamartine (1849), Stern (1862), and Tocqueville (1971).

16. Although this enlargement of the suffrage may seem modest in retrospect, at that time only 250,000 of the 9,000,000 adult males in France qualified for the electoral rolls.

17. According to Carter and Middleton (1908: 744), there were no fewer than seventy banquets in all, involving some 170,000 participants.

18. Ledru-Rollin, like Blanc and Marrast, was associated with *La Réforme* and was seen as a radical. His subsequent role in the Provisional Government would, however, be more that of intermediary between moderate and radical factions. Albert was the *nom de guerre* of Alexandre Martin, a buttonmaker and veteran of Parisian secret societies and one of the founders of the workers'

newspaper *l'Atelier* (McKay 1933: 7; Duveau 1967: 55). Aside from seconding Blanc as Vice Chairman of the Luxembourg Commission, he played no prominent role in subsequent events.

19. A victory in terms of the demonstrators' expressed aim, that is. Various analysts have attributed the radicals' defeat in the 23 April elections to the postponement they won in the protest of 17 March. The leftists' chances would have been better, their argument contends, either if the elections had been scheduled earlier, when revolutionary fervor was still at its peak, or if the elections had been held much later, giving the democrats time to mount a more effective campaign in the provinces. I find, first, that this reasoning rests on a number of questionable assumptions and, second, that the actual difference of two weeks' time in the scheduled date of the elections is too small to have had a decisive effect.

20. The point is significant, since even the most astute recent commentators on the period like Price (1972) and Sewell (1980), while correctly placing the *beginnings* of class consciousness in France in the early 1830s, do not consistently emphasize how incomplete this transformation remained in 1848. It need hardly be pointed out that Marx and Engels incorporated the same kind of bias in their writings. The systematic study of the elections of 23 April 1848 (and, to a lesser extent, the by-elections of early June) offers the opportunity to assess the state of class consciousness among French workers at this crucial juncture. Systematic research on this question has yet to be done.

21. The actual range of contemporary estimates of the number of participants in the June insurrection extends from 12,000 to 60,000. The lowest figure is, interestingly enough, provided by Lefrançais (1902: 58), a radical who fought on the June barricades and cites this number as if in explanation of the rising's failure. Many later authors (e.g., Stearns 1974: 89-90; Ponteil 1955: 144) assert that the rebels numbered roughly 15,000 without explaining the basis of their estimate. It seems likely that they have taken the number of arrestees as an indication of the number of participants, clearly a questionable assumption. The contemporary accounts by Pagès-Duport (1848: 125) and the Parisian weekly *l'Illustration* (1848: 225) each specified a total of 40,000. The Commission of Inquiry (France, Assemblé nationale 1848: I, 358) cites the testimony of Trouvé-Chauvel, Prefect of Police at the time of the June Days, to the effect that there were between 40,000 and 50,000 insurgents.

The Baroness Bonde (1903: 206), probably relying on word of mouth, set the number at 45,000. Blanc (1858: 436) placed the figure at 50,000. Cavaignac, the Minister of War invested with martial powers to suppress the insurrection, gave 50,000 as the highest estimate he had received (*le Moniteur*: 4 July 1848; Stern 1862: II, 482-83). Quentin-Bauchart (1901: 49), who was placed in charge of the Assembly's Commission of Inquiry, reported that no fewer than 50,000 had participated. Faucher, whom McKay describes as a "naturally prejudiced witness," is responsible for the highest estimate of insurgent strength, 60,000 (McKay 1933: 145). The discrepancies surely result in part from the difficulty of making systematic assessments of forces dispersed among several hundred barricades scattered throughout the city. In addition, however, there seems to have been some tendency for the higher estimates to adopt general measures of participation that included those who helped construct barricades and those who provided medical and logistical support. The lower figures usually consider only the core of combatants active on the final day of hostilities when the outcome was already obvious. Perhaps the best grounded retrospective estimate of the number actually bearing arms is Tilly and Lees's (1975: 186) figure of 10,000 to 15,000 active participants.

CHAPTER TWO

1. Crémieux (1912); Stern (1862); Bouniols (1918); Duveau (1967). Here I have followed the standard sources that attribute much of the responsibility for the outcome in February to the personal indecision of the king or to cabinet-level machinations. I believe that such explanations are ultimately unsatisfactory because they fail to account for the conditions under which the fraternization and subsequent defection of social control forces took place, let alone to come to grips with the more indirect mobilizing effects of the reform campaign. What is unfortunately lacking is an in-depth study of the February Days that analyzes the determinants of participants' political orientation much as the present work attempts to understand those affecting the June combatants.

2. Garnier-Pagès (n.d.: I, 320). The Municipal Guard had earned a reputation for brutality well before the February Days. Its members were so detested by the people that after the change of regimes

they dared not appear in uniform on the streets of Paris (Langer 1966: 98; Chalmin 1948: 38-39). Many of these men were eventually taken into the National Workshops but, because of friction with the other workers, had to be assigned to a special work project outside Paris. After the June Days, the corps was revived as a police force (Thomas 1848: 128-33).

3. The anger and suspicion of the people were based in part on the army's role in the massacre of the Boulevard des Capucines, which left fifty dead. The view of the Provisional Government, represented by Marie, was that

> The army was not worth considering. [The *journée* of] February 24 had dispersed it. It was not so much defeated as annulled, disbanded in a sense, by events. What it cost Arago, Charras, and later General Cavaignac in worry and energy to reorganize it, reestablish its discipline, and revive the idea of subordination and obedience, contemporary accounts have already told and history will repeat. For myself, I can only affirm a single fact: that Paris no longer possessed a military force. (Cherest 1873: 208)

The lack of *esprit de corps* that followed the February Days is described by Tocqueville:

> Soldiers were the commonest sight in those empty streets, some alone, all unarmed and homeward bound. Their recent defeat had left an acute sense of shame and anger in their souls, as became obvious later, but at the time it did not show. (1971: 88; see also Chalmin 1955: 46-47)

It was the desire to recover the army's lost sense of military pride that dictated Cavaignac's strategy in June. Whereas in February, General Sebastiani had dispersed his forces, thus allowing the insurgents to exploit the opportunities for fraternization and street-fighting tactics (Stern 1862: I, 305-306), Cavaignac insisted on massing his troops, often using them in combination with artillery, even though this permitted the insurrection to gain initial possession of large areas of the city without opposition.

4. Marie complained that

> The National Guard was powerless. We had called upon it in the first days. It answered our summons, then dispersed. (Cherest 1873: 209)

For comments by another member of the Provisional Government, see Garnier-Pagès (n.d.: I, 320).

Despite the National Guard's benevolent attitude in the February Days and the government's attempt at democratization, it was never entirely trusted by popular elements because of its still disproportionately bourgeois or petty-bourgeois composition (Daumard 1963: 596).

5. Caussidière (1849: I, 189-90). Tocqueville concurred:

> Throughout this day [of 25 February] in Paris I never saw one of the former agents of authority: not a soldier, or a gendarme, or a policeman; even the National Guard had vanished. The people alone bore arms, guarded public buildings, watched, commanded and punished; it was an extraordinary and a terrible thing to see the whole of this huge city, full of so many riches, or rather the whole of this great nation, in the sole hands of those who owned nothing. (1971: 90)

This view, however, was far from universal, and Tocqueville himself notes a selectivity in the elaboration of

> a particular kind of morality of disorder and a special code for days of riot. . . . These exceptional laws tolerate murder and allow devastation, but theft is strictly forbidden. (1971: 91)

6. Lavisse (1921: 10); Schmidt (1948: 9). Lamartine was acting on a suggestion attributed to Dubourg, who in 1830 had organized the *volontaires de la Charte* (Stern 1862: I, 443; Chalmin 1948: 40-42). This corps of irregulars, which served as a model for the Mobile Guard, was used in Africa as part of the French colonial army and was later absorbed into the army of the line as the 67th regiment. Duvivier, first commanding general of the Mobile Guard, had served as commander of one of the auxiliary battalions of the *volontaires de la Charte*.

7. This was considered a premium wage for military service. By contrast, the simple soldier in the regular army was paid a mere 25 centimes per day. Though their nominal compensation was initially to be the same as that of members of the National Workshops, Mobile Guardsmen in fact received nearly half again as much in pay and greater subsistence benefits as well.

8. *Le Moniteur universel* (26 and 27 February). Each Mobile Guard company was to consist of 120 simple soldiers, a drummer, four corporals, two sergeants, one quartermaster, one second lieutenant, one lieutenant, and one captain. Eight such companies constituted a battalion with ten general officers at its head. Figures to be presented below will show that in fact only about 16,000 men had signed up (and perhaps 14,000 remained active) by the time of the June Days.

9. In the very first days, students from St. Cyr, the French military academy, were pressed into service as provisional officers.

10. The new corps was named the "Garde nationale mobile" to distinguish it from what would henceforth be officially designated as the "Garde nationale sedentaire." We have followed the convention of referring to these groups as the Mobile Guard and the National Guard, respectively.

11. The founding decree circumscribed its movements to within 1,000 meters of the detached forts of Paris in the absence of an explicit order from the government. Units were to be rotated among these forts on the outskirts of the city so that none spent more than a month separated "from the interior of Paris and from their families" (Archives historiques F1 2, 26 February).

12. I do not wish to prejudge the issue of how fundamental this shift was in political terms. After all, the February insurrection was directed against a monarchy, however bounded by constitutional constraints; the June insurrection, for its part, attacked a duly constituted republican regime elected by universal manhood suffrage, whatever its failings in the view of the ultra-democratic left. The behavior of Mobile Guard members in these different situations is by no means self-evidently inconsistent. My point here is simply that in February the Parisian lower class was unified, in June divided. In the interim, members of the Mobile Guard had undergone a political evolution different from that of the radical activists with whom they had joined in the February Days. It is precisely in order to assess the *relative* extent of change in political orientation that the comparative case of the National Workshops will be examined in later chapters.

13. Archives historiques (Xm 32, 17 March). The Minister requested two battalions of Mobile Guardsmen "to assure the liberty of the workers involved in the Fête de la Concorde." (This occasion is not to be confused with the 21 May celebration of the same name.)

The Mobile Guard had already assumed regular patrol duties in the city, but this was the first exceptional use of the corps that I have been able to document aside from a premature and abortive attempt to arm and deploy a few Mobile Guard battalions on the morning of 17 March (House 1975: 159, 168).

14. Regnault (1850: 296-97); Lamartine (1849: II, 317-19); Stern (1862: II, 176). Mobile Guard orders (Archives historiques Xm 49, Nos. 123-125, 16 April: 25 *bis*) show that Duvivier also sent reinforcements to the Mobile Guard units already stationed at the Hôtel de Ville as well as small contingents to guard the Ministries of Foreign Affairs and Finance.

15. His speech was reprinted in *le Moniteur universel* (19 April, 1848: 860).

16. Lamartine (1849: II, 336-38), who incorrectly placed this *journée* on the 21st rather than the 20th of April.

17. The exception was a small detachment sent to guard the Ministry of Finance at the request of the Undersecretary of State who feared a possible attack (Archives historiques Xm 32, 19 April). In the next chapter, we shall see that some units of the Mobile Guard had threatened not to attend the review as a form of protest against delays in the delivery of their uniforms. In the event, they decided against this act of insubordination, and when uniforms began arriving one week later their resentment quickly dissipated.

18. This placed him ahead of the radical members of the Provisional Government (Albert, Ledru-Rollin, Flocon, and Blanc, in order of their total number of votes) as well as such prominent leftists as Caussidière and Lamenais. For a complete compilation of the votes received by all major candidates, see Stern (1862: II, 580-81).

19. Archives historiques (Xm 34); Caspard (1974: 102). Also significant was the behavior of the 5th battalion, stationed in Amiens since 11 April on orders from Ledru-Rollin for the purpose of subduing royalist agitation against the local commissar. The workers of that city adopted these Mobile Guardsmen as their political allies. When, however, a riot broke out on 29 April, the Mobile Guard "fought without noticeable hesitation" on the side of order, and the rebellion was quickly put down (Caspard 1974: 102-103).

20. Buchez, President of the National Assembly, issued the original command summoning four battalions of the Mobile Guard (Archives historiques Xm 32, 14 May; France, Assemblé nationale 1848: I, 196). The reports of battalion commanders indicate, how-

ever, that at least seven battalions (the 2d, 3d, 5th, 8th, 9th, 13th, and 15th) took an active part in events while still others were kept on alert (Archives historiques F1 15). Mobile Guard units were assigned key positions on the Pont de la Concorde, the principal approach to the chamber, and on the Esplanade des Invalides to protect against attacks from the rear; others were held in reserve behind the grillwork of the Palais Bourbon itself (Archives historiques F1 15; Stern 1862: II, 250-51).

21. Archives historiques (F1 15, especially the report of Bassac, commander of the 5th battalion). Courtais's version of these events differed substantially. He complained of the inaction of Tempoure, who he claimed was seen standing about in the chamber as a spectator. As a result of this testimony, Tempoure was removed from command of the Mobile Guard, pending the outcome of an inquiry. Though ultimately exonerated of all wrongdoing, Tempoure was never reappointed. Concerning this controversy, see France, Assemblé nationale (1848: I, 198-203).

22. The figure is that cited by Lamartine (1849: II, 454; see also Doumenc 1948: 257), who gives the following breakdown of the rest of the 40,000-man government force said to have been under arms in Paris at that time: 2,600 Republican Guards; 2,000 Gardiens de Paris; and 20,000 army troops quartered in local barracks. In addition, there were army units with a total strength of some 15,000 men stationed in the area surrounding Paris (Vidalenc 1948: 99-100). In principle, a vast number of National Guardsmen were also available, but few responded to the *rappel* in the working-class sections of the city, and many of those from bourgeois quarters merely patrolled the streets in their own neighborhoods. Of 237,000 nominally enrolled by June, a mere 12,000 participated actively (Caspard 1974: 82). Once word of the uprising reached the provinces, a massive influx of departmental National Guardsmen began, but with few exceptions (Vidalenc 1948: 117) these men were held in reserve or arrived too late to take part in actual combat.

23. Stern (1862: II, 387), who also cites Lamoricière to this same effect (1862: II, 393).

24. Lamartine (1849: II, 478, 480); *le Moniteur universel* (24 June, 1848: 1480); Ménard (1904: 150); Vidalenc (1948: 117); Luna (1969: 166). Merimée's recollection was that the National Guard led on the Mobile Guard and regular army in the first clashes, but

he went on to state that the Mobile Guard "behaved admirably and accomplished miracles" (Schmidt 1948: 60). Lamoricière, one of the three generals appointed by Cavaignac to head the repression, felt that the Mobile Guard had to be "cleverly compromised" in the early fighting in order to secure its allegiance (Schmidt 1926: 56; Stern 1862: II, 389; Duveau 1967: 138). Lamoricière's own statements, however, suggest that this represented the blanket suspicion of the professional military officer toward militias of every variety. For his part, Engels made the converse claim, namely that by 25 June the National Guard was relatively inactive and the bulk of the fighting was being done by the army of the line and the Mobile Guard (Marx and Engels 1976: VII, 142). In the same passage, Engels credits the Mobile Guard with the "worst" (i.e., most energetic and savage) conduct. A typical report is that of the secretary to the Prefect of Police who recounted the capture by the Mobile Guard of a barricade that had previously resisted the concerted efforts of the army and the National Guard (Archives historiques F1 9, Nos. 1 and 27, 26 June).

25. Caspard (1974: 103), using figures from Archives historiques (F1 15). He has also pointed out that army casualties were about the same even though a substantially greater number of soldiers of the line were deployed. Chalmin, drawing upon *le Moniteur universel* of 22 July, counted 114 Mobile Guard dead, 476 wounded, and 161 missing. He compared the rate of attrition with the bloodier battles of contemporary international wars (1948: 68-69). Balleydier (1848: 113-28), also using early and therefore incomplete information, lists 592 wounded in addition to 100 dead. Obviously, one key to reconciling these various estimates is to establish how many individuals who were initially categorized as wounded subsequently died of their injuries.

26. Compare the judgement of Girard (1964: 321): "The infatuation of the public first fell upon the members of the Mobile Guard in proportion to the degree to which their conduct was an agreeable surprise."

27. Stern (1862: II, 164). On bourgeois fears, see also Garnier-Pagès (n.d.: II, 219). Exceptions to this consensual view were rare. Chalmin (1948: 50) cited the case of the publicist Delaplace who, virtually at the moment of the corps' formation, qualified it as "a dangerous militia, apt to become the blind instrument of a regime which seeks to oppress liberty." It was not entirely clear, at that

early date, whether Delaplace was more concerned that the result would be too reactionary or too revolutionary for his taste. Amann (1962: 415-16) took note of the perceptive delegate of the Club of Clubs who correctly predicted as early as April that the Mobile Guard would remain loyal to the moderate Provisional Government.

28. Stern (1862: II, 269). Compare the testimony of Achard (1872: 117), a member of the National Guard assigned to the Place de la Concorde on 15 May:

> We were anything but reassured concerning the attitude of the Mobile Guard, whose members had been recruited from the mob. Issued from the barricades, would they not return to them?

Compare also Merimée (quoted in Schmidt 1948: 60) and the aristocratic Rémusat (1962: 299) who, in reviewing the probable allegiances of the various social control forces then in Paris, frankly conceded that "We did not know what to think of the Mobile Guard."

29. Tocqueville (1971: 162). The hesitant attitude of the representatives present is further evidenced by the fact that many came armed to this "Festival of Harmony" (1971: 158-59).

30. Archives nationales (C 930, No. 685, report of 9 June 1848: 2). See also France, Assemblé nationale (1848: II, 202), which reprinted this report but incorrectly substituted *vous* for *nous*.

31. Falloux (1925: 313). For further illustrations of the currency of this opinion among contemporaries associated with the party of order, see Barrot (1875: 264) and Tocqueville (1971: 178).

32. Stern (1862: II, 381). See also the police report (Archives nationales C 930, No. 686; France, Assemblé nationale 1848: II, 203) according to which delegates from the Mobile Guard battalion commanders had already met on 10 June to decide whether they would refuse to take up arms to disperse crowds in the city.

33. Marx and Engels (1976: VII, 142). It is worth noting that this change of attitude toward the Mobile Guard corresponded with the very first instance in which the label "lumpenproletariat" was applied to it. It seems significant that the argument that the Mobile Guard was composed primarily of lumpenproletarians should surface only *after* its anti-insurgent attitude had been definitely established. This suggests that the lumpenproletariat thesis, to which

Marx and Engels had referred on only four occasions prior to June
1848, relies not simply on a loose and empirically ungrounded
assessment of the objective class position of participants but on a
post hoc interpretation of the historical consequences of their actions (Traugott 1980b; Bovenkerk 1980).

Lefrançais, the career revolutionary, member of the National
Workshops, and June insurgent, offered an alternative view in his
memoirs. According to this version, the scruples that, he alleged,
the Mobile Guard manifested in the early fighting were removed
only because the insurrection was portrayed as a Bonapartist plot
(Lefrançais 1902: 55). Although Bonapartist sentiment was widespread among the lower classes by June, notably in the National
Workshops, Lefrançais's argument appears suspect. The intensity
of Bonapartist influence within the Mobile Guard was frequently
remarked upon by contemporary observers, and it therefore seems
unlikely that such a claim would have proved an effective lever.

34. This reputation appears to have sparked the assassination of
General Bréa. Taken prisoner after passing behind the barricades
to parley with the insurgents, he was shot when his captors pan-
icked at cries of "Here comes the Mobile" (*l'Illustration* 1848:
204).

35. Caussidière (1849: II, 223). Renard, another leftist commen-
tator, concurred (1907: 10).

36. Ménard (1904: 149). Ménard went on to claim first that many
Mobile Guardsmen went over to the insurrection in June and
second that the reactionary behavior of the militia at large was
perhaps due to the inclusion of lumpen elements in its ranks. (Both
of these assertions will be examined subsequently.) Yet he also
noted, in a passage reminiscent of Marx, that "when the People
saw these young guards, among whom it recognized many children
of the barricades, passing in the street, it greeted them with cordial
acclamations. Woe to the People!" (1904: 42).

37. Rébillot (1912: 47). Balleydier (1848: 15) renders much the same
judgment:

> The organization of this young guard had for a moment alarmed
> the peaceful citizens, friends of order, who believed they were
> witnessing the military formation of twenty-four battalions
> recruited from the barricades out of essentially revolutionary
> and subversive elements.

210

Further statements by contemporaries linking members of the Mobile Guard with the February insurgents can be found in Achard (1872: 117, 194), Rittiez (1867: II, 9), and Stern (1862: I, 443). A host of later analysts uphold this view, among them Girard (1964: 291), Gossez (1956b: 446-47), House (1975: 157), Luna (1969: 97, 134), Renard (1907: 10), and Schmidt (1926: 23). There appears to be no way of identifying specific individuals as having participated in the February Days due to the lack of documentation. The lack of suitable evidence is explained by the fact that a *successful* insurrection typically produces poorer records than a failure such as the one in June. It is true that there exist incomplete lists of disability pensions or other compensation awarded to those wounded or to the survivors of those killed in the February Days (cf. Archives nationales F1d III, 84-98 and Archives de la Préfecture de Police, Série Aa). As these casualties of the February fighting were inherently unlikely to become members of the Mobile Guard, however, these sources are of little use in establishing the degree of continuity between the two groups.

38. There were, notably, avowed Bonapartists both in the ranks and in positions of high authority. The ultrademocratic strain was exemplified by the Club de la Garde nationale mobile. At the same time, police reports show that Orleanist and even legitimist influence was suspected from an early date. There were, however, numerous indications that the great majority of members identified with the moderate republic or at least with the higher echelons of the Mobile Guard administration, which was strongly progovernment. Caspard (1974: 100), for example, cited the profession of faith addressed to Commanding General Damesne and signed by the virtual entirety (465 men) of the 17th battalion on 11 June. It underscored their commitment to

Respect their officers and obey them in all circumstances;

assure by all available means the maintenance of order so necessary to the nation and the inviolability of the laws;

show devotion without limits to the National Assembly, faithful representation of the will of the nation;

maintain the progressive republic which assures to everyone the freedom that any democratic government owes its citizens.

39. Marx and Engels (1976: VII, 143). For another contemporary version of this thesis, see Audiganne (1854: 195). A number of later analysts have echoed this line of argument, among them Schmidt (1926: 21), Chalmin (1948: 57), Gossez (1956b: 446), and Luna (1969: 134).

40. Control by age seems crucial more in the determination of geographical than of class origin because of important fluctuations in the rate of in-migration from the provinces over the previous two decades. Though Chevalier (1950: 45-46) has stated that "the proportion of people born in Paris and of people born in the departments was fairly constant," this generalization holds only for the second half of the nineteenth century. Chevalier himself cited data that show the proportion of Parisian natives falling from 50 percent in 1833 to 36 percent in 1866. But in the intervening period and particularly during the July Monarchy, the net rate of in-migration was very uneven.

41. Chambre de Commerce (1851). This inquiry, for which the data were collected in the late spring and early summer of 1848, is an outstanding example of the precocity of nineteenth-century statistical social science in France. Carried out at the request and with the partial financial support of the new republican government, which was anxious to assess the extent of economic collapse, it provided detailed descriptive statistics on the sociological as well as economic characteristics of workers. This information is broken down by ward of the city, sector of the economy, and occupational group. It constitutes a precious resource for anyone working in the period. The greatest weakness of the study is that it covers only the "industrial" population—that is, those employed in the actual manufacture of commodities—and thus leaves out those in commerce, transportation, and service occupations.

Audiganne (1854: 171, 177, 180) criticized the Chamber of Commerce study on methodological grounds. He argued that because its data were based on returns from shop owners, it exaggerated the decline in the value of trade in 1848, the number of workers employed in 1847, and the level of Parisian wages (see also Molok 1952: 62). Tilly (1972: 228-29), on the other hand, has suggested that it understated the size of the labor force in sectors that involved large numbers of single, self-employed workers and those where many were unemployed. Despite these and other possible sources of error, the overall assessment of Markovitch (1965a: 256) seems accurate. He called it a "masterful inquiry . . . of capital importance."

Caspard (1974: 83) acknowledged the desirability of comparisons with the Parisian population at large but was stymied by the fact that the categories supplied in the Chamber of Commerce survey did not fit with his classification of the Mobile Guard data. I found that 1,812 of 3,845 individual Mobile Guardsmen could be classified as to the sector of the economy in which they worked, the greater part of the missing cases being due to the restricted definition of the industrial population employed by the Chamber of Commerce. Most of those coded by sector could also be situated within a specialized occupational group as well. The system that Caspard developed presumably aimed at increasing the proportion of Mobile Guardsmen who could be coded, though he does not report the relevant figures. He also made use of sectoral distinctions but achieved increased inclusiveness in part by removing unskilled laborers into a separate category independent of sectoral affiliation. This, and the fact that certain of the sectoral categories employed by the Chamber of Commerce were either lumped together or subdivided in Caspard's system, makes it impossible to effect direct comparisons of his data with those of either the Chamber of Commerce or of Tilly and Lees. These methodological differences, incidentally, appear to be the primary explanation of the discrepancies noted by Tilly and Lees (1975: 207) concerning the occupational distribution of June insurgents reported in the two studies.

42. Tilly and Lees (1975) and the book by Price (1972), which must have appeared between the drafting and publication of Caspard's work.

43. This classification system can be reliably applied thanks to a carefully detailed description of its categories (Lees and Tilly n.d.) made available to me by the authors.

44. Archives historiques (Série Xm, uncatalogued). There are, in addition, three volumes of registers of officers in this same series. Also held in the Archives historiques de la Guerre are the miscellaneous correspondence and internal documents of the Mobile Guard (Série F1, cartons 1 to 15). Carton F1 15 is of special interest as it contains reports prepared by battalion commanders on the participation of their units in the events of 15 May and the June Days. The personal papers of General Duvivier, who commanded

the Mobile Guard during the first two months of its existence, are likewise held in the Archives historiques in Série Xm 39. The French National Archives contain important primary sources that are, however, widely scattered. Among the most useful of the cartons I have consulted are: C 920A, C 920B, C 921, C 925, C 930, C 932A, C 932B, C 933, C 934, C 941, C 942; and series F9, cartons 1072, 1119, 1120, 1121, and 1150.

45. This information was explicitly requested on the sign-up form and is therefore available for virtually all members of the Mobile Guard. Additional information not specifically requested—for instance, the individual's most recent residence in Paris—is provided for a highly variable proportion of recruits according to the whim of the recording officer.

46. The approximate date on which this practice began can be interpolated from data provided in the registers themselves. A careful examination demonstrates that in any given battalion no soldier who left the corps by a specifiable date in August or September ever has his occupation recorded. In contrast, in battalions where records were conscientiously maintained, the occupation of most of those who left the corps after that date is listed (regardless of the date on which they enrolled). On the uneven quality of occupational data among battalions, see Archives historiques (Xm 35, 17th battalion, letter of 25 August).

47. Some battalions finessed the issue by simply recording an age in years rather than a precise date of birth. As Caspard has pointed out, despite this occasional bending of the regulations, the insistence of the popular press after the June Days on the number of heroes of the repression who held the "fateful age of fifteen years" was very much exaggerated.

48. Potts does not appear to have been an isolated case. It might be thought that the presence of foreigners in the Mobile Guard is remarkable and even lends indirect support to the lumpenproletariat thesis. Since information on nationality was not collected in the enlistment records, no precise account of foreign nationals can be obtained. If we base an estimate on the conservative criterion of place of birth of Mobile Guard volunteers, however, that proportion appears to have been no greater than the 6 percent of all Parisians who were of foreign nationality in 1848 according to Canfora-Argandoña (1976: 177) or the 6.1 percent of the insurgents whom Lees and Tilly classified as foreign-born (n.d.: 7-9).

49. Bibliothèque nationale (n.d.). The information from the poster corresponds with that found in *l'Illustration* (1848: 210), but the battalion register is correct, if we are to trust the recruit's own signature.

50. Price (1972: 165) reported that 163 Mobile Guardsmen were among the June arrestees. My own research revealed a total of 154 Mobile Guardsmen suspected of having gone over to the rebels (Archives historiques Série J). The vast majority of these were released without being charged and, given the severity with which armed men suspected of siding with the insurrection were treated, it seems likely that many were vouched for by members of their Mobile Guard units from which they had become separated in the confusion of the fighting.

51. The reader will better appreciate the methodological difficulty when it is pointed out that in this sample of 3,845 Mobile Guardsmen, only nineteen individuals could be identified with the "Leather" sector. In addition to the purely statistical unlikelihood that such small numbers of workers would be as evenly distributed among the wards of Paris as the much larger numbers engaged in the highly populous sectors, there were often systematic factors at work as well. Tanning operations, for example, were generally located downwind from residential centers—from bourgeois quarters at any rate—and thus tended to be concentrated in the eastern part of the city.

52. The one disturbing exception occurs in the category of "Fancy goods" workers, those employed in the luxury trades of which Paris was the recognized center. They are seriously underrepresented in our Mobile Guard sample in comparison with their prevalence in the capital as a whole. The fact that columns 1 and 2 of Table 2.2 coincide almost exactly indicates that in this specific case the six-battalion sample appears to have missed a significant local concentration. In effect, the Chamber of Commerce survey reported that a disproportionate share of "Fancy goods" workers were located in the 5th and 6th wards, areas not covered in our sample.

Data on literacy, construed as a very imprecise indicator of socioeconomic status, confirm the overall identity of these populations. The rate of illiteracy among sampled Mobile Guardsmen whose occupations could be classified within the Chamber of Commerce system was 12.8 percent. The Chamber of Commerce (1851:

68-69) found that in all Paris, of 169,000 male members of the "industrial" work force for whom this information was available, the rate of illiteracy was 13.1 percent. This convergence exists despite variations in illiteracy among sectors of the economy that ranged from 3 percent to 40 percent.

53. I have calculated these percentages from their Table 3 (Tilly and Lees 1975: 190) because the data given there refer to Paris proper rather than to the larger group of all arrestees (including many residents of the suburbs) to which their Table 2 (1975:189) refers. I have used the Tilly and Lees data in preference to those of Price for a number of reasons, the most important of which is the availability of detailed documentation on their coding system, including subcategorical distributions (Lees and Tilly n.d.). Some differences between the two data sets are noted in Tilly and Lees (1975: 206). The use of Price's less convenient system, though it would have precluded the discussion of the correlates of participation undertaken below, would not have materially affected the conclusions presented here. A slight reclassification of Price's data (1972: 165) yields the following results (see Table 2.A), consistent with my general argument. Note that the degree of fit between the classifications of Price and of Tilly and Lees, based on the same set of records, is not a great deal closer than that between my Mobile Guard sample and either of these studies.

54. The use of the thirteen-sector scheme reduces the number of Mobile Guardsmen who could be coded to 1,812. Reliance on this more restricted base is unavoidable, as only the Chamber of Commerce survey provides data, indispensable for the calculation of rates, on the total number of workers per sector. Note that the rates for insurgents reported here are not the same as those reported in Tilly and Lees (1975: 190), though they are derived from Tilly and Lees's raw data. The reason is that I take exception to their practice of basing rates on the total number of Parisian workers of *both* sexes employed in a given sector. They presumably included women because 2.4 percent of all arrestees were female. This procedure, however, appears questionable inasmuch as women, while representing only a tiny fraction of arrested insurgents, constituted a substantial minority of all "industrial" workers (35.5 percent).

The use of the total labor force, men and women, as a base for calculating rates of participation thus tends to underrepresent the

Table 2.A

Occupational Distribution: Arrested Insurgents

Sector	Percentage
Food	3.9
Construction	15.3
Furniture	8.9
Clothing and shoes	10.9
Thread and textiles	3.1
Leather	1.4
Carriage-making	2.0
Chemicals, ceramics	1.0
Base metals	11.7
Precious metals	2.1
Cooperage, basketry	0.6
Fancy goods	—*
Printing	3.8
Transport	4.6
Services and others	20.0**
Liberal professions	3.3
Commerce	4.0
Military	3.4
TOTAL	100.0
(N)	(11,251)

Source: Raw data from Price (1972).
Note: Reprinted, by permission of the publisher, from Traugott (1980a: 719).
* Not ascertained.
** Probably somewhat inflated relative to Tilly and Lees because it contains more residual categories.

rates for men alone by averaging them with the systematically lower rates for women. This would be unproblematic for purposes of comparison if the effect were evenly distributed across sectors of the economy. Two-thirds of all employed Parisian women, however, were concentrated in just two sectors ("Thread and textiles" and "Clothing and shoes") where, moreover, they constituted an absolute majority of workers (66.5 percent and 64.2 percent respectively). As a consequence, rates that fail to differentiate between the sexes seriously distort the relative levels of participation among different sectors.

For example, if, in dealing with those employed in the manufacture of clothing, one takes into account the sex-composition of
the labor force and the fact that virtually all arrestees (97.7 percent)
are male, then one would expect 858 total arrests in that sector:

(arrestees) / (male adult workers) × (male adults in "Clothing")
= (5,808) / (204,825) × (30,274)
= 858

But if one's calculations fail to distinguish the sexes, implicitly
anticipating that men and women would be arrested at equivalent
rates, then one would expect 1,549 of the arrestees to originate
in that sector:

(arrestees) / (adult workers) × (adults in "Clothing")
= (5,808) / (317,716) × (84,672)
= 1,549

The fact that 863 clothing workers were actually arrested in
June 1848 means that the clothing sector participated proportionately if sex ratios are taken into account but at only half its
anticipated rate if sex ratios are ignored. The corresponding figures
for the sector devoted to "Thread and textiles" are 313 anticipated
arrests based on males alone, 601 based on both sexes, and 274
actually recorded.

These discrepancies are of considerable substantive importance
in debates about the determinants of participation, since the sectors
in which women were concentrated were precisely those in which
skill levels and wages were lowest and in which the labor force
had been most subject to the effects of proletarianization. If one
adopts a base that includes both sexes, it appears that these more
proletarianized sectors were underrepresented among insurgents
when in fact, as our figures based on males alone clearly show,
they were represented neither above nor below the level of other
sectors, given that arrests were largely confined to the male population. In the light of recent controversy over the interpretation
of the thesis of "artisanal activism" (Stedman Jones 1983; Calhoun
1983b) these initially technical questions assume great substantive
significance.

It might be objected that in using a base of male workers only,
I have myself introduced a converse distorting influence by failing
to extract female arrestees from the totals for each sector. But

although I would ideally want to base rates on males only in both numerator and denominator, the form of the available data makes this impossible. Since, however, female arrestees represent only 2.4 percent of the total, the resulting distortion is very much less serious than the one that results from the converse practice.

Two further methodological points should be briefly noted. First, whereas Tilly and Lees (1975: 190) also report rates for "non-industrial" sectors based on the 1856 census, I have chosen not to rely on this source because it employs as its unit of analysis the head of household rather than the individual and because of the sometimes dramatic changes that occurred in the composition of the Parisian labor force between 1848 and 1856. Some commentators have suggested that these changes were in part the result of government policies aimed at the removal from the capital of precisely those groups that had been most active in the June insurrection. Part of the discrepancy was due to naturally occurring shifts—for example, the decline in the number of carpenters residing in Paris and its immediate suburbs from 7,500 in 1845 to 3,000 in 1856 as a result of the conversion from wood to iron in the building trades. Regardless of cause, many of these changes were of such a magnitude as to render comparisons meaningless, as Table 2.B is intended to show.

It should also be noted that the number of arrestees included in Tilly and Lees's data differs from the number used by other analysts in part because the former retained only those residing in Paris proper. Although this was a constraint imposed upon them by the form of the Chamber of Commerce data that they also used, it has proved invaluable for the purpose of effecting comparisons with the Mobile Guard.

55. High levels of proletarianization in this sector are indicated by a number of variables. For example, the Chamber of Commerce (1851: 68-69) reports that only 67 percent of all "Thread and textiles" workers were literate (73 percent of men, 64 percent of women), the lowest rate of any sector and well below the 84 percent average (87 percent for men, 83 percent for women) for Paris as a whole. The same source (1851, Table 3) reported that shops of more than ten workers were appreciably more common in textile production (18.4 percent) than in the Parisian economy as a whole (11.0 percent). It is not possible to calculate the overall level of salaries in "Thread and textiles," but the Chamber of

Table 2.B
Occupational Distribution of the Adult Male
Parisian Population, 1848 and 1856
(Percentage)

Sector	1848 Chamber of Commerce Inquiry	1856 Census
Food	3.9	12.3
Construction	19.6	12.1
Furniture	14.0	7.4
Clothing and shoes	14.8	31.6
Thread and textiles	5.4	9.0
Leather	2.1	1.1
Carriage-making	5.2	1.8
Chemicals, ceramics	3.2	1.7
Base metals	10.8	5.3
Precious metals	5.3	3.5
Cooperage, basketry	2.0	2.2
Fancy goods	8.6	6.4
Printing	5.3	5.5
TOTAL	100.2	99.9

Note: Reprinted, by permission of the publisher, from Traugott (1980a: 716).

Commerce (1851: 49-50) data show that they were ranked twelfth
of thirteen sectors for men and tenth of thirteen for women.
56. The size of these occupational groups ranged from "lacemaking," which employed a single male worker (who happened to fall
into the Mobile Guard sample!), to shoemaking in which there
were 13,782 male practitioners. The Mobile Guardsmen in the
six-battalion sample could be assigned to just 134 of these occupational groups, but the number used in the calculations reported
here was further pared for methodological reasons. To reduce the
"noise" that results from the inclusion of occupational groups
represented in the Mobile Guard sample, but which employed
extremely small numbers of Parisian males, I required that an
occupational group involve at least 100 men. This reduced to 117

the number of occupational groups on which the correlations were based. Had I not taken this precaution, I would have been confronted with such nonsensical results as a projected rate of 10,000 participants for every 10,000 workers in lacemaking.

57. For reasons previously discussed, I based rates of participation on the numbers of male workers only. As a rule, this presented no problem since the Chamber of Commerce data on salaries, literacy, residence *en garni*, and so on are listed separately for each sex. In the case of two variables—average number of workers per *patron* and rate of unemployment—, however, the Chamber of Commerce data make it impossible to distinguish between males and females. If I have made use of these variables regardless, it is for lack of a suitable alternative and because I have found that the percentage of males in an occupational group is not significantly correlated with either of them: $r = -.066$ ($p = .24$) in the case of average shop size; and $r = .127$ ($p = .09$) in the case of unemployment rates.

58. Two further methodological considerations justify this confidence in the results reported here. The first is that whereas Tilly and Lees's (1975) conclusions are based on a comparison of sectors, I have used occupational groups. This smaller and more homogeneous unit of analysis helps limit the potential for ecological fallacy inherent in the comparison of large and internally diverse economic sectors. The second is that by basing comparisons on 117 occupational groups rather than thirteen sectors, I was able to use correlations in the place of Tilly and Lees's crosstabulations, thus taking full advantage of the interval-level data of the Chamber of Commerce study.

59. The expression *en garni* refers to the nineteenth-century practice, widespread among transients and the poor, of renting furnished rooms, often by the day or week. Lodgers typically shared cramped accommodations in large, densely packed complexes that became congregation points for the floating population of the capital. The Chamber of Commerce study referred to the inhabitants of *garnis* as "the most miserable and degraded portion of the Parisian population" and, in a turn of phrase that almost perfectly mirrored the sentiments of Marx and Engels concerning the lumpenproletariat, as "people who only rarely conserve the right to be counted among [true] workers" (Chambre de Commerce 1851: 950, 70). In an appendix devoted to residents *en garni*, the Chamber of

Commerce offered a classification according to level of mores in four categories ranging from "good" to "very bad." The key to the classification system explained that the third category included "individuals who frequently abandoned themselves to laziness, drunkenness, and debauchery" as well as "openly prostituted women." The fourth category was reserved for the "most degraded, abject, and dangerous part of the population . . . those whose life is merely a succession of misdeeds and excesses of every kind" (1851: 979).

60. This is another finding that appears to set my characterization of the Mobile Guard somewhat at odds with Tilly and Lees's portrayal of the June insurgents. They reported, for example, that small shop sizes were associated with low rates of participation in the June Days (Tilly and Lees 1975: 193). Although the rest of their findings concerning the determinants of rates of participation are phrased in terms of the interaction of several variables (shop size, ratio of male to female workers, and proportion of domestic production by sector), making direct comparisons extremely complex, there are several simpler explanations for the apparent discrepancies other than the existence of substantive differences between the two groups. The first is that I have used, for reasons previously discussed, rates of participation based on the number of male workers rather than on the number of workers of both sexes, as was the case for Tilly and Lees. This dramatically affects all relations between participation and sex-related occupational characteristics. Thus, Tilly and Lees report that

> Crafts with large amounts of domestic production and/or many females in the trade were not as politically active as crafts based upon medium sized or large workshops where the labour force was predominantly male.

In my view, this finding must be understood as a misleading artifact of Tilly and Lees's methodological procedures.

Yet, even if the question of the appropriate base were set aside, certain difficulties would remain. Tilly and Lees (1975: Table 3, 190) report two rates of June participation for each sector of the economy, the first based on the 1848 Chamber of Commerce survey, the second on the 1856 census. In most cases, the two rates are in close agreement. In others, however, they are clearly discrepant. To take the most extreme example, the "Food" sector produced the third highest rate of arrests by industry according to the Chamber of Commerce data but only the second lowest according to the 1856 census. Yet Tilly and Lees appear to treat "Food" as a sector that yielded a low rate of June participation. My previously expressed reservations concerning the use of the 1856 census data incline me in the opposite direction.

A third reason, also mentioned above, is that I have used a correlation based on 116 occupational groups rather than a high/low categorization of thirteen sectors, and this finer unit of analysis may also account for part of the difference. If, however, I were to impose my choice of data base on Tilly and Lees's basic methodology by generating a simple cross-tabulation of shop size and rate of June arrests (based on the number of male workers only, as established in the 1848 Chamber of Commerce survey), the results would be those presented in Table 2.C. In this form, the

Table 2.C
Participation by Sector in the June Insurrection
and Shop Size

Shop Size[a]	Rate of June Arrests[b]	
	Low	High
High	Carriage-making Chemicals Precious metals	Construction Leather Base metals
Low	Furniture Cooperage Fancy goods	Food Clothing

Sources: Chambre de Commerce (1851: Table 3); Tilly and Lees (1975).
Note: Two sectors, "Printing" and "Threads and textiles," were not included because they had median values on the variables "Shop Size" and "Rate of June Arrests" respectively and could not be categorized either high or low.
[a] Shop size was based on the number of workers of all kinds per *patron* according to the 1848 Chamber of Commerce data.
[b] The rate of June arrests (Paris only) per 10,000 male workers is based on my calculation from raw data provided in Tilly and Lees (1975: Table 3, 190).

pattern of the data would not appear to justify a firm conclusion concerning the relation between these two variables.

61. Price (1972: 165-66). In my view, the very presence of this small percentage of certifiable lumpenproletarians within the Mobile Guard is reassuring, since it shows that occupations of this sort would actually find their way into the records rather than being censored by a recording officer or by the individuals in question.

62. Ménard (1904: 42) asserted that the lower age of Mobile Guardsmen was politically significant because it made them "easy to direct according to the views of the authorities." This psychologically reductionist approach cannot in itself, however, provide a satisfactory explanation of their June behavior. If, on the one hand, one believes that the effect of youth is specific (i.e., it leads only to reactionary and not to insurgent loyalties), then one should be able to outline the causal chain that produces this asymmetric result, something that Ménard does not attempt. If, on the other hand, one believes that youth simply makes the individual more pliable (i.e., it can lead to either a reactionary *or* a radical stance depending on the surrounding circumstances), then the problem of explaining political orientation is merely pushed back one step, for one must still uncover the determinants of the observed outcome.

63. For the sake of the comparison to be made in subsequent chapters, recall that pay in the National Workshops, though initially set at the same level, ultimately worked out to just 1 franc 15 centimes per day without the advantage of the supplemental subsistence benefits. In addition, most of the members of the workshops, unlike Mobile Guardsmen, had families to support on this meager sum.

64. Tocqueville, for example, referred to them as "young men, or rather children" (1971: 162), and Stern (1862) repeatedly employed the term *gamins*.

65. See Lees and Tilly (n.d.: 11-12). The respective figures for the median ages of Mobile Guardsmen and insurgents were twenty and thirty-two years; for the mode, eighteen and twenty-eight years.

66. Despite claims to the contrary, the minimum age limit was rarely infringed. Chalmin (1948: 42-43) exaggerated the extent to which the sixteen-year requirement was violated, and Lamartine (cited in Caspard 1974: 89) is certainly wrong when he speaks of Mobile

Guardsmen as "children or adolescents of twelve to twenty years."
Contrary to the impression conveyed by the popular press (cf.
l'Illustration 1848: 212), only a handful of fifteen-year-olds managed to gain entry to the corps. In questionable cases, recording
officers verified the age of volunteers by requesting birth certificates
from authorities in the individual's home town. Where these documents are appended to battalion registers, they rarely indicate
that the volunteer in question had been underaged at the time of
enlistment. Indeed, I was able to locate only seven fifteen-year-
olds among 3,615 recruits for whom age was indicated, or 0.2
percent of the total sample. Mobile Guard records (Archives historiques F1 3, letter from Duvivier of 12 March; Xm 32, letter
from the mayor of the 9th ward of 1 March) make it clear that it
was the failure to respect the upper age limit that was the more
frequent problem. At the same time that measures were adopted
to end these abuses, a compromise provision extended eligibility
to men up to forty years of age if they were military veterans
(Archives historiques Xm 32, *dossier* for 2 June). In brief, with
only minor exceptions at both ends of the spectrum, the range of
ages of those inducted into the Mobile Guard was circumscribed
by law.

67. These documents, contained in Archives historiques (F1 15, 5th
battalion), were produced in the course of inquiries conducted
preliminary to the payment of indemnities. Though based on a
very limited number of cases, this figure probably overestimates
the proportion of married men, since the pension-granting process
required a survivor to initiate a claim in the case of Mobile Guardsmen killed in action and this would obviously be less likely in the
case of individuals without spouse or dependents.

68. Figures for the insurgents are based on the 2,860 individuals for
whom this information was available in Lees and Tilly (n.d.: 12).
Of course, this distribution was *not* merely the result of self-selection among volunteers. The stipulation that recruits be unmarried appears initially to have been informal, since the Provisional
Government's decree of 26 February (Archives historiques F1 2)
constituting the Mobile Guard mentioned no such restriction. The
June decree of the Executive Commission (Archives historiques
Xm 32, *dossier* for June), however, specifically limited eligibility
to "bachelors, sixteen to thirty years of age." The testimony of
Lefrançais, then a young radical vacillating over the decision whether

or not to enlist in the Mobile Guard, is illuminating. After calling attention to the other main alternative open to unemployed Parisian workers—enrollment in the National Workshops—he goes on to say: *"As for the younger men,* they had the option of signing on in the battalions of the Mobile Guard" (1902: 29, emphasis added).

69. As noted previously, most of these men were immediately released when inquiries proved that they had taken part as loyal members of their Mobile Guard units. In some cases, they had actually been wounded in the defense of the moderate republic and were suspected only because, in the wake of the insurrection, any armed man separated from his unit was subject to detention. But the innocence of most members of this group does not invalidate the comparison, since it does not fundamentally distinguish them from the majority of June arrestees on whom descriptions of insurgents are based. Of more than 16,000 individuals initially taken into custody, nearly 5,000 were released immediately and less than 4,000 were ultimately convicted of wrongdoing (Tilly and Lees 1975: 190-91).

70. Archives historiques (Série AA). From these documents a list was prepared of all arrestees specifically noted to have been members of the Mobile Guard. Of 154 original names, sixteen could not be associated with a specific battalion or verified in the Mobile Guard enlistment records as members of the corps. To ensure strict comparability, the remaining 138 cases were scrutinized according to the same criteria used to construct the Mobile Guard sample on which the calculation of average age was initially based. I therefore eliminated such individuals as Douillet and Gouthier, who were released from the 23d battalion for medical reasons just before the June Days; Dietrich, Moulin, and Mellinger, all of whom were officers detached from the regular army rather than Mobile Guard volunteers; and those men attached to units inactive in June. Of the 129 names then remaining, no age was given in five cases. The average age reported for "disloyal" Mobile Guardsmen is thus based on a carefully pared list of 124 individuals.

71. There were, however, minor differences in those he used. The average ages he gives for both loyal Mobile Guardsmen and insurgents (21.5 and 34 years respectively) are slightly different from those derived from the data collected here and by Tilly and Lees (22.1 and 33.4 years respectively). Perhaps more important is the

fact that his figure for the average age of disloyal Mobile Guardsmen was 24 years as against the 22.8 years reported here. This difference is due in part to the methodological procedures mentioned in the previous footnote, which led to different rules for the inclusion/exclusion of cases, and in part to the fact that in order to ensure strict comparability I have calculated disloyal Mobile Guardsmen's ages from the time of enlistment (rather than the age recorded in their judicial dossiers some six months later). By the same token, the appropriate comparison figure for the average age of insurgents, corrected for this lapse of time, would be approximately 33 years. Caspard also reported that the average age of Mobile Guardsmen subsequently *convicted* of participation in the insurrection was 25.3 years (based on thirty-nine individuals). Unfortunately, no one appears to have reported comparable data on the average of *convicted* insurgents as a whole.

CHAPTER THREE

1. Caussidière (1849: I, 222). It should be noted that the radical Prefect of Police, who possessed a finely honed, intuitive political sense, was no admirer of the Mobile Guard and that his relations with Commanding General Duvivier were consistently antagonistic. See, for example, Archives historiques (Xm 32, letters of 14, 17, and 21 April).
2. Most notably, the army's humiliation in February had deeply troubled its internal discipline and produced an exceptional rate of desertion and insubordination, a point that Chalmin himself has made elsewhere (1955: 47, 50). The National Guard was also in a state of turmoil, in part the result of the democratizing reforms instituted by the Provisional Government, in part in response to these same, diffuse political and social forces. But because the infractions of these part-time soldiers were not subject to military discipline, they were not usually associated with their status as members of the National Guard and therefore tended to remain invisible from an organizational point of view.
3. Archives historiques (Xm 32, 13 April). In the same letter, however, he counseled patience rather than an inflexible attitude toward these "children's games," for fear of inciting a sharp reaction. He also defended the Mobile Guardsmen accused of disorderly conduct by the director of a Paris hospital, pointing out that sol-

diers from all corps, most of whom had been admitted after contracting venereal disease, shared the blame for the recent disciplinary problems in that institution.

4. The objection of the Prefect of Police, however, was less to the possible political intent of those speeches than to the immediate threat that such assemblies might become the pretext for disorders (Archives historiques Xm 32, 8 June). Note that the cry being raised in the first of these incidents was for the "democratic republic," not for the "democratic and social republic" (the slogan usually adopted by the more radical opponents of the conservative National Assembly). The document does not make clear, in the case of the second incident, to which side of the emerging conflict officers were being asked to swear allegiance.

5. The further evidence of Mobile Guard indiscipline that Chalmin offered—the uncontrolled enthusiasm with which it joined battle—admits of alternative interpretations. Depending on the observer's point of view, either it betokened the extent to which Mobile Guard loyalties had been cemented to the cause of the moderate republic or it betrays the facility with which its members' youthful passion could be swayed in one direction or another. Chalmin cited Stern concerning the excesses and atrocities, especially the execution of prisoners, allegedly committed by Mobile Guardsmen. But Stern's testimony was ambiguous on this score since at various points in her narrative she reported that Mobile Guardsmen did carry out impromptu court-martials and summary executions (1862: II, 403, 435-36); that no such atrocities ever occurred (1862: II, 447); and that the total number of prisoners executed by regular army *or* Mobile Guard units reached as high as 150 (1862: II, 479). On this subject, other authors are divided, largely according to political prejudices. For their equally categorical, if contradictory, assertions, see for example Ménard (1904: 152, 156, 162-67, 170-71, 180-81, 188-93, 208-209); Pagès-Duport (1848: 97, 102-103); and Castellane (1896: IV, 85–87).

6. Archives nationales (C 940, Nos. 7286, 7287, 7290, 7292-7294). I would like to thank Peter Amann for calling these documents to my attention as well as for the invaluable aid provided by his work on 1848 and the Parisian club movement (especially 1960, 1963, 1970, and 1975).

7. It is also important to distinguish, both theoretically and empirically, between the sentiments of cadres and those of the rank and

file. A police report of 13 June (Archives nationales C 930, No. 689) shows how different their respective attitudes could be. It described an encounter on the square before the Hôtel de Ville where three sympathetic Mobile Guardsmen were being questioned by a group of workers as to the likely action of their corps should serious fighting break out. Before the trio had a chance to reply, a Mobile Guard commander who had held himself inconspicuous on the fringes of the crowd intervened with this provocative retort: "You should know that we don't fire on scum." The reaction of his audience was spirited enough to oblige him to retire from the scene.

8. According to Archives historiques (Xm 32, 1 March, p. 3), students from St. Cyr, the French military academy, were also used in the early stages, offering, as will be apparent in later chapters, a remarkable parallel to the use of students of the Ecole centrale in the National Workshops. That the regulations were at first literally applied by the military establishment is indicated by a letter to General Duvivier (Archives historiques Xm 32, 29 February) rejecting two of his recommendations for commissions on the grounds that regular army officers were not eligible under the terms of the Provisional Government's decree.

9. The ambiguity of Duvivier's position at this early stage can be further documented. On 18 March, a captain-major detached to the Mobile Guard requested written confirmation, to be addressed to the mayor of the 6th ward, of what he took to be the general's assurance that detached officers could be elected to positions of authority on a provisional basis. Duvivier preferred to reply orally at the next day's assembly rather than commit to paper anything more than the marginal note: "Very imperfect translation of the verbal information which I gave" (Archives historiques Xm 35, 12th battalion, 18 March). A letter from David d'Angers, mayor of the 11th ward, indicated that although Duvivier instructed him on 24 March to proceed according to the formal terms of the decree of 26 February, it was with the qualification, "pending a resolution of this issue at higher levels" (Archives historiques Xm 32, 27 March). Duvivier's reluctance to overturn the regulations on his own authority may have derived from his democratic principles, but an added reason is suggested by the complaint of a quartermaster in the 24th battalion (Archives historiques Xm 36, n.d.), indignant at the brazen attempts of detached officers to

secure positions in the Mobile Guard, who seemed prepared to defend the interests of qualified volunteers by appealing to higher authorities.

10. Archives historiques (Xm 49, 25 March). These well-documented maneuvers flatly contradict Rittiez's (1867: II, 13) assertion that the authorities played no role in Mobile Guard elections. That statement was true only in the most limited sense that they were not present during the actual balloting.

The major bureaucratic obstacle to the election of regular army officers—the fear that the latter would be able to rise quickly in the Mobile Guard and later have to be reintegrated into their original units at a much higher rank—was overcome with the proviso that detached officers would rejoin their regular units at their former rank regardless of promotions received within the Mobile Guard.

11. Thus, the elevated rate of dismissals is also a measure of the care taken in reviewing the files. Mobile Guard records offer innumerable examples of the aggressive exercise of administrative discretion (cf. Archives historiques F1 4, 8 March, 25 March; Xm 32, 8 May, 20 June; Xm 46, No. 915; and many others). At the same time, the Mobile Guard general staff was successful in blocking the requests of regular army units that valued officers be returned (cf. Archives historiques Xm 32, 31 May, 31 June, and others). The documents show that most of those returned to their units of origin were either disciplinary cases or low-level non-commissioned officers (cf. Archives historiques Xm 35, 14th battalion).

12. This preference was so strong as to elicit this caustic comment by Chalmin (1948: 43-44, 49): "The ballots designated especially soldiers, former soldiers, or charlatans who managed to convince people that they had once worn uniforms."

13. By mid-April, le Moniteur (16 April: 4) was able to report that the outfitting of the Mobile Guard with percussion rifles was complete.

14. We shall see, for example, that young cadres in the National Workshops, recruited from among the students of the Ecole centrale, insisted on smart uniforms styled to match those of their traditional rivals of the Ecole polytechnique (Comberousse 1879: 114, 118-19). Nor were the radical defenders of the common man immune from the lure of ceremonial dress. Caussidière's monta-

gnard police earned the sobriquet "the swallows of the republic" because they wore a brilliant crimson scarf and sash in the style made popular in the Revolution of 1789 (Achard 1872: 74). Remember, too, that the demonstration of 16 March in protest of the democratization of the National Guard was dubbed the "march of the *bonnets à poil*" or "bear-skin hats," for these conspicuous elements of dress were the mark of pride of the elite bourgeois companies threatened with dilution. For an illustration of the analytical use to which styles of dress may be put as indicators of social origin and political orientation, see Tocqueville's account of the review of 21 May, 1848 (1971: 162).

15. Archives historiques (Xm 39, 5th *liasse*). A companion poster resumed this idea with emphasis on broken promises and the need to protest in strong terms, inviting Mobile Guardsmen to terminate outside duties "until such time as we can let others see that we are really soldiers."

16. Duvivier seemed well aware of the gravity of the situation and placed much of the blame on the noncooperation of his superiors. In the note that accompanied his resignation from command of the Mobile Guard, he took a parting shot at the unnamed bureaucrats who had made his job so difficult: "I am giving back to the fatherland twenty-four organized battalions of the finest, whom training and discipline have already made powerful and who would have made still further progress if they had been assisted more regularly" (*l'Illustration* 1848: 214).

17. Compare Rébillot (1912: 48): "Not only did these majestic tailors not want to do anything, but they presumed to forbid work to those who were not part of their association. They threatened to descend from their Olympus to give a thrashing to those who would steal from them the business of clothing the young Mobile Guardsmen." See also Rittiez (1867: II, 14-15); Renard (1907: 35); and the *Revue des deux mondes* (Anonymous 1848: 482).

18. For example, on 21 June Trouvé-Chauvel informed Duvivier of the participation of two sergeants-major of the 22d battalion at a meeting of the Club Blanqui (Archives historiques Xm 32). Duvivier directed their battalion commanders to place the men in question under constant surveillance.

19. Archives historiques (Xm 32, 17 June, report of under-secretary of the Interior Carteret). This incident was the nearest approximation I have uncovered to a collective revolt within the ranks of

the Mobile Guard, though it never went beyond insubordination and had been resolved by the evening of that same day, apparently without any ensuing disciplinary action.

20. A Mobile Guard memo (Archives historiques F1 5, 8 April) details the daily and weekly succession of duties. See also the more general schedule outlined by the mayor of the 9th ward (Archives historiques Xm 32, 1 March).

21. The official rationale for the policy of quartering all Mobile Guardsmen in barracks is provided in the government decree of 26 February (Archives historiques F1 2):

> The *Garde nationale mobile* must, as its name implies, be available for immediate mobilization at any time; this requires that its battalions be virtually always assembled. Consequently, the battalions will be established in the various buildings which will serve them as lodgings.

Provision was made for a limited number of exemptions from this regulation in the case of men whose family situation required residence in private dwellings; it was not, however, widely exercised except in the first days when beds and bedding were lacking.

22. Archives historiques (Xm 32, 15 June, "Etat des 25 bataillons de la Garde national mobile"); Caspard (1974: 98). This deployment should not be confused with the policy of detaching Mobile Guard units from Paris to *provincial* towns, which Duvivier initially resisted on the grounds that the decrees establishing the corps prohibited such action. See Seignobos's (1905: 586) account of this controversy, based on the minutes of the sessions of the Provisional Government.

23. I am particularly skeptical in the case of these two stories. The first is taken from an official history of the Mobile Guard by Balleydier, generally an apologist for its every action. Pardigon, on the other hand, was a revolutionary who fought with the insurgents in the June Days and who tended to paint the forces of repression in the darkest colors. That the situation was not unique to the Mobile Guard and did not always lead to such defensive reactions is indicated by an anecdote from Bonde (1903: 218). She told of a National Guardsman who first tried to get killed and, failing in that effort, resigned because he had discovered his father and brothers behind the first barricade he stormed.

24. Cherest (1873: 262); Archives historiques (Xm 32, 22 June, order of the Executive Commission to General Damesne, then Commander-in-Chief of the Mobile Guard; and a separate communication of the same date and in the same file, from the chief of the secretariat of the Executive Commission to General Damesne); Pardigon (1852: 70).

25. France, Assemblé nationale (1848: II, 212); Stern (1862: II, 394). The policy of confinement to barracks seems to have dated back at least as far as 15 May (Bonde 1903: 137). Of course, these attempts to tighten control over the Mobile Guard were never entirely effective. For example, a police report on the eve of the June Days stated that Sergeant Martin of the 7th company of the 11th battalion had been observed in frequent relations with men identified as montagnards and alleged that Martin had supplied the latter with cartridges. Duvivier, however, refused to initiate disciplinary action on the basis of this report alone and instead arranged for surveillance of the officer in question. The general's restraint seems to have been justified if one is to rely on battalion records, for they reveal that Martin loyally accomplished his duty as part of the June repression.

26. Archives historiques (Xm 34, 8th battalion). Officers of these same formations took this opportunity to dine out together.

27. Archives historiques (F1 7, 18 May). Duvivier had actually resigned his post as commander-in-chief some two weeks earlier, but the general staff continued to receive reports from this unnamed source for a time.

28. The following report is of note in this regard:

> On the Place du Carrousel at midnight, many commissioned and noncommissioned officers as well as soldiers of the National Guard come to fraternize with the Mobile Guard. These National Guardsmen belong to the first legion. Officers and soldiers of the National Guard, the Mobile Guard and the regular army were seen linking arms, all swearing that they would unite to repress the slightest disorder. (France, Assemblé nationale 1848: II, 223)

The first legion was among the first of those few National Guard units that openly declared their allegiance to the government in the June Days. The same report mentioned another banquet offered by the National Guard for the Mobile Guard and regular army

units. Mixed groups leaving this function at 10:30 P.M. were heard
to shout in unison, "Long Live Union; Long Live the Republic!"

Chapter Four

1. Blanc (1939). Blanc objected vehemently to the misattribution,
after June, of this institution to him. He claimed, with justice, that
the National Workshops "were founded and organized not by me
but against me, or, more properly, against the social science of
which circumstances had made me the official exponent" (1858:
156). Social workshops, as Blanc had described them, were to have
a decentralized structure; they were to be cooperatively organized
among workers in a single trade with the role of the state limited
to providing initial loans of capital. Members would thus assume
collective control over the productive process. Although Blanc's
formulation remained abstract, it can clearly be distinguished from
the National Workshops as actually instituted. The latter were
purely a stopgap measure, not intended to have a lasting impact
on the organization of production. They indiscriminately assembled workers from all trades, employing them at subsistence wages
and under the supervision of outsiders on make-work projects that
bore no connection to members' occupational skills.

Though participation was limited by statute to residents of Paris
(see Cherest 1873: 192), the workshops were "national" in the
sense that the central government provided both the funds and the
administrative authority for their operation. Thus, contrary to
Blanc's proposals, the state retained the primary role in the National Workshops, and political rather than social considerations
remained paramount in the minds of their creators, who had taken
to heart the lesson of the previous century that revolution in France
begins in the streets of Paris.

2. *Chantiers* or *ateliers de charité* were a device used to counter
economic crisis as early as the sixteenth century (Renard 1907:
10). Perhaps the best known were those that functioned on Mont-
martre prior to and through the early phase of the French Revolution of 1789. The most recent example, the *ateliers de secours*
of 1830, offered many parallels to the National Workshops. They
were established to head off popular unrest. Their creation in Paris
attracted many unemployed provincials, and they quickly placed
a burden on the treasury. Attempts to control conditions of en-

rollment, limit the number of participants, and ultimately phase them out produced a lively reaction among workers, but their disestablishment was accomplished early in 1831 without major incident (Pinkney 1965).

3. The initial link between the workshops and the Ecole centrale arose through the fact that the son of Higonnet, the director of the clearinghouse in the rue Bondy, was one of its students. Higonnet had called upon the services of his son's friends in an unofficial capacity.

Thomas's own connection with the Ecole centrale dated from 1839 when at the age of sixteen he had matriculated along with his younger brother Pierre. They left only the barest record of their passing in that institution's archives, as neither was to graduate. Emile lasted only a year and a half, due, by his own account, to the "fear inspired in him by the aridity of higher mathematics" (Thomas 1848: 9). His academic record was far from outstanding, as suggested in letters addressed by his father to the school's director (Archives de l'Ecole centrale des arts et manufactures, *dossier individuel*). An early one discussed arrangements for private tutoring. A later one adopted an enigmatic tone to announce that

> I am very sorry to tell you that I have decided to withdraw my son Emile from the Ecole centrale. I never had anything but praise for his attitude toward work before his admission to the Ecole, but I am forced to recognize that this attitude has not been maintained in his new studies. I know the reason for this, and if I refrain from making it the object of recriminations which would be painful both to me and to you, my motive is based in my respect for the Ecole and in the sincere desire which I have for his continuing welfare.

With the help of his uncle, the chemist Payen, Emile next entered the Conservatoire des arts et métiers, ultimately to start a chemical engineering firm. He nonetheless maintained contact with his former classmates at the Ecole throughout this period.

4. Cherest (1873: 204). Thomas frequently contradicted himself on dates. For example, his first meeting with Marie was variously set on 3 March (pages 35 and 29) and 4 March (page 33).

5. Thomas repeatedly denied that the centralization of the National Workshops originated with him. (See, however, Thomas 1848: 52 where centralization is one of the special virtues Thomas claimed

for his original plan.) The military organization he created none-theless followed strict hierarchical lines. It took as its basic unit the "squad" of ten men headed by a squad leader. A "brigade" consisted of five squads plus a brigadier, or fifty-six men in all. Four brigades were joined to form a "company" of 224 men under the orders of a company commander or captain. As enrollments outstripped the number of available cadres, a new administrative level, the "lieutenancy," was added between the brigade and com-pany, each consisting of 225 men headed by a lieutenant. As the membership continued to grow, the company was expanded from two to four lieutenancies or a total of 900 men. Three companies constituted a "service" (675, 1,350, and 2,700 men at various points in time), under a service commander. Services were grouped by ward—for the workshops remained tied to the internal geog-raphy of Paris—and the number of services under the fourteen ward commanders (one from each true ward and, later, two rep-resenting the suburbs) was therefore variable. In general, all ranks higher than lieutenant were reserved for students of the Ecole centrale.

6. Thomas (1848: 45). Thomas's account would appear to have been composed with an eye to self-justification and in the light of subsequent events. It receives, however, general confirmation from the recollections of Garnier-Pagès (n.d.: II, 26).

7. Thomas (1848: 146-47). Still according to Thomas, Marie took him aside one week later to insist "on the necessity of having the workers available on a given day. He asked me if they were armed and told me it was important to see that they be; that, if necessary, he would provide the means" (1848: 158). The arming of work-shops' members was accomplished de facto through their enroll-ment in the National Guard. This was encouraged by a policy under which members were paid by the workshops for days spent on duty in their Guard units. Girard (1964: 294, 309), the major chronicler of the National Guard, indicated that "most of the workers of the National Workshops were members of the Guard."

8. "No one believed that this figure would grow much, and the mayor of the eighth ward was accused of exaggeration for thinking that he alone could furnish 8,000 workers. Who would have thought, at that stage, that this figure, far from being in excess, amounted to only one-third of the true number! The eighth ward's share of

the National Workshops came to more than 22,000 men" (Thomas 1848: 54).

9. McKay (1933: 159-60) has compiled this concordance of bi-monthly membership totals from a variety of official and semi-official sources. On the question of numbers, see also Thomas (1848: 54, 76, 79, 85, 87, 89, 147, 164, 181, 187, 195, 207); Lalanne (1848); Barrot (1875: 234); Garnier-Pagès (n.d.: II, 26, 125, 275); and Archives nationales (C 920B, No. 256, no. 9).

10. "Some of the foremen and the delegates of the national work-shops tried by every possible means to stop us going off to the provinces. They urged on us the need to stand firm against the first attack" (deposition of M. Jarry, member of the National Workshops, to the Commission of Inquiry, cited in Price 1975a: 110).

11. Tilly and Lees's (1975: 194) examination of these records pro-duced a figure of 43 percent. They used a 10 percent sample ($N = 123$) obtained by reading every fifth *dossier* in every twentieth *carton*. My own calculations, based on a similar sample of 104 individuals, indicated a somewhat higher incidence of 53.8 percent (Archives historiques Série AA). Although I was attempting to recreate Tilly and Lees's sample, the system by which arrest rec-ords, many of them multiple files, are indexed is not sufficiently stable to ensure precise replication. The difference in the reported incidence of National Workshops' membership, however, is more likely due to my exclusive focus on the single issue of National Workshops' participation. This allowed me to pick up a number of indirect indications not only in the interrogations of prisoners but in the supporting documents solicited from relatives, character witnesses, officials, and so forth.

Of course, these percentages apply to those arrested and not to actual insurgents, and it could be argued that these groups differ significantly. For example, following studies of revolutionary ac-tivists that suggest that militants are more likely to evade arrest because they are able to take advantage of the information and contacts that their networks afford, one might believe the pro-portion of workshops' members to be higher among insurgents than among arrestees. But it is also plausible to speculate that in the political climate of the time, membership in the workshops may in itself have increased the probability of being arrested. All one can know for certain, is what is demonstrated by Table 4.A,

Table 4.A

Legal Disposition of Arrestees According to
Membership in the National Workshops ($N = 104$)

Membership status	Legal disposition	
	Later freed	Later convicted
Members	30	26
Nonmembers	40	8

Source: Archives historiques (AA).

namely, that among those arrested, workshops' members were more likely to be convicted than were nonmembers.

12. This range roughly coincides with contemporary estimates. Lalanne (France, Assemblé nationale 1848: I, 303-304), who as Director of the National Workshops in June had every reason to minimize the number of members who took part in the fighting, claimed that only 5,000 to 6,000 had actually fought with the insurgents, though he conceded that the rest were sympathetic and that his opinion was mere conjecture. Quentin-Bauchart, who bears a prime responsibility for the myth that the National Workshops had from their inception been an institutional front for the forces of disorder, erred in the opposite direction, by setting at 25,000-30,000 the number of insurgent workshops' members, as noted above. The precise figures will never be known.

13. The minutes of the 29 May session of the Assembly's Comité du Travail asserted that there were 8,000 to 10,000 escaped or liberated criminals enrolled in the National Workshops (Archives nationales C 928). Statements made on the floor of the Constituent Assembly set the number as high as 40,000 (Lefrançais 1902: 47). If it were even necessary to dispute such obvious fabrications, however, the testimony of Carlier, director of the Ministry of the Interior's secret police and no friend to the workshops, set the matter to rest by specifying that there were only 25,000 released convicts in France as a whole, of whom he estimated half at most, were in Paris (France, Assemblé nationale 1848: I, 246).

14. The evidence consists primarily of memos originating in the
Ministry of the Interior and calling upon regional commissars to
help stem the flow (Archives nationales C 930, Nos. 666 and 668).
The minutes of the 24 May session of the Comité des Travaux
publics (Archives nationales C 928, No. 561, no. 14: 6-8) give the
following, probably apocryphal, breakdown of 100,000 men then
supposed to be enrolled in the workshops:

> 11,000 foreigners
> 39,000 provincials
> 38,000 Parisians
> 12,000 rebels and ex-convicts

15. Garnier-Pagès (1872: X, 110); see also Thomas (1848: 336).
The passage is remarkably similar to Marx's characterization of
the Mobile Guard as a body of men drawn from the lower class,
yet distinct from it in that they were not "real workers." Thomas
himself seems to have sensed the parallel between the two organizations:

> Alongside the Mobile Guard, a praetorian guard enrolled at
> 30 sous a day . . . a new corps of official lazzaroni [i.e., his
> own National Workshops!] was now created and paid the
> same 30 sous a day because the republic cried out for "Equal-
> ity!" (Thomas 1848: 30)

16. Renard (1907: 62). He went on to assert that children as young
as ten and twelve years were admitted and claimed that the population of the Parisian *garnis* had tripled between February and
May:

> Only too happy to live as paid lazzaroni, professional do-
> nothings (to use a phrase) of the type which exists in all eras
> came to demand work with an insistence which was all the
> greater for the fact that they knew none was to be had.

His estimate of the increase in the population living *en garni*—
from 10,000 to 30,000—is probably based on Thomas (1848:
172, 208).

17. This survey was administered on 7 June and verified by visits
to workers' residences on 20 June. The only surviving census document of real interest that I have been able to locate merely provides the subtotals by ward and suburb without any further break-

down (Archives nationales C 932B, No. 2099). It gives a grand total of 103,243 members, virtually the same as the figure reported by Lalanne (1848: V, 2; Archives nationales C 932B, No. 2068). There are also a few fragmentary individual returns, indicating that a great deal of useful data was collected, but these documents are far too incomplete to provide an overall picture of the workshops' composition. The last mention of the composite survey is Lalanne's statement indicating that at the moment when insurrection broke out the returns were in the hands of ward mayors for verification. Other missing sources that might help specify the social composition of the workshops are a census of 25,000 members that Thomas (1848: 264) said he delivered to Marie on 10 April; the complete register of workers that Thomas insisted (and Lalanne denied) was maintained at the central office; and the relief lists drawn up periodically by workshops' delegates. Unless and until one or more of these sources is brought to light, the best available information on the workshops' composition will remain the occupational distribution on which I have based the results reported below.

18. It should be pointed out that part of the discrepancy is purely the result of a methodological artifact. Thomas's data were based on returns from 87,913 individuals (not 87,942 as he mistakenly claimed due to a computational error). What he actually reported, however, was the aggregated number of workshops' members exercising each of 186 trades. For purposes of comparison, these had to be recoded into the Tilly and Lees eighteen-category classification scheme. The absence of individual-level data comparable to those used in the categorizations of insurgents and Mobile Guardsmen sometimes made it difficult or impossible to proceed. For example, Thomas provided a subtotal for "painters" that did not distinguish among "house painters," "sign painters," "curio painters," "landscape painters," and so on. Sometimes I was able to apportion members among the obviously appropriate sectors. Often my only solution was to assign, for example, *all* painters to the single sector ("Construction" in this case) to which most of them belonged. Similarly, all locksmiths were categorized as "Base metals" workers even though some were employed in furniture-making, carriage construction, or fancy goods manufacture. Two distortions of the table's figures result. The first is that this method makes "big" sectors appear bigger and "small" sectors appear

smaller. That is, since "Construction" is a populous sector employing *most* painters, *all* painters were assigned to it in the process of recoding, and the numerical importance of "Construction" was exaggerated. Conversely, less populous sectors like "Fancy goods," which nonetheless employed some painters, were ignored. This was particularly true if a small sector was also highly diverse in its internal structure. Second, rubrics that amount to residual categories (notably "Services and others") were inflated simply because Thomas's system failed to provide enough information to classify many workers in an unambiguous way. These effects are readily apparent in the National Workshops' data in Table 4.2 and probably explain much of the variation from the distributions observed in the comparison groups where classifications could be based on specific, individual information.

19. Again, it is the aggregated form of the Thomas data that prevented me from using the 345 finely divided occupational categories from the Chamber of Commerce study that proved so helpful in my consideration of the Mobile Guard. Given the manipulations to which the data have been subjected, even an examination of the crude variations among the thirteen sectoral categories would be suspect.

20. These are, of course, the same ones used to organize the account of Mobile Guard political evolution. The reader will recall that the first spans the period from the overthrow of Louis Philippe to the demonstrations of mid-March. The second witnessed a further polarization, culminating in the *journée* of 16 April. The succeeding month, in which legislative elections returned an unexpectedly conservative Constituent Assembly, produced the aborted coup attempt of 15 May. Political tensions reached the breaking point in the fourth and final phase leading to the outbreak of the June Days.

21. Ironically, in view of their June behavior, the first project undertaken by workshops' members was to replace paving stones and remove the stumps of trees cut down by barricade builders in February.

22. France, Assemblé nationale (1848: I, 352). Thomas has, of course, confused his dates again. His account is consistent with the best external evidence and corroborated by both Garnier-Pagès (n.d.: II, 125) and Stern (1862: II, 67-68, 77-78, 153). Contrary to the politically motivated contention of the Commission of Inquiry that

the workshops were at the center of the events of 17 March, no more than a handful of members could have been in attendance.

23. Thomas himself complained of the difficulty of locating on short notice the 500 brigadiers and 3,000 squad leaders required by an enrollment of nearly 30,000 men by 31 March. In most cases he was forced to rely on the often untrustworthy recommendations of ward mayors (Thomas 1848: 147).

24. The suggestion was made following a meeting of late March at which the Minister of Public Works thanked workshops' members for their consistent show of support for the government, counseling them to "remain calm as you have been and avoid marches and meetings which disturb industry and commerce" (Thomas 1848: 153-56). On the origins of this body, see also Garnier-Pagès (n.d.: II, 125).

25. The theme of respect for law and order was reinforced in the speech of Jaime (Thomas 1848: 178-84), an assistant director whom Lefrançais (1902: 30) described as "a vaudevillist from the Palais-Royal." Initially the Réunion centrale, or "Club of delegates" as it was known, comprised some 350 men. The roll of delegates rose with the membership until it listed nearly 2,000 names, and the council had to be reorganized under a system of multitiered, revolving representation.

26. Thomas (1848: 200-201). According to the same source (1848: 184, n. 1), three-fourths of all workshops' members belonged to the National Guard. This same footnote, incidentally, contains yet another of Thomas's misattributions of date. He is referring to the 16 April and not, as stated, the 15 May demonstration. This is clear from the context as well as from the date of the letter being discussed. McKay (1933: 73), however, has followed him in this confusion.

27. Cherest (1873: 235). Confirmation from the right is provided by Garnier-Pagès (n.d.: II, 214, 221); from the left by Renard (1907: 38). McKay (1933: 50), following Stern (1862: II, 174), noted that an additional group of workshops' members assembled at the Hippodrome with the intention of converging with the column from the Champ de Mars. He made of this the beginning of an entire trend toward disaffection (1933: 51). The notice (*le Moniteur*, 18 April) cited as evidence, however, was based on a statement by workshops' delegates at a 17 April meeting and made reference to the initial presence of workshops' members at the

Hippodrome without mentioning whether they were also in attendance at the demonstration proper. It is not clear whether Thomas dispatched his lieutenants to the Hippodrome gathering as well—he made no mention of it, in any case—but here, too, the majority of members appear to have responded to the *tambours* and played no part in the actual demonstration.

28. Thomas asserted that he "suffered no electoral maneuver whatever in the hierarchical order of our brigades," but in the next breath he gave as his reason that he wished to "maintain all my independence in order better to place obstacles in the path of the conspiracies of the Luxembourg" (1848: 218-19). In practice, this meant that while refraining from open endorsement of any slate he did everything in his power to sway opinion against radical candidates, as his own account made clear (1848: 216-17). For three days running, the Minister of Public Works placed 500 men from the workshops' payroll at the disposal of a moderate coalition supporting the slate of a club called the Union des travailleurs (Thomas 1848: 217-18). They were paid special wages to distribute lists of approved candidates at the polls. The entire membership was originally to be given the day off with a 50-centimes bonus on top of their normal pay (McKay 1933: 57-58; Renard 1907: 48), though this plan was later abandoned. The students from the Ecole centrale were sent to all points of the city to turn workers away from leftist rallies and succeeded in causing the collapse of a mass meeting scheduled by the Luxembourg for the morning of the 23d (France, Assemblé nationale 1848: II, 179). On the rivalry between the National Workshops and the Luxembourg Commission, see Thomas (1848: 210-23); Blanc (1850: 130ff.); Cherest (1873: 236-39).

29. See the letter from Marrast reproduced in Thomas (1848: 245-46).

30. Thomas (1848: 252-53). The purpose of this assembly was to express to Lamartine the gratitude of the left for his support of the nomination of Ledru Rollin (still in the good graces of most radicals) to the Executive Commission. Thomas not only instructed his company commanders to gather their units and convey each collectively to its own quarter of the city, so as simultaneously to regiment and disperse the mass of workers; but he also headed for the Place de la Concorde, accompanied by his service commanders, to harangue the groups rallying there and persuade them

to disband (1848: 252-53). Thomas also made the merest mention (1848: 247-48) of a failed demonstration of 13 May. This forerunner of the 15 May rally, similarly organized to show support for Poland, collapsed despite the presence of Blanqui.

31. According to the estimates of Carlier (Archives nationales C 932A, No. 1467) and Thomas (1848: 262), respectively.

32. This confusion resulted in part from the efforts of opponents of the workshops to discredit the organization by convincing their contemporaries that it had been deeply implicated in the coup attempt. It should be pointed out, however, that some highly sophisticated later commentators have accepted similarly early dates for the onset of the workshops' disaffection. Gossez (1967: 301), for example, claimed that the masses were already being unified by the spread of unemployment and that workshops' members joined in the events of 15 May (undifferentiated) in defiance of their officers. Yet it was Gossez himself (1967: 301) who called attention to the march of 21 May at which workshops' members snubbed the representatives of the radical camp, as noted below.

33. Thomas (1848: 257-58). McKay (1933: 73) contrasted this lack of preparation with the administration's vigilance in the two preceding *journées* and ascribed the difference to the ambivalence awakened in Thomas by the government's new policy toward the workshops. In effect, on 12 May Trélat, who had just replaced Marie as Minister of Public Works, informed Thomas of the government's desire to curtail the organization. Elsewhere Thomas estimated the number of workshops' demonstrators at 12,000 (1848: 260) and 10,000 (France, Assemblé nationale 1848: I, 352). Carlier's more conservative figure is 8,000 to 10,000 (Archives nationales C 932A, No. 1467). It will be recalled that approximately 113,000 workers were then enrolled.

34. Unfortunately, we possess virtually no direct evidence concerning the motivation that led this minority of workshops members to participate in the rally. Also in attendance, however, was a sizable representation of provincial National Guardsmen who had come to the capital some days before to take part in the Fête de la Concorde. Lévy-Schneider's (1910: 231) description of the latter's frame of mind would seem to apply equally well to the National Workshops contingent:

There is nothing surprising in the fact that they went, especially since the demonstration had been presented as solely intended to affirm their sympathy in favor of Poland. No doubt many also went as onlookers. But to suppose from this day that they are in complete agreement with the insurgents is a great leap.

On the attitude of his men, compare also Thomas in a note to the president of the Assembly written before its invasion:

As for the workers, they are of good faith and are thinking only of Poland. (1848: 259)

McKay (1933: 72, n. 100) draws the same conclusion from a 16 May article in *la Liberté*. It is important to recall that, from all indications, the organizers of the demonstration had purposely selected this innocuous pretext in order to draw the largest crowd possible, in the hope that in the heat of the moment its members could be engaged upon a more radical course of action.

35. The text is to be found not in his self-justificatory book but in Archives nationales (C 932A, No. 1189).

36. Renard (1907: 63). Renard's position on the precise dating of the reorientation of workshops' support is, however, somewhat difficult to pin down. On the one hand, he is not only one of the few commentators who make explicit the crucial distinction between the two phases of the 15 May events, but he has provided one of the most perceptive assessments of the National Workshops' counterrevolutionary role in the first two months of the Second Republic:

In political affairs, they were an instrument in the hands of the moderate faction which made their battalions into a conservative force. They were used to divide the Parisian proletariat, to set one part of the people against another, to neutralize the socialist workers with malleable and submissive workers. (1907: 59-60)

Yet elsewhere Renard (1907: 63) has indicated that a rapprochement between the membership and the Luxembourg Commission was already underway by mid-May.

37. This effort to pinpoint the moment and thus explicate the process of workshops' disaffection will only indirectly be concerned with the extremely active course of elite politics. The rivalries that de-

veloped among the Assembly, the Executive Commission it created, and a variety of special subcommittees and oversight bodies as they struggled now to advance, now to retard the timing of dissolution are of interest to us primarily in terms of the reaction they incited among the lower classes. A particularly clear presentation of these baroque political machinations is provided by Renard (1907: 64-78). McKay (1933) has best captured the spirit of destructive and opportunistic competition among power-holders. A detailed, though excessively self-justificatory version is provided by Garnier-Pagès (1872: X, 419-43).

The confused political status of the workshops resulted in part from the ambiguity in the jurisdictional boundaries between the Assembly and the Executive Commission; the further division in bureaucratic authority over the "National" Workshops between the office of the mayor of Paris, the French Ministry of Public Works, and, to a lesser extent, the Ministry of the Interior; the change in policy and ministerial personnel that occurred after the Provisional Government gave way to the Executive Commission (particularly the appointment of a Minister of Public Works whose attitude toward the workshops was consistently hostile); and the different political agendas of the several subcommittees of the National Assembly simultaneously attempting to chart the institution's future.

38. McKay (1933: 78) not only called attention to this "concerted attack" but went so far as to suggest that "the government's actions during the day of 15 May also point in the direction of a conscious policy aiming to discredit the Workshops."

39. The source is Gossez (1967: 301) who appears to be relying on Renard (1907: 63).

40. Thomas (1848: 368-70). The author of the report, Peaucellier, qualified this judgment only to the extent of remarking that some workers were complaining that their officers were not enough in evidence on certain worksites.

41. This may have been the end that Trélat had in mind from the beginning. Though he called upon Thomas to render his highest service to the Republic by "helping to destroy that which you have created" (Thomas 1848: 285), the interview of 12 May had already made it obvious that Thomas would oppose precipitate measures that violated the spirit of understandings painstakingly negotiated with the workers. Since the *journée* of 15 May had made the

elimination of the workshops politically feasible, the installation of a more pliant director had assumed a critical importance. Renard (1907: 65) claimed that Thomas's removal was motivated by the fact that his plans for the workshops had increasingly come to resemble the ideas of Blanc. Lavisse (1921: II, 93) indicated that it was on 22 May that Thomas proposed the cooperative reorganization of the National Workshops. It remains more likely, however, that Thomas's hesitant attitude during the preliminaries of 15 May had caused concern over his reliability in an ultimate test. That Thomas's uncertain loyalty was the real issue is indicated in a note by Marie, no longer Minister of Public Works but a member of the Executive Commission: "27 May: Dismissal of Emile Thomas. He was sent to Bordeaux because we feared his resistance to the plans for dissolution" (Cherest 1873: 230-31).

42.   In his memoirs, Thomas cited Alexandre Dumas's account of this confrontation as if it were based on independent sources (Thomas 1848: 286-308). In fact, it seems to represent information obtained in large part from Thomas and his close associates. Both its broad outlines and many telling details, however, were confirmed in the parliamentary debates provoked by the incident and in the later investigation of the Commission of Inquiry. Indeed, the testimony of Boulage, the secretary to the Minister of Public Works who was present at the interview, actually supported Thomas on specific points where the latter disagreed with Trélat, Boulage's immediate superior (France, Assemblé nationale 1848: I, 242).

43.   The announced object of this mission was a study of the lengthening of provincial canals. Thomas protested that as a chemist with no real engineering expertise, he was unqualified and would be forced to decline. To this Trélat replied that in the interest of Thomas's personal security, he, Trélat, was prepared to order Thomas from the capital (1848: 289). That the original description of the mission was merely part of a ruse to justify his absence is further indicated by the fact that the next morning Trélat gave a totally different version of the exchange to Thomas's supporters at Monceaux (Thomas 1848: 301; McKay 1933: 98, n. 58).

44.   From the report of Flachat and Polonceau, cited in the account of Dumas, itself reproduced in Thomas (1848: 302-303). See also the account of Jaime's position in Archives nationales (C 930, No. 610; C 932A, Nos. 1819 and 1846).

45. Beauplan's second report (undated, but written at 3 A.M., presumably on the 28th) noted that the National Guard *rappel* could be heard in various parts of the city and mentioned five separate assembly points for meetings later that day aimed at freeing Thomas. According to Beauplan, "the lieutenants of the workshops are recruiting men everywhere and exciting the minds of the workers." Compare also Archives nationales (C 932A, No. 1747): "The students of the *Ecole centrale*, of whom a large number are employed in the National Workshops, are generally reported to be hostile to the government."

46. Some impression of the magnitude of the change can be gleaned from the reports of paid agents to the Prefect of Police (France, Assemblé nationale 1848: II, 185-215) and from the reports of both Carlier and Trouvé-Chauvel (France, Assemblé nationale 1848: II, 226-36). Unfortunately, these documents do not constitute a sufficiently complete series on which to base a systematic, quantitative measure of insurgence over time, and sources on which to ground a comparison with the period immediately preceding 26 May are even less satisfactory.

47. See, for example, France, Assemblé nationale (1848: II, 193) and a police report of 22 June, according to which:

> Two or three hundred individuals, headed by flags bearing the inscription "National Workshops," crossed the bridge at the Tuileries. . . . When they passed in front of the barracks occupied by the Mobile Guard, they shouted "Long Live the Mobile Guard!" (France, Assemblé nationale 1848: C 930, No. 698)

According to Stern (1862: II, 394), the insurgents continued efforts to win over the Mobile Guard even after the fighting began. Although this corps proved immune to such urgings for reasons detailed in the preceding chapters, large numbers of National Guardsmen, less insulated from popular agitation, appeared on the barricades, often in leadership roles.

48. France, Assemblé nationale (1848: II, 201ff.) This source detailed 750 arrests on 11 June alone.

49. Compare Barrot (1875: 244). According to Garnier-Pagès (1872: XI, 160-61), certain representatives continued to argue for immediate dissolution even after outbreak of hostilities, with the consequence of prolonging and intensifying the crisis.

50. According to Marie (as reported in Garnier-Pagès 1872: XI, 73), Pujol had participated in the 15 May attack on the Assembly and had in fact been one of the first to gain passage through the iron grillwork protecting the chamber. If so, he is the one member of the National Workshops whose presence I have been able to document. The judicial dossier compiled on Pujol is, as one might expect, extremely detailed. It is, however, difficult to interpret in many respects not only because of differences between Pujol's account of events and that of the authorities but also because of the many internal contradictions among the documents assembled. These include, for example, everything from inconsistent accounts of his whereabouts on 22 and 23 June to an erroneous report of his death (see Archives historiques Série AA). The file often refers to Pujol as a "worker" of the National Workshops, but the internal passport with which he came to Paris from Toulouse in March 1848 listed his occupation as "merchant" (*négociant*). Thus he also appears to be a rare documentable example of that phenomenon that the government never tired of decrying, an individual who had migrated from the provinces to join the Parisian National Workshops. According to a note appended by the editor to the minutes of the Executive Commission of 22 June (France, Comité nationale du centenaire de 1848 1950: 406), Pujol had once been a seminarist and an enlistee in the African cavalry and in 1848 had published an "apocalyptic" pamphlet titled *Prophéties des Jours sanglants*.

51. This is, in a sense, to place the most positive construction on the decision to bring an end to unemployment relief. For many observers on both right and left, the government's actions represented a provocation, pure and simple. The conscious desire to precipitate an armed resolution to the basic social conflict was expressed in the increasing currency of the conservative watchword of June: "*Il faut en finir!*"

Chapter Five

1. Thomas (1848: 53). Thomas voiced his concerns even more forcefully in a memo of early April (1848: 192).
2. Thomas (1848: 190; at page 144, Thomas gives the figure 12,000).
3. Their resistance seems to have been the result of a longstanding rivalry. Thomas himself and the cadres he recruited to staff the

higher echelons of the National Workshops were associated with the Ecole centrale, the institution responsible for training civil engineers in France. The public engineers of the Ministry of Public Works on whom Thomas was dependent were products of the more prestigious Ecole polytechnique. As early as mid-March, Thomas complained of the latter's recalcitrance. Even Marie, the minister with direct authority over them, was unable to gain their cooperation (Thomas 1848: 87ff., 190, 203). An indirect indication that rivalry between the two schools was the source of many of the early difficulties is provided by the fact that the situation improved somewhat after the installation as director of Léon Lalanne, a graduate of the Ecole polytechnique and career engineer in the department of "bridges and highways." According to Delessard (1900: 27), however, the new administration's efforts were directed primarily toward preparations for dissolution, and those students of the Ecole centrale who elected to remain associated with the National Workshops after Thomas's departure had to fend for themselves in finding work for their men.

4. Excerpted from a poster of 20 June riposting to the accusations of Representative Dupin, this passage was written by Auguste Siebert, a brigadier in the National Workshops, and is reproduced in France, Assemblé nationale (1848: II, 294-96).

5. From a response to a speech by Representative Goudchaux, Minister of Finance. This poster, issued on 18 June and signed by National Workshops' delegates from all Parisian wards, is reproduced in France, Assemblé nationale (1848: II, 293-94).

6. Thomas (1848: 139-40) mentioned the growth of the membership, the lack of work, and the threat of disorder as reasons and cited the example of 1830 as precedent for such measures. Marie replied that such a plan was impractical because of the political opposition it would encounter from the Luxembourg Commission (Thomas 1848: 141-42).

7. Thomas's concrete proposals included (1) the construction of housing for Parisian workers on undeveloped land and (2) the digging of canals and the improvement of railways in the basin of the Seine River (Thomas 1848: 190-92).

8. The women's workshops were organized separately from the men's. A number of factors made the formation of producers' cooperatives more practicable there: a more restricted scale of operations (peak enrollment of 25,000); a very much narrower range of occupations due to the sectoral concentration of women workers;

and the fact that the type of manual labor used in the men's workshops was from the beginning deemed inappropriate for women. The proceeds from the sale of goods underwrote the cost of these workshops, so well in fact that the cost per member, per day was held to a mere 15 centimes. The comparable figure for the men's workshops was at least ten times as great.

9. Twenty-three sous equal 1 franc 15 centimes. This passage is extracted from a 27 May letter to the editors of *le Constitutionnel* signed by 400 to 500 members of the National Workshops. It is reproduced in Garnier-Pagès (1872: X, 113).

10. In a study that focuses primarily on the Mobile Guard and the National Workshops as opponents in a bloody insurrection, it is surely worth remarking, if only in passing, on the irony of history that nearly joined the two organizations. When in late May and early June the authorities considered ways of diverting the members of the workshops, a plan was drawn up (though never put into effect) calling for the younger members to be enrolled in the Mobile Guard. This militia had never, after all, reached the full complement of 25,000 volunteers that the Provisional Government had envisioned. The records do not make it clear whether the block of 10,000 men that the Mobile Guard could have absorbed was judged too small or whether the opponents of the National Workshops simply preferred to route them to the army and thus remove them from the capital altogether. It is interesting to note, however, that one of the original proposals made a point of the fact that any workshops' members inducted into the Mobile Guard should be spread indiscriminately among all twenty-four battalions rather than being distributed on a geographical basis, as had been the case with the initial recruits. Although this provision was justified in terms of maintaining the numeric equality of the various battalions, it obviously would also have helped prevent the concentration of workers within local networks of personal and political relations. See, for example, Archives historiques (Xm 32, 10 June, letter from Carteret to General Bedeau).

11. This sense of solidarity may actually have been enhanced by the Ecole centrale students' pride in having usurped a role much like that played by graduates of the Ecole polytechnique in previous revolutions. As in the case of the Mobile Guard, uniforms assumed an exaggerated importance as symbols of the finer gradations of revolutionary fervor. On this issue, see Delessard (1900: 17), Lefrançais (1902: 30), and Thomas (1848: 45).

12. Thomas (1848: 41). Nowhere is the number of Ecole centrale students and alumni participating in the National Workshops specified. One can make crude estimates for three discrete points in time based on the distribution of ranks then filled by students from that school, the number of members commanded by each such rank, and the total number of members then enrolled. Thus, for "the first month" of the workshops' operation (1848: 59, 81), using 20,000 as an approximation of the number of members Thomas is referring to, the calculation yields the following results:

> 5 directors and assistant directors
> 14 ward commanders
> 30 service commanders leading 675 men each
> 89 company commanders leading 225 men each
> <u> 0</u> lieutenants (rank then nonexistent)
> 138 total students

As of 1 April (Thomas 1848: 164), calculations differ depending on whether one uses Thomas's contextual estimate of the membership as 40,000 or the figure of 30,000 that, according to McKay, approximated the enrollment on that date. If one splits the difference, the results are the following:

> 5 directors and assistant directors
> 14 ward commanders
> 26 service commanders leading 1,350 men each
> 78 company commanders leading 450 men each
> —(a small but indeterminate number of
> <u>   </u> lieutenants leading 225 men each)
> 123 + total students

Later, "when the number of workers became larger still" (Thomas 1848: 165; see also 58)—a number that can be set at approximately the 89,000 enrolled at the end of the Thomas regime—the corresponding figures would be:

> 5 directors and assistant directors
> 14 ward commanders
> 33 service commanders leading 2,700 men each
> 99 company commanders leading 900 men each
> 0 lieutenants (since students were by then
> <u>   </u> reserved for higher offices)
> 151 total students

The range—from 123 to 151—is great, and the detailed assumptions implied by any one of these calculations are subject to question, but they at least provide an order of magnitude estimate on which to base comparisons with the size of the non-Ecole centrale cadres of the lower administration.

13. At least between 22 March and 4 April, police security officers detached to the National Workshops attempted to conduct inquiries into the background and trustworthiness of nominees for these low-level positions (France, Assemblé nationale 1848: II, 177). These resulted in the rejection of about 20 percent of the 231 nominations investigated. These figures included, however, only a portion of the total number of appointments made in that period, and this review procedure does not appear to have been continued beyond the beginning of April. Thomas gave some idea of the abuses to which the original system lent itself when he complained of one nominator from whom he received 700 written recommendations and of the mayor of the 7th ward who "sent me more brigadiers and squad leaders than workers" (1848: 85).

14. Picattier (1899: 36) confirmed both that all brigadiers and squad leaders were originally appointed by the administration and that the transition to elections was made at the insistence of the rank and file.

15. Thomas (1848: 60, 173); Garnier-Pagès (1872: X, 428). As Lalanne (1848: III, 2) described the system, a would-be brigadier would actively seek out 55 men from his neighborhood or among his contacts in the workplace and convince them to enroll, with the understanding that they would vote for their patron once admitted.

16. *Vraie République*, 3 May (reproduced in Gossez 1967: 301); Picattier (1899: 101-105). Thomas introduced the revised electoral criteria immediately after his 20 April confrontation with the Luxembourg delegates and without consulting the membership. Surprisingly, it does not appear to have produced any appreciable dissension within the National Workshops.

17. Thomas (1848: 148, 156-58, 174-80). The Réunion centrale underwent several subsequent reorganizations, largely because its membership, reflecting that of the workshops in general, grew by leaps and bounds.

18. In a proclamation reproduced in Picattier (1899: 80), Thomas made it clear that his explicit intention had been to dilute the

political influence of the approximately 400 delegates he originally expected.

19. "Cooptation is the process of absorbing new elements into the leadership or policy-determining structure of an organization as a means of averting threats to its stability or existence" (Selznick 1949: 13). To be more precise, Thomas practiced *formal* cooptation in which "the public symbols or administrative burdens of authority" are shared "without the transfer of substantive power." As Selznick pointed out, this "requires informal control over the coopted elements lest the unity of command and decision be imperiled" (1949: 261).

20. Lalanne had recently served as a member of the extraparliamentary committee on the National Workshops, which in all its brief career had never been more than a rubber stamp for the policies of the Minister of Public Works (McKay 1933: 117-18). It is interesting that the vita in Lalanne's dossier in the national archives (Archives nationales F14, 2254) does not list among his services to his country the four weeks spent as director of the National Workshops. An added reason why Trélat may have felt he could rely on complete obedience is that Lalanne was his brother-in-law (Lavisse 1921: 93).

21. As noted above, secret police reports (Archives nationales BB30 313, 2d *liasse, dossier* 445) implicating them in anti-government plots had called their loyalty into question. The Executive Commission issued warrants for the arrest of Pierre Thomas and Jaime, among others. Although the government was no doubt correct in reading their sympathies, their judicial pursuit was apparently abandoned for lack of evidence. Lalanne, incidentally, claimed that the assistant directors' positions were "suppressed" (1848: V, 2). If true, however, this change clearly must have taken place after their resignation en masse.

22. On his pivotal role in the mass meetings of 22 and 23 June, see, for example, Stern (1862: II, 365-69).

23. In *Mémoires d'un révolutionnaire* (1902: 47-55), Lefrançais recounted the progressive disillusionment of one young cadre in the face of organizational chaos and political treachery. Lefrançais's autobiographical account is of added interest because he confided that in February his first temptation had been to enlist in the Mobile Guard. Only after he had been dissuaded by his father and a few old friends did he end up joining the National Workshops where

he was ultimately elected a squad leader. His personal experience thus suggests, even if only anecdotally, the near equivalence in the social status of the members of these groups in February and the almost incidental circumstances on which the choice between them often hinged.

24. Thomas (1848: 339; cf. also 157-58). Lalanne not only did not share Thomas's reformist and conciliatory attitude toward the workers but also lacked the latter's personal instinct for exploiting the institution's cooptive potential. He refused to attend the Club of Delegates' first meeting after he had assumed office. He attended the second with a bodyguard of policemen and only after stipulating a format in which he spoke without interruption or questions (Thomas 1848: 339). Lalanne's attempt to replace the broad-based Réunion centrale with a committee of fourteen hand-picked ward delegates was never taken seriously by the general membership.

25. Though perhaps overstated, Audiganne's characterization is apt:

> In this corps, racked by a thousand worries, accessible to every provocation, and whose members scattered every evening to the various corners of the city, it was never possible to realize the least guarantees of subordination. (1854: 196-97)

On the difficulties of achieving isolation, see also Delessard (1900: 18).

26. Thomas (1848: 81). Of course, this highly structured daily routine remained an unrealized ideal. In practice, the lack of any useful work meant that the two hours originally allocated for meals and relaxation were gradually expanded to fill the entire day. As there were not enough nooks and crannies in all Paris to secrete 100,000 men, ten at a time, large and boisterous congregations sometimes resulted.

27. Caussidière (1849: II, 214), for example, reported that several brigadiers has told him they were threatened with dismissal unless they helped elect the candidates designated by the Director's office.

28. The reader will recall that the Luxembourg had been officially disbanded immediately after 15 May, and one of Lalanne's first acts as director had been to dissolve the Réunion centrale.

29. Amann (1960) has given the best account of the episode and its part in the political evolution of June. I would only take issue with the extent to which he played down the role, direct and indirect, of the National Workshops (1960: 438, 443). In a later article,

Amann revised his initial view. First, he acknowledged that the banquet resulted from the merger of two mobilizing efforts, the more important of which originated in the National Workshops with the assistance of the radical newspaper *le Père Duchêne*. Second, he explicitly associated the launching of the banquet campaign with the protest resulting from Thomas's ouster (Amann 1968; see also Molok 1952: 67).

The date of the banquet was first moved from 4 June to 11 June; next to an unspecified date later in the month; finally to Bastille day. With the intervention of the June Days, the entire project was abandoned.

30. Archives nationales (C 932B, No. 1918). According to the Commission of Inquiry (France, Assemblé nationale 1848: II, 197), they were successful; this appears to be contradicted, however, by a subsequent report from the same source (1848: II, 198).

31. France, Assemblé nationale (1848: II, 286), where this notice is mistakenly dated 9 May instead of 29 May.

32. On 5 June he vowed "to do everything in my power either to prevent the National Workshops from taking part or even to abort it" (Archives nationales C 932B, No. 1971). Called to an interview with Lalanne, Thomassin and Deshayes—spokesmen for the organizing committee—protested that their intentions were in no way hostile to the government and that they would proceed only with its approval.

Chapter Six

1. I have not included the work of Moss (1976) on the French labor movement between 1830 and 1914. This is because Moss tended to minimize the significance of variations in levels of skill, autonomy, and work organization as determinants of political activity. His one-sided insistence on the continuity between artisans and proletarians over a period in which the industrialization of the French economy made substantial progress devalued precisely those distinctions that constitute the essence of the theme of artisanal activism.

Whereas Moss used the term "skilled workers" indiscriminately to designate both artisans and proletarians, it might be objected that in this manuscript I have inappropriately used the same term as a synonym for "artisans." Although it is true that not all skilled workers are artisans, in the conditions that prevailed in mid-nine-teenth-century Paris (and with the partial exception of specific trades that I have tried to call attention to whenever the effects of skill level were at issue), my tendency to equate the two constitutes a minor distortion.

2. The pattern of artisanal activism now has so rich a documentary basis as to constitute what could be termed the "new orthodoxy" of the social history of the nineteenth century (Traugott 1983a). Although this perspective serves as a useful counterpoint to the claims of simplistic Marxist analysis, it is by now ripe for critical examination in its own right. For an original, if inconclusive, dissenting view, see Stedman Jones (1983).

3. By implication, virtually all the research used to ground the thesis of artisanal activism needs to be reexamined in order to establish whether in addition to an absolute predominance of skilled workers and petty entrepreneurs, movements of popular protest were also characterized by a *proportional* preponderance of these same groups relative to, most obviously, more proletarianized strata. Rates expressed in terms of the relevant segment of the general population have now become indispensable to further progress in explaining the central role of artisans to which so many authors have pointed.

4. In addition to the indications noted below, the reader will recall that in Chapter Two the rate of unemployment by trade was found to be among the best predictors of the occupational distribution of the group of Mobile Guard recruits that has proved to be so similar to the group of June insurgents in all its other socioeconomic characteristics.

5. Tilly and Lees (1975: 199). Unfortunately, the published version of this paper omitted the footnote in which a more detailed discussion of this evidence might have been expected.

6. Almost by definition, those enrolled in the workshops were unemployed. As to the other half of the June arrestees, I have made the conservative assumption that they suffered from a rate of joblessness equal to that of the general population. One might object that, once the membership of the workshops has been accounted for, this general rate would have been much lower. Contemporary observers have suggested, however, that the ranks of the insurgents were in fact filled out by the mass of 50,000 to 60,000 unemployed Parisian workers who were unable to gain admission to the work-

shops due to the new policy limiting enrollments (cf. Bouniols 1918: 229).

7. It is at least plausible to suggest, for example, that contrary to the cohort hypothesis, the unmarried members of the Mobile Guard may well have been *less* economically vulnerable in certain respects, both objective and subjective, than older workers with family responsibilities.

8. Systematic estimates of the age of National Guardsmen specific to the crucial months of 1848 are, to my knowledge, lacking. These assertions can nonetheless be made without real fear of contradiction. In addition to the impressionistic evidence of contemporaries, it is known that the enlistment requirements of the National Guard specified that male citizens from twenty to fifty-five years of age were eligible (Girard 1964: 294) and that more than 190,000 men were enrolled by June, among whom were at least 60,000 members of the National Workshops (Stern 1862: II, 164). Given the high proportion of all Mobile Guardsmen who were under twenty and the enormous share of all male Parisians over twenty who were distributed throughout the National Guard on a geographic basis, it is virtually certain that *any* sampling of the National Guard would be appreciably older than any sampling of the Mobile Guard.

METHODOLOGICAL APPENDIX

1. Note that there also existed a 25th battalion of "marine guards," created in April, and several smaller units of mounted guards. These were, however, unlike the twenty-four regular battalions in that they were recruited from the city at large rather than from a specific ward. It is the ability to link ward characteristics with those of the recruits who resided there at the time of their enlistment that permits us methodologically to ground many of the comparisons between the Mobile Guard and relevant reference groups. I have therefore eliminated these special units of the Mobile Guard from consideration.

2. The data shown in column 2 Table A.1 represent 100 times the ratio of the number of citizens with a property qualification of 1,000 francs or more to the number of citizens with a property qualification of less than 300 francs. Although labeled as a "prosperity measure," it would be more accurate to say that these figures

indicate the relative proportion of each ward's population living in relative poverty. On the coexistence of affluence and poverty in all Parisian wards, however, see Daumard (1963: 184ff.).

3. The dichotomous categorization of the conduct of National Guard legions is based on accounts found in Stern (1862: 382-86, 403); Schmidt (1926: 50, 52); Pagès-Duport (1848: 11); Girard (1964: 313-14); Levy (1961); and Doumenc (1948: 264). Map A.1 (which follows the Notes) not only depicts the east/west distribution of sampled wards but provides a useful comparison with Tilly and Lees's cartographic representation of the physical distribution of those convicted for participation in the June Days (1975: 199).

4. The average was 7.8 fatalities per battalion for those included in our sample, 8.1 for all twenty-four battalions.

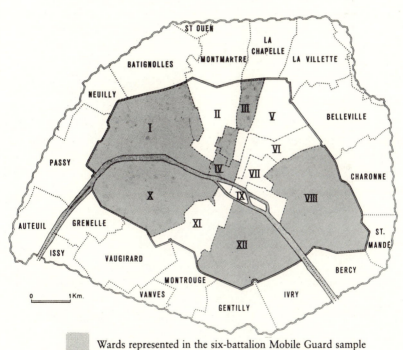

Wards represented in the six-battalion Mobile Guard sample

Map A-1: Paris and Its Outskirts in 1848

BIBLIOGRAPHY

I. ARCHIVAL SOURCES

A. *Archives historiques du Ministère de la Guerre (Vincennes)*

Série AA: Justice militaire
Série F1: République de 1848
    1-15
Série J: Insurrection de 1848
Série Xd: Armament de la Garde nationale mobile
    385
Série Xm: Garde nationale mobile
    32-49; also, noncatalogued volumes that include the twenty-five battalion registers and three volumes on officers

B. *Archives nationales (Paris)*

Série C: Assemblés nationales
    920A, 920B, 921-922, 925, 928, 930, 932A, 932B, 933-934, 940, 941, 942
Série F: Versements des Ministères
    F1d III: Récompenses honorifiques
        83-98
    F7: Police générale
        2585-2586
    F9: Affaires militaires
        1072, 1075-1076, 1089, 1119-1122, 1150
    F14: Travaux publiques
        2254
    F20: Statistique
        760
Série BB: Ministère de la Justice
    BB18: Correspondance générale de
    la Division criminelle
        1463

BIBLIOGRAPHY

BB24: Grâces demandées et accordées ou refusées
BB30: Versements divers
   313

C. *Archives de la Préfecture de Police de Paris*

Série Aa:
   427-431, Evènements de 1848
   432, Sociétés ouvrières

D. *Bibliothèque historique de la Ville de Paris*

Série 25: 1055, 1057

E. *Bibliothèque nationale (Paris)*

Série Lb53: Gouvernement provisoire de 1848

F. *Archives de l'Ecole centrale des arts et manufactures*

II. Newspapers Consulted

le Constitutionnel (Paris)
l'Illustration (Paris)
la Liberté (Rouen)
le Moniteur universel (Paris)
le National (Paris)
la Réforme (Paris)

III. Books and Articles

Achard, Amedée. *Souvenirs Personnels d'Emeutes et de Révolutions.* Paris: Michel Lévy, 1872.
Acomb, Evelyn M., and Marvin L. Brown, Jr., eds. *French Society and Culture Since the Old Regime.* New York: Holt, Rinehart & Winston, 1966.
Agulhon, Maurice. *1848 ou l'apprentissage de la république, 1848-1852.* Paris: Editions du Seuil, 1973.
Allen, Christopher. " 'Lumpenproletarians' and Revolution." In *Political Theory and Ideology in African Society*, 91-115. Proceedings of a seminar held in the Centre of African Studies, University of Edinburgh, 1970.
Amann, Peter. "Prelude to Insurrection: the Banquet of the People." *French Historical Studies* 1, no. 4 (December 1960): 436-44.

Amann, Peter. "Recent Writings on the Second French Republic." *Journal of Modern History* 34, no. 4 (December 1962): 409-29.

Amann, Peter. "The Changing Outlines of 1848." *American Historical Review* 68, no. 4 (1963): 938-53.

Amann, Peter. "*Du neuf* on the 'Banquet of the People,' June, 1948." *French Historical Studies* 5, no. 3 (Spring 1968): 344-50.

Amann, Peter. "A *Journée* in the Making: May 15, 1848." *Journal of Modern History* 42, no. 1 (March 1970): 42-69.

Amann, Peter H. *Revolution and Mass Democracy: the Paris Club Movement in 1848.* Princeton, N.J.: Princeton University Press, 1975.

Aminzade, Ronald. *Class, Politics, and Early Industrial Capitalism: A Study of Mid-Nineteenth Century Toulouse, France.* Albany, N.Y.: State University of New York Press, 1981.

Anonymous. "Chronique." *Revue des deux mondes* 22 (April-May-June 1848).

Apponyi, Rodolphe. *De la Révolution au coup d'Etat, 1848-1851.* Genève: La Palatine, 1948.

Audiganne, A. "l'Industrie française depuis la révolution de février." *Revue des deux mondes* 2 (June 1849): 979-1006.

Audiganne, A. *Les Populations ouvrières et les industries de la France dans le mouvement social du dix-neuvième siècle.* Paris: Capelle, 1854.

Balleydier, Alphonse. *Histoire de la Garde mobile depuis les Barricades de Février.* Paris: Pillet, 1848.

Barrot, Odilon. *Mémoires Posthumes.* Paris: Charpentier, 1875.

Bertaut, Jules. *1848 et la Seconde République.* Paris: Librairie Arthème Fayard, 1948.

Bezucha, Robert J. "The 'Preindustrial' Worker Movement: The Canuts of Lyon." In *Modern European Social History*, edited by Robert J. Bezucha, 93-123. Lexington, Mass.: Heath, 1972.

Bezucha, Robert J. *The Lyon Uprising of 1834: Social and Political Conflict in the Early July Monarchy.* Cambridge, Mass.: Harvard University Press, 1974.

Bezucha, Robert J. "The French Revolution of 1848 and the Social History of Work." *Theory and Society* 12, no. 4 (July 1983): 469-84.

Blanc, Louis. *Pages d'histoire de la révolution de février 1848.* Paris: Nouveau Monde, 1850.

263

Blanc, Louis. *1848. Historical Revelations.* London: Chapman and Hall, 1858.

Blanc, Louis. *Organisation du travail.* Paris: Société de l'industrie fraternelle, 1939.

Bonde, Baroness [née Robinson]. *Paris in '48: Letters from a Resident Describing the Events of the Revolution.* New York: James Port, 1903.

Bonnell, Victoria E. *Roots of Rebellion: Workers' Politics and Organizations in St. Petersburg and Moscow, 1900-1914.* Berkeley: University of California Press, 1983.

Bouniols, Gaston. *Histoire de la Révolution de 1848.* Paris: Delagrave, 1918.

Bovenkerk, Frank. "Rehabilitatie van het rapalje: hoe en waarom Marx en Engels het lompenproletariaat ten onrechte hebben afgeschilderd als een reactionaire kracht." *Sociologische Gids* 27, no. 3 (May-June 1980): 191-224.

Brogan, D. W. *The French Nation from Napoleon to Pétain, 1814-1940.* New York: Harper, 1957.

Calhoun, Craig. *The Question of Class Struggle: Social Foundations of Popular Radicalism During the Industrial Revolution.* Chicago: University of Chicago Press, 1982.

Calhoun, Craig. "The Radicalism of Tradition: Community Strength or Venerable Disguise and Borrowed Language?" *American Journal of Sociology* 88, no. 5 (March 1983a): 886-914.

Calhoun, Craig. "Industrialization and Social Radicalism: British and French Workers' Movements and the Mid-Nineteenth-Century Crisis." *Theory and Society* 12, no. 4 (July 1983b): 485-504.

Canfora-Argandoña, Elsie. "La répartition de la population à Paris au dix-neuvième siècle." In *La répartition de la population, les conditions de logement des classes ouvrières à Paris au dix-neuvième siècle*, edited by Elsie Canfora-Argandoña and Roger H. Guerrand, 105-325. Paris: Centre de Sociologie Urbaine, 1976.

Carter, Edward, and J. S. Middleton. "The Paris National Workshops of 1848." *The Socialist Review: A Monthly Review of Modern Thought* 2 (September-February 1908-1909): 743-57.

Caspard, Pierre. "Aspects de la lutte des classes en 1848: le recrutement de la garde nationale mobile." *Revue historique* 511 (July-September 1974): 81-106.

Castellane, Maréchal de. *Journal du Maréchal de Castellane, 1804-1862*. Paris: Plon, 1896.

Caussidière, Marc. *Mémoires de Caussidière, ex-préfet de police et représentant du peuple*. Paris: Michel Lévy Frères, 1849.

Chaboseau, A. "Les constituants de 1848. Notes de statistique démographique, professionnelle, etc." *La Révolution de 1848* 7 (1910-1911): 287-305, 413-25; and 8(1911-1912): 67-80.

Chalmin, Commandant P. "Une Institution militaire de la seconde république: la garde nationale mobile." *Etudes d'histoire moderne et contemporaine* 2 (1948): 37-82.

Chalmin, Commandant P. "La crise morale de l'armée française." In *l'Armée et la seconde république*, vol. 18 of *Bibliothèque de la révolution de 1848*, 28-76. La Roche-sur-Yon: Imprimerie Centrale de l'ouest, 1955.

Chambre de Commerce de Paris. *Statistique de l'industrie à Paris, résultant de l'enquête faite par la chambre de commerce pour les années 1847-1848*. Paris: Guillaumin, 1851.

Chassin, Ch.-L., and L. Hennet. *Les Volontaires nationaux pendant la Révolution*. Paris: Léopold Cerf, 1899.

Chauvet, Paul. *Les Ouvriers du livre en France de 1789 à la Constitution de la Fédération du livre*. Bibliothèque d'Histoire économique et sociale. Paris: Librairie Rivière, 1946.

Cherest, Aimé. *La Vie et les oeuvres de A.-T. Marie*. Paris: Durand et Lauriel, 1873.

Chevalier, Louis. *La Formation de la population Parisienne au dix-neuvième siècle*. Institut National d'études démographiques, Travaux et Documents, no. 10. Paris: Presses Univérsitaires de France, 1950.

Chevalier, Louis. *Class laborieuses et classes dangereuses à Paris pendant la première moitié du dix-neuvième siècle*. Paris: Plon, 1958.

Chevalier, Louis. *Laboring Classes and Dangerous Classes in Paris During the First Half of the Nineteenth Century*. Princeton, N.J.: Princeton University Press, 1981.

Chorley, Katherine. *Armies and the Art of Revolution*. London: Faber and Faber, 1943.

Clapham, John Harold. *The Economic Development of France and Germany, 1815-1914*. Cambridge, England: Cambridge University Press, 1961.

Clark, T. J. *The Absolute Bourgeois: Artists and Politics in France, 1848-1851.* Greenwich, Conn.: New York Graphic Society, 1973.

Clough, Shepard Bancroft. *France: A History of National Economics, 1789-1939.* New York: Octagon Books, 1964.

Cobb, Richard. *The Police and the People: French Popular Protest, 1789-1820.* London: Oxford University Press, 1972.

Cobban, Alfred. *The Social Interpretation of the French Revolution.* Cambridge, England: Cambridge University Press, 1965.

Comberousse, Charles de. *Histoire de l'Ecole Centrale des Arts et Métiers.* Paris: Gauthier-Villars, 1879.

Comité français des sciences historiques. *Actes du congrès historique du centenaire de la révolution de 1848.* Paris: Presses Univérsitaires de France, 1948.

Coornaert, E. "La pensée ouvrière et la conscience de classe en France de 1830 à 1848." In *Studi in Onore di Gino Luzzatto,* 12-33. Milano: Giuffre, 1950.

Crémieux, Albert. *La Révolution de Février: étude critique sur les journées des 21, 22, 23, et 24 février.* Paris: E. Cornely, 1912.

Dansette, Adrien. *Deuxième République et Seconde Empire.* Paris: Librairie Arthème Fayard, 1943.

Dansette, Adrien. *Louis-Napoléon à la conquête du pouvoir.* Paris: Hachette, 1961.

Daumard, Adeline. *La Bourgeoisie parisienne de 1815 à 1848.* Paris: S.E.V.P.E.N., 1963.

Dautry, Jean. *1848 et la IIe République.* Paris: Editions Sociales, 1957.

Dayot, Armand Pierre Marie. *Journées révolutionnaires, 1830, 1848; d'après des peintures, sculptures, dessins, lithographies, médailles, autographes, objects . . . du temps.* Paris: E. Flammarion, 1897.

Delessard, Ernest. *Souvenirs de 1848: l'Ecole Centrale aux Ateliers Nationaux.* Paris: E. Bernard, 1900.

Doumenc (Général). "L'armée et les journées de juin." In *Actes du congrès historique du centenaire de la révolution de 1848,* Comité français des sciences historiques, 255-66. Paris: Presses Univérsitaires de France, 1948.

Draper, Hal. "The Concept of the 'Lumpenproletariat' in Marx and Engels." *Economies et Sociétés* 6, no. 12 (December 1972): 2285-312.

Dubief, Lise. *Tables analytiques des publications de la Société d'histoire de la révolution de 1848*, vol. 17 of *Bibliothèque de la révolution de 1848*. La Roche-sur-Yon: Imprimerie Centrale de l'Ouest, 1957.

Duveau, Georges. *La Vie Ouvrière en France sous le Second Empire*. Paris: Gallimard, 1946.

Duveau, Georges. "l'Ouvrier de quarante-huit." *La Revue socialiste* 17-18 (1948): 73-79.

Duveau, Georges. *1848: The Making of a Revolution*. New York: Vintage Books, 1967.

Edwards, Stewart. *The Paris Commune, 1871*. London: Eyre and Spottiswoode, 1971.

Engels, Friedrich. *The German Revolutions*. Chicago: University of Chicago Press, 1967.

Eyck, Frank, ed. *The Revolutions of 1848-49*. New York: Barnes and Noble Books, 1972.

Falloux, Comte de. *Mémoires d'un Royaliste*. Paris: Perrin, 1925.

Fasel, George W. "The French Election of April 23, 1848: Suggestions for a Revision." *French Historical Studies* 5, no. 3 (Spring 1968): 285-98.

Flaubert, Gustave. *Sentimental Education*. London: Penguin Books, 1964.

France. Les Archives nationales. *Etat général des Fonds. Tome II: 1789-1940*. Paris: Archives nationales, 1978.

France. Assemblé nationale. *Rapport de la Commission d'Enquête sur l'insurrection qui a eclaté dans la journée du 23 juin et sur les évènements du 15 mai*. Paris: n.p., 1848.

France. Bibliothèque nationale. *La Révolution de 1848: Exposition Organisée par le Comité National du Centenaire*. Paris: Bibliothèque nationale, 1948.

France. Bureau de la Statistique Générale. *Répertoire technologique des noms d'industries et de professions*. Paris: Berger-Levrault, 1909.

France. Comité national du centenaire de 1848. *Procès-verbaux du Gouvernement Provisoire et de la Commission du Pouvoir Exécutif (24 février-22 juin 1848)*. Paris: Comité national du centenaire de 1848, 1950.

Franklin, Bruce. "The Lumpenproletariat and the Revolutionary Youth Movement." *Monthly Review* 21, no. 8 (January 1970): 10-25.

Freycinet, C. de. *Souvenirs, 1848-1878*. Paris: Delagrave, 1912.

Garnier-Pagès, Louis Antòine. *Histoire de la Révolution de 1848.* Paris: Degorce-Cadot, n.d.

Garnier-Pagès, Louis Antoine. *Histoire de la Révolution de 1848.* Paris: Pagnerre, 1872.

Geraudel, P. "Les Sources manuscrites parisiennes de l'histoire de la deuxième république." In *Actes du congrès historique du centenaire de la révolution de 1848,* Comité français des sciences historiques, 85-87. Paris: Presses Univérsitaires de France, 1948.

Girard, Louis. *Etude comparée des mouvements révolutionnaires en France en 1830, 1848, et 1870-71.* Paris: Les Cours de Sorbonne, 1960.

Girard, Louis. *La Garde nationale, 1814-1871.* Paris: Plon, 1964.

Girard, Louis. *La Deuxième République, 1848-1851.* Paris: Calmann-Levy, 1968.

Godechot, Jacques. *Les Révolutions de 1848.* Paris: Editions Albin Michel, 1971.

Gossez, Rémi. "Notes sur la composition et l'attitude politique de la troupe." In *l'Armée et la second république,* Société d'histoire de la révolution de 1848, 77-110. La Roche-sur-Yon: Bibliothèque de la révolution de 1848, 1955.

Gossez, Rémi. "A propos de la carte des troubles de 1846-1847." In *Etudes de la Société d'histoire de la révolution de 1848,* 1-3. Paris: C.N.R.S., 1956a.

Gossez, Rémi. "Diversité des antagonismes sociaux vers le milieu du dix-neuvième siècle." *Revue économique* 5 (May 1956b): 439-58.

Gossez, Rémi. "Pré-syndicalisme ou pré-coopération? L'organisation ouvrière unitaire et ses phases dans le département de la Seine de 1834 à 1851." *Archives internationales de sociologie de la coopération* no. 6 (1959): 67-89.

Gossez, Rémi. *Les Ouvriers de Paris. Livre premier: l'Organisation, 1848-1851,* vol. 24 of *Bibliothèque de la révolution de 1848.* La Roche-sur-Yon: Imprimerie Centrale de l'Ouest, 1967.

Gouldner, Alvin. *The Two Marxisms: Contradictions and Anomalies in the Development of Theory.* New York: Seabury Press, 1980.

Greenberg, Louis. "The Commune of 1871 as a Decentralist Reaction." *Journal of Modern History* 41 (March-December 1969): 304-18.

Guillemin, Henri. *La Tragédie de Quarante-huit.* Paris: Milieu du Monde, 1948.

Guillet, Léon. *Cent ans de la vie de l'école centrale des arts et manufactures, 1829-1929.* Paris: de Brunoff, 1929.

Hamerow, Theodore S. *Restoration, Revolution, Reaction: Economics and Politics in Germany, 1815-1871.* Princeton, N.J.: Princeton University Press, 1958.

Hammen, Oscar J. *The Red '48ers: Karl Marx and Friedrich Engels.* New York: Scribner, 1969.

Hanagan, Michael P. *The Logic of Solidarity: Artisans and Industrial Workers in Three French Towns, 1871-1914.* Urbana, Ill.: University of Illinois Press, 1980.

Hanagan, Michael, and Charles Stephenson. "The Skilled Worker and Working-class Protest." *Social Science History* 4, no. 1 (Winter 1980): 5-13.

Herzen, Alexander. *My Past and Thoughts: The Memoirs of Alexander Herzen.* New York: Knopf, 1973.

Herzen, Alexandre. *Lettres de France et d'Italie, 1847-1852.* Geneva: n.p., 1871.

Hobsbawm, E. J. *The Age of Revolution, 1789-1848.* New York: New American Library, 1962.

House, Jonathan M. "Civil-Military Relations in Paris, 1848." In *Revolution and Reaction: 1848 and the Second French Republic,* edited by Roger Price, 150-69. New York: Barnes and Noble, 1975.

Illustration, Journal universel, l'. Journées Illustrées de la Révolution de 1848. Récit historique de tous les évènements. Paris: Plon, 1848.

Johnson, Christopher H. "Economic Change and Artisan Discontent: the Tailors' History, 1800-48." In *Revolution and Reaction: 1848 and the Second French Republic,* edited by Roger Price, 87-114. New York: Barnes and Noble, 1975.

Kamenka, Eugene, and F. B. Smith. *Intellectuals and Revolution: Socialism and the Experience of 1848.* New York: St. Martin's Press, 1980.

Kuhn, Thomas S. *The Structure of Scientific Revolutions.* Chicago: University of Chicago Press, 1970.

Labrousse, Ernest. "1848-1830-1789: comment naissent les révolutions." In *Actes du congrès historique du centenaire de la révolution de 1848,* Comité français des sciences historiques, 1-29. Paris: Presses Univérsitaires de France, 1948.

Labrousse, Ernest. "Panoramas de la Crise." In *Aspects de la crise et de la dépression de l'économie française au milieu du 19e siècle, 1846-1851*, edited by Ernest Labrousse. Vol. 19 of *Etudes de la Société de la Révolution de 1848*, iii-xxiv. La Roche-sur-Yon: Imprimerie Centrale de l'Ouest, 1956.

la Gorce, Pierre de. *Histoire de la Seconde République française*. Paris: Plon, 1904.

Lalanne, Léon. "Lettres sur les Ateliers Nationaux, I-VI." *Le National* (14, 15, 19, and 23 July; 6 and 16 August, 1848).

Lamartine, Alphonse de. *Histoire de la révolution de 1848*. Paris: Perrotin, 1849.

Langer, William L. "The Pattern of Urban Revolution in 1848." In *French Society and Culture since the Old Regime*, edited by Evelyn M. Acomb and Marvin L. Brown, Jr., 90-118. New York: Holt, Rinehart & Winston, 1966.

Langer, William L. *Political and Social Upheaval: 1832-1852*. New York: Harper Torchbooks, 1969.

Lavisse, Ernest. *Histoire de France contemporaine depuis la révolution jusqu'à la paix de 1919*. Paris: Hachette, 1921.

Lees, Lynn, and Charles Tilly. *Analysis of Arrests in Paris: June, 1848*. Codebook available through The Inter-university Consortium for Political and Social Research, Ann Arbor, Michigan, n.d.

Lefebvre, Georges. *The Coming of the French Revolution*. Princeton, N.J.: Princeton University Press, 1976.

Lefrançais, Gustave. *Souvenirs d'un révolutionnaire*. Brussels: Bibliothèque des Temps nouveaux, 1902.

Le Play, Ferdinand. *Les Ouvriers de l'Occident: populations ébranlées*. Tours: Alfred Mame et fils, 1878.

Levasseur, E. *Histoire des classes ouvrières et de l'industrie en France de 1789 à 1870*. Paris: A. Rousseau, 1904.

Lévy, Claude, "Les Journées parisiennes de juin 1848 d'après des études récentes." *Etudes de la Région Parisienne 35*, nos. 112-13 (July-December 1961): 19-26.

Lévy-Schneider, L. "Les préliminaires du 15 mai 1848." *La Révolution de 1848* 7 (1910-1911): 219-32.

Ligne, Princesse Ch. de. *Souvenirs de la Princesse de Ligne*. Brussels: G. Van Oest, 1923.

Luna, Frederick A. de. *The French Republic under Cavaignac, 1848*. Princeton, N.J.: Princeton University Press, 1969.

McKay, Donald Cope. *The National Workshops: A Study in the French Revolution of 1848*. Cambridge, Mass.: Harvard University Press, 1933.

Margadant, Ted. "Modernisation and Insurgency in December 1951: A Case Study of the Drôme." In *Revolution and Reaction: 1848 and the Second French Republic*, edited by Roger Price, 254-79. New York: Barnes and Noble, 1975.

Margadant, Ted W. *French Peasants in Revolt: The Insurrection of 1851*. Princeton, N.J.: Princeton University Press, 1979.

Markovitch, T. J. "La crise de 1847-1848 dans les industries parisiennes." *Revue d'histoire économique et social* (1965a): 256-60.

Markovitch, T. J. "L'Industrie française de 1789 à 1964: Sources et méthodes." *Cahiers de l'Institut de Science Economique Appliquée* Series AF4, no. 163 (July 1965b).

Markovitch, T. J. "L'Industrie française de 1789 à 1964: Analyse des faits." *Cahiers de l'Institut de Science Economique Appliquée* Series AF6 (May 1966a).

Markovitch, T. J. "L'Industrie française de 1789 à 1964: Conclusions générales." *Cahiers de l'Institut de Science Economique Appliquée* Series AF7, no. 179 (November 1966b).

Marx, Karl. *Political Writings*, Vol. II: *Surveys from Exile*, edited by David Fernbach. New York: Random House, 1973.

Marx, Karl, and Friedrich Engels. *Basic Writings on Politics and Philosophy*, edited by Lewis S. Feuer. Garden City, N.Y.: Anchor Books, 1959.

Marx, Karl, and Friedrich Engels. *Werke*. Berlin: Dietz Verlag, 1961-1968.

Marx, Karl, and Friedrich Engels. *La Nouvelle Gazette Rhénane*. Paris: Editions Sociales, 1963.

Marx, Karl, and Frederick Engels. *The Revolution of 1848-49: Articles from the Neue Rheinische Zeitung*. New York: International Publishers, 1972.

Marx, Karl, and Frederick Engels. *Collected Works*, Vol. VII: *1848*. New York: International Publishers, 1976.

Mauco, Georges. *Les Etrangers en France: Leur rôle dans l'activité économique*. Paris: Colin, 1932.

Ménard, Louis. *Prologue d'une Révolution*. Paris: Cahiers de la Quinzaine, 1904.

Merriman, John M., ed. *1830 in France*. New York: New Viewpoints, 1975.

Molok, A. I. "Le Problème de l'insurrection de juin 1848." *Questions d'Histoire* 2, no. 12 (1952 or 1954): 58-100.

Moore, Barrington, Jr. *Injustice: The Social Bases of Obedience and Revolt*. White Plains, New York: M. E. Sharpe, 1978.

Moss, Bernard H. *The Origins of the French Labor Movement: The Socialism of Skilled Workers, 1830-1914*. Berkeley: University of California Press, 1976.

Moulin, Charles, ed. *1848: Le Livre du Centenaire*. Paris: Editions Atlas, 1948.

Newman, Edgar Leon. "What the Crowd Wanted in the French Revolution of 1830." In *1830 in France*, edited by John M. Merriman, 17-40. New York: New Viewpoints, 1975.

Normanby, The Marquis of. *A Year of Revolution: From a Journal kept in Paris in 1848*. London: Longman, Brown, Green, Longmans, and Roberts, 1857.

Noyes, P. H. *Organization and Revolution: Working-class Associations in the German Revolutions of 1848-1849*. Princeton, N.J.: Princeton University Press, 1966.

O'Brien, Patricia. "The Revolutionary Police of 1848." In *Revolution and Reaction: 1848 and the Second French Republic*, edited by Roger Price, 133-49. New York: Barnes and Noble, 1975.

O'Brien, Patrick, and Caglar Keyder. *Economic Growth in Britain and France, 1780-1914: Two Paths to the Twentieth Century*. London: Allen and Unwin, 1978.

Pagès-Duport, M. A. *Journées de Juin: Récit complet des évènements des 23, 24, 25, 26 et des jours suivants*. Paris: Pitrat et fils, 1848.

Palmade, Guy P. *French Capitalism in the Nineteenth Century*. New York: Barnes and Noble, 1961.

Palmer, R. R., and Joel Colton. *A History of the Modern World*. New York: Knopf, 1963.

Pardigon, F. *Episodes des journées de juin 1848*. London: Jeffs, 1852.

Picattier, Eugène. *Les Ateliers Nationaux en 1848*. Thèse pour le doctorat presentée le Jeudi 26 Janvier 1899 à 10 heures du matin. Saint-Etienne: Société de l'Imprimerie Théolier, 1899.

Pinkney, David H. "The Crowd in the French Revolution of 1830." *American Historical Review* 70, no. 1 (October 1964): 1-17.

Pinkney, David H. "Les Ateliers de Secours à Paris (1830-1831):

Précurseurs des Ateliers Nationaux de 1848." *Revue d'histoire moderne et contemporaine* 12 (January-March 1965): 65-70.

Pinkney, David H. *The French Revolution of 1830*. Princeton, N.J.: Princeton University Press, 1972.

Ponteil, Félix. *1848*. Paris: Librairie Armand Colin, 1955.

Price, Roger. *The French Second Republic: A Social History*. Ithaca, N.Y.: Cornell University Press, 1972.

Price, Roger, ed. *1848 in France*. Ithaca, N.Y.: Cornell University Press, 1975a.

Price, Roger, ed. *Revolution and Reaction: 1848 and the Second French Republic*. New York: Barnes and Noble, 1975b.

Proudhon, P.-J. *Les Confessions d'un Révolutionnaire pour servir à l'histoire de la Révolution de février*. Vol. 9 of *Oeuvres complètes de P.-J. Proudhon*. Paris: Librairie Internationale, 1868.

Quentin-Bauchart, Pierre. *Etudes et souvenirs sur la deuxième république et le second empire (1848-1870)*. Paris: Plon, 1901.

Quentin-Bauchart, Pierre. *La Crise Sociale de 1848: Les Origines de la révolution de février*. Paris: Hachette, 1920.

Rébillot, le Général Baron. *Souvenirs de Révolutions et de Guerre*. Paris: Berger-Levrault, 1912.

Regnault, M. Elias. *Histoire du Gouvernement Provisoire*. Paris: Victor Lecon, 1850.

Rémusat, Charles de. *Mémoires de Ma Vie: Les Dernières Années de la Monarchie; La Révolution de 1848; La Seconde République (1841-1851)*. Paris: Plon, 1962.

Renard, Georges. *La République de 1848, (1848-1852)*. Vol. 9 of Jean Jaurès, ed., *Histoire Socialiste (1789-1900)*, Paris: J. Rouff, 1907.

Rittiez, F. *Histoire du gouvernement provisoire de 1848*. Paris: Librairie Internationale, 1867.

Robertson, Priscilla. *Revolutions of 1848: A Social History*. Princeton, N.J.: Princeton University Press, 1967.

Rougerie, Jacques. "Composition d'une population insurgée: l'exemple de la commune." *Le Mouvement social* (July-September 1964): 31-47.

Rudé, George. *The Crowd in the French Revolution*. New York: Oxford University Press, 1973.

Schmidt, Charles. *Les Journées de juin 1848*. Paris: Hachette, 1926.

Schmidt, Charles. *Des Ateliers Nationaux aux Barricades de juin*. Paris: Presses Univérsitaires de France, 1948.

Sebastiani, Général. "Rapport sur les journées de février adressé à Villemain." *La Révolution de 1848* 8 (1911-1912): 320-30.

Seignobos, Charles. "Les Procès-verbaux du Gouvernement provisoire et de la Commission du pouvoir exécutif de 1848." *Revue d'histoire moderne et contemporaine* 7 (1905-1906): 581-97.

Seignobos, Charles. *La Révolution de 1848; Le Second Empire (1848-1859)*. Vol. 6 of Ernest Lavisse, ed., *Histoire de France contemporaine depuis la révolution jusqu'à la paix de 1919*. Paris: Hachette, 1921.

Selznick, Philip. *TVA and the Grassroots: A Study in the Sociology of Formal Organization*. Berkeley: University of California Press, 1949.

Senior, William Nassau. *Journals Kept in France and Italy from 1848 to 1852*. New York: Da Capo Press, 1973.

Sewell, William H., Jr. "Social Change and the Rise of Working Class Politics in Nineteenth Century Marseille." *Past and Present* 65 (November 1974): 75-109.

Sewell, William H. "*Corporations Républicaines*: The Revolutionary Idiom of Parisian Workers in 1848." *Comparative Studies in Society and History* 21, no. 2 (April 1979): 195-203.

Sewell, William H., Jr. *Work and Revolution in France: The Language of Labor from the Old Regime to 1848*. Cambridge, England: Cambridge University Press, 1980.

Shorter, Edward, and Charles Tilly. "The Shape of Strikes in France, 1830-1960." *Comparative Studies in Society and History* 13 (1970): 60-86.

Skocpol, Theda. *States and Social Revolutions: A Comparative Analysis of France, Russia, and China*. Cambridge, England: Cambridge University Press, 1979.

Soboul, Albert. *The French Revolution, 1787-1799*. London: New Left Books, 1975.

Soboul, Albert. *The Sans-Culottes: The Popular Movement and Revolutionary Government, 1793-1794*. Princeton, N.J.: Princeton University Press, 1980.

Stadelmann, Rudolph. *Social and Political History of the German 1848 Revolution*. Athens, Ohio: Ohio University Press, 1975.

Stearns, Peter N. *1848: The Revolutionary Tide in Europe*. New York: W. W. Norton, 1974.

Stedman Jones, Gareth. "The Mid-Century Crisis and the 1848 Revolutions: A Critical Comment." *Theory and Society* 12, no. 4 (July 1983): 505-20.

Stern, Daniel [Comtesse d'Agoult]. *Histoire de la Révolution de 1848.* Paris: Charpentier, 1862.

Thomas, Emile. *Histoire des Ateliers nationaux.* Paris: Michel Lévy, 1848.

Thompson, E. P. *The Making of the English Working Class.* New York: Vintage Books, 1963.

Thompson, E. P. "The Moral Economy of the English Crowd in the Eighteenth Century." *Past and Present* 50 (February 1971): 76-136.

Tilly, Charles. "Reflections on the Revolutions of Paris: An Essay on Recent Historical Writing." *Social Problems* 12, no. 1 (Summer 1964): 99-121.

Tilly, Charles. "How Protest Modernized in France, 1845-1855." In *The Dimensions of Quantitative Research in History,* edited by William O. Aydelotte, Allan G. Bogue, and Robert William Fogel, 192-255. Princeton, N.J.: Princeton University Press, 1972.

Tilly, Charles, and Lynn H. Lees. "The People of June, 1848." In *Revolution and Reaction: 1848 and the Second French Republic,* edited by Roger Price, 170-209. New York: Barnes and Noble, 1975.

Tilly, Charles, Louise Tilly, and Richard Tilly. *The Rebellious Century, 1830-1930.* Cambridge, Mass.: Harvard University Press, 1975.

Tocqueville, Alexis de. *Recollections.* Garden City, N.Y.: Anchor Books, 1971.

Traugott, Mark. "The Mobile Guard in the French Revolution of 1848." *Theory and Society* 9, no. 5 (September 1980a): 683-720.

Traugott, Mark. "Determinants of Political Orientation: Class and Organization in the Parisian Insurrection of 1848." *American Journal of Sociology* 86, no. 1 (July 1980b): 32-49.

Traugott, Mark. "Introductory Comments." *Theory and Society* 12, no. 4 (July 1983a): 449-53.

Traugott, Mark. "The Mid-Nineteenth-Century Crisis in France and England." *Theory and Society* 12, no. 4 (July 1983b): 455-68.

Tucker, Robert C., ed. *The Marx-Engels Reader.* New York: W. W. Norton, 1978.

Tudesq, A. J. "La Crise de 1847, vue par les milieux d'affaires parisiens." In *Aspects de la crise et de la dépression de l'économie française au milieu du 19ᵉ siècle, 1846-1851.* Vol. 19 of *Etudes de la Société de la Révolution de 1848,* 4-36. La Roche-sur-Yon: Imprimerie Centrale de l'Ouest, 1956.

Vidalenc, Jean. "La Province et les Journées de juin." *Etudes d'Histoire moderne et contemporaine* 2 (1948): 83-144.

Weiss, John. "Karl Marlo, Guild Socialism, and the Revolution of 1848." *International Review of Social History* 5 (1960): 77-96.

Williams, Roger L., ed. *The Commune of Paris, 1871.* New York: Wiley, 1969.

Zeldin, Theodore. *France, 1848-1945.* Vol. 1: *Ambition, Love, and Politics.* London: Oxford University Press, 1973.

AUTHOR INDEX

INDEX

Provisional Government (*cont.*)
    See also under names of members
    Mobile Guard created by, 36
    National Workshops created by, 4, 115
    response to major events, 19, 22
Pujol, Louis
    in *journée* of 15 May, 249 n. 50
    in June Days, 28, 145, 160-61, 254 n. 22

Raspail, François Vincent, 39, 165
ratio of male to female workers, 74-75, 216-19 n. 54, 222 n. 60
reform campaign of 1847-1848, 13-15, 166, 200 n. 17, 202 n. 1
Réforme, la, 13, 16-17, 200 n. 18
Republican Guard. See *montagnards*
Reunion centrale des Ateliers nationaux. *See* National Workshops, Club of Delegates
revolutionary crowd, 17, 18, 21, 34-35, 115-16, 189-90, 204 n. 5
Revolutions of 1848. *See* European revolutions; French Revolution of 1848
riffraff thesis, xiv, 169
right of association and assembly, 17, 116, 143
right to work, 18, 115, 116, 137, 145, 151, 154, 174
Rouen insurrection of April 1848, 40, 100, 108, 132, 165, 191
Rumania, 197 n. 1
Russia, 172

Sebastiani, General, 203 n. 3
Second Empire, French, xii-xiii
Second Republic, French. *See*

French Revolution of 1848
Sénard, Antoine, 63
shop size, 8, 75, 198 n. 8, 219 n. 55, 221 n. 57, 222-23 n. 60
Skocpol, Theda, 184
Soboul, Albert, 182-84
social republic. *See* democratic and social republic
social workshops, 116-17, 152, 234 n. 1. *See also under* Blanc, Louis; National Workshops
socialism, 12, 152, 173
sociological analysis, distinctiveness of, 52, 81, 114, 169, 186-87, 190
Sologne, 154
state, xiii, 152, 234 n. 1
suffrage
    reform of, 13, 200 n. 16
    universal, 17, 22-23, 205 n. 12
Switzerland, 197 n. 1

Tempoure (Commanding General, Mobile Guard), 41, 207 n. 21
textiles sector, 6-7, 9, 71, 73, 217-18 n. 54, 219-20 n. 55
Thiers, Louis Adolphe, 16
Thomas, Emile, 20-21, 135, 151-53, 155-61, 163-64, 174, 235 n. 3, 236 n. 6, 240 n. 17, 242 n. 23, 244 n. 33
    cooptive strategy of, 128-33, 163-64, 253-54 nn. 16, 18, 19
    dismissal of, 26, 42, 136-41, 146, 152, 160, 165, 246-47 nn. 41, 43, 248 n. 45, 256 n. 29
    proposes reorganization of National Workshops, 117-20, 149, 190, 191
Thomas, Pierre, 140, 155, 235 n. 3, 254 n. 21
Thomassin (member, National Workshops), 256 n. 32

292

LIBRARY OF CONGRESS CATALOGING IN PUBLICATION DATA

Traugott, Mark.
Armies of the poor.

Bibliography: p.
Includes index.
1. Paris (France)—History—June Days, 1848.
2. France—History—February Revolution, 1848.
3. Labor and laboring classes—France—Paris—
Political activity—History—19th century.
4. France. Armée. Garde nationale mobile.   I. Title.
DC273.T73   1985   944.04   85-3511
ISBN 0-691-09414-4 (alk. paper)
ISBN 0-691-10173-6 (pbk.)